REPRODUCING SCHOLTEN & BAIJINGS

In collaboration with **maharam**

SCHOLTEN & BAIJINGS IN CONTEXT

Michael Maharam in conversation with Louise Schouwenberg

Scholten & Baijings was born in 2000 from a clear ambition: Stefan Scholten and Carole Baijings wanted to design functional products, collaborate with the best professionals in the world, and create a balance between industrially produced series and experimental projects. Fourteen years later the Dutch designers can look back on an extensive body of work that distinguishes itself by its singular use of colour and the exceptionally high quality of workmanship. The designers have won several awards, their designs are part of prestigious collections, and they have worked for a variety of leading international companies, including Maharam, one of their most recent clients.

This collaboration deserves an interview with Michael Maharam, who is particularly celebrated for the precision with which he makes choices for his collection, and has the reputation for working with only the best designers and producers in the world.

Louise Schouwenberg
What made you decide to initiate a book about Scholten & Baijings, a decision that evolved from a small booklet, intended to accompany a specific project, into a monograph?

Michael Maharam
The question of how it all comes together is the one most unanswered. This subject has been of interest for some time and we had previously considered various formats, including a comparative overview of designers working in the present day, and a retrospective of those at the twilight of celebrated careers predicated on materials and techniques that now seem nostalgic contrasted against the new digital standard.

The world certainly doesn't need another coffee table tome or self-aggrandizing product catalogue thinly disguised as a monograph. As this project evolved from the initial inevitable self-serving agenda to the broader and relevant question of what serves the reader, we returned to the need to document design research.

In the end, we felt the diversity demonstrated in the work of Scholten & Baijings, with their highly defined aesthetic vocabulary overlaid across varied product types, their hands-on approach, and the fact that they were a small office reliant on the distilled thinking of few versus many, would provide the necessary fundamentals for this exercise.

This coupled with our desire to work with Joost Grootens, whose skills at book design enable him to document and portray information in the most elegantly legible and expressive manner, as well as the photographic documentation of Scheltens and Abbenes, made this project whole.

LS: Why now?

MM: As we are in the midst of developing our first products with Scholten & Baijings and in the process of getting acquainted, the explanatory demands of a new medium (textiles) and the initial rites of courtship create an intensity of dialogue and observation that suits this sort of exploration. It is also interesting to observe the nature of these collaborations as they evolve from the innocence of early idealism to thinking grounded in experience and knowledge of the category, the user and the partner. I cannot say that our mature collaborations run independently, but the first conversations with a new collaborator are often the most meaningful in leading us to challenge the status quo. We devote many hours to discussing the details. Those discussions lead one to ask why things are done a certain way, as new collaborators may not understand our business and are therefore inclined to ask many naive though intelligent questions.

LS: What happens once you know each other?

MM: Over time you gain the benefit of more comfortable and confident dialogue and the spontaneity and rhythm that come with intuitive understanding. At the same time, inquisitiveness and curiosity about a new medium are replaced by expertise, and with this expertise comes a point of view and a resulting vocabulary that defines work stylistically but also can reduce creative agility. This is not to say that a narrowly defined aesthetic vocabulary equals limited creative bandwidth... it is the difference between deep and wide, and we appreciate each.

LS: Do you make mistakes in choosing the designers you get involved with?

MM: I would characterize these as unmet expectations, and both parties can be held accountable and suffer the result. One would like to think that the wisdom of experience would lead to precise knowledge of what is needed from a working relationship. Despite this, chemistry and circumstance can conspire to undermine the best prospects.

Naturally, courtship is the test. Carole and Stefan are bright, charming and funny people. They have an impressive and profound process and are extremely engaged. Their office is fascinating... a little candy shop for the curious eye. Ilse Crawford introduced me to them in Eindhoven at the annual student project presentation, which is an incredible incubator. At the time they were working for MINI and doing a very good job of it, so obviously they had the skills. The Netherlands has such an abundance and diversity of design talent that one cannot help but draw comparisons, and Carole and Stefan stand tall in their own rigorous and modern way. They are clever organizers and excellent makers. Our project was fully conceptualized and produced from start to finish as an artisanal one-off, utilizing remnant yarns woven on rented looms, all beautifully photographed and carefully documented in a single edition published specifically for their presentation to us. They even developed and modelled a seating design intended to complement their textiles… a flattering bit of cart before the horse. They understand theatre, and they are very convincing costume designers, set designers and players.

Scholten & Baijings might be described as the Dutch Muji on the basis of the pleasantly universal and useful character of their designs. Importantly, they bring unexpected and striking colour to the mix and couple it with a studied approach to pattern. Though one could say that their palette and pattern language is narrow, we find this focus to be a fascinating point of exploration and a great strength.

LS: So you were convinced that Scholten & Baijings would be a valuable addition to the Maharam collection.

MM: We were first attracted to Scholten & Baijings' palette in combination with their early work in colour-blocking, which heralded the extreme success of Phoebe Philo at Céline, who brought this theme to broad public attention.

With every designer and project, the transition from concept to production is the greatest leap. As these textiles would be essentially graphic in nature, we felt a flat construction would be appropriate. With Scholten & Baijings, colour was the greater challenge, as we rely upon the sometimes limited yarn banks of the weavers we work with, and the production of new yarn colours can be costly… often with minimums as high as 500 to 1000 pounds, which amounts to miles of a lesser used accent colour, or untold amounts of unsold inventory. Since colour dominates the Scholten & Baijings theme, this was a point of great concern. In the end Carole and Stefan built the programme around an existing yarn palette and we did not produce any new yarn colours. In retrospect, we might have invested in a more daring approach to colour or a more dimensional construction, but this is all part of the learning experience and guides us as we look ahead. Of course we're always self-critical… complacency leads nowhere… but this does not mean I think the products are not good. More so, I think the concept of a composed sofa is so perfectly clever in its simplicity that the rest is somewhat secondary, albeit beautiful.

LS: Who's responsible for a design trajectory?

MM: In the first round, we claim majority responsibility… a crisp brief is the critical foundation of a successful project. The brief can be explicit, poetic, or simply a set of markers. It differs from project to project and reflects the nature of the collaborator and the need. In this case, the designers worked with numerous particulars that we stipulated… a yarn system, a construction, a weaver, and our desire for large-scale colour-blocking. Scholten & Baijings brought the concept to the table and coupled it with a composition and a palette. At the beginning the commissioner must take the lead. We have the market knowledge and the product expertise, and we're paying the bill. In a first effort, our tendency is to want to be part of every decision and to command the situation. In the end you have to take responsibility for this. Thankfully, as the relationship evolves the designers become much more independent. The ultimate hope is that our collaborators generate the ideas, understand and govern the production, and feel a sense of ownership in our mutual success. And then it all becomes a pleasurable dialogue and a partnership.

LS: How critical are you during a process?

MM: Some relationships allow antagonism from the start, though Carole and Stefan are polite and willing to bend and perhaps this is based on the newness of it all. We have no doubt that they will become pleasantly feisty at some point in the future. I'd be concerned if they didn't… we like a good fight!

LS: In which phase of the courtship are you?

MM: Murray Moss once commented to me that with some people you have a one-night stand, with others you have a romance, and with others still, you have a marriage. Thankfully, Murray and I became an old married couple and it resulted in a lot of good work and a lasting friendship. With Scholten & Baijings it's a happy romance at the moment. Who knows what the future will bring, but we are hopeful. In general I see a shift in the design world. It seems that the days of the usual suspects are passing. The short list of 'all-stars'—Jasper Morrison, Hella Jongerius, Konstantin Grcic—is being supplanted by a far longer list of lesser-known and less monogamous players. Companies and designers seem to be unable to commit themselves to long-term design relationships. It's project to project, limited attention span, flavour of the month. It's no longer acceptable for companies to insist that relationships with collaborators be exclusive, and vice versa, as young designers thrive on variety—across media, product categories and geography. Perhaps the bright side of this trend could be a transition away from the collaboration set on a pedestal as a promotional device. Wouldn't it be ideal if all companies just did thoughtful work with capable people and didn't tout 'design' as some sort of panacea?

Sadly, design patronage does not exist on the same level as it once did. Design is now a managed process led more by managers than by the entrepreneurs who embraced this activity as a cultural cornerstone, a hobby, a passion, a joy and an investment of themselves and their money in people and things they believed in. To truly be good in the 'design' business is to know and appreciate the applied arts; this creates opportunity and lifts the bar universally. Unfortunately, most companies view this as a cost rather than an investment.

LS: Maharam has a rich tradition, a long history and a strong reputation for working with the best designers in the world and producing high-quality products.

MM: I would say we're focused on finding interesting people to work with. We also insist on working with people we like, people we like to dine with, people with whom we could envision taking holidays. It is very personal, and very much not about grandstanders.

LS: You speak of 'we', but isn't it 'I'? What is your specific influence within the company?

MM: The 'I' is the entrepreneurial 'I'. I guide an excellent and capable staff of people, the 'we' that shapes the product. My role is to ascribe values and define the character of the what, why and how at Maharam. I know my limitations. I want to accomplish many things, but I only have a general feeling for how to do this. My colleagues have expertise, patience and experience that I do not possess. I'm good at conceptualizing and I'm good at critiquing... I know what feels right.

LS: Over the course of time you have had to make many choices and I assume you have had to find the right balance between cultural and historical responsibility and expected economic profit. Can you describe how you accomplish this?

MM: The initial balance starts with the very practical and essential matter of distribution. Without it, the best products remain idealistic dreams. Our good fortune as a company has been our diverse foundation of well-distributed quotidian products in a broad range of prices and subcategories. These are workhorses intended to address the pragmatic everyday needs of our clients and their clients. These products support exploratory and cultural investments... the 'stars' that become the public persona of the company despite the fact that they generally account for only a small percentage of sales. On occasion they do strike a chord commercially, but on the whole they are the legacy products we love to love.

In the case of this first project with Scholten & Baijings the investment has been considerable and involves a fair amount of risk… a large collection of costly textiles with a very particular aesthetic and perhaps a limited application and audience. That said, we prefer to introduce a new collaborator to our clientele with a dramatic statement that represents their work archetypally through a strong and clear narrative, and then follow up with products that can be more readily used… in this case, Tones, the third textile we are working on with Scholten & Baijings.

LS: So distribution is one of the key elements for a successful product that balances cultural value and economic profit. What else?

MM: It's imperative to recognize that the things that we make have to be a point of personal interest and conviction. If one is not committed to exploration in earnest, it becomes evident through careless superficial choices and poorly executed products, which are unconvincing. The audience is not easily fooled and few companies can stomach the amount of time, energy and money involved in being meticulous and truly interesting over time without a traditional monetary return on investment. We have always viewed association, visibility and risk as the critical means to achieve our version of healthy profitability… they are structural pillars at Maharam, not occasional attention-getting devices.

Forgive the soapbox, but the twentieth century introduced the populace to material aspiration and America led the charge. There is so much junk out there, and the world is not hurting for another product. As this is a contraption of our own making and since most of us have to earn a living, we must create–and creating good things that have lasting character and quality is the most hopeful aspiration if we seek to make a better world. The American appetite for variety is enormous and ours has been a dispose-and-replace mentality. Europeans tend to have a greater respect for sustainability and to buy better quality products and to look after them. We have lessons to learn, and it is heartening to see this movement in play.

LS: You are an educator?

MM: To have a set of values that are demonstrated philosophically through a corporate culture and realized physically through the development and presentation of products that seek to transform and elevate the perception of a product category is the noblest objective in business. Just making things to make money is a wasted opportunity on so many levels… it is a shame. The painful inherent obsolescence of personal electronics was made irrelevant by Steve Jobs, perhaps the most successful pedagogue of our generation. It is such a thrill to find a craftsperson, a website, a shop, a company that makes it easy to choose with the knowledge that you are buying something good and smart and believable… something that answers a question and a need convincingly. We aspire to be that company in textiles.

In our industry, Vitra does this with seeming effortlessness. I have been greatly influenced by Rolf Fehlbaum, and by the notion of the European family-business tradition with its holistic embrace of all the elements that add up to the fully dimensional definition of being good… one in which the cultural basis of the activity, the product, the presentation, and all the people including the gardener and the chef who cooks for the staff, are regarded with equal esteem as parts of a whole, regardless of rank. Unfathomable as this is becoming in our tightly stretched world, this is the way to run a business in my view.

None of us wants to be associated with work in which we cannot take pride. Though very successful, my father was a practical man generally selling things that were sensible but not particularly inventive. This held no appeal for me or my brother. We were incredibly fortunate to be able to completely reinvent his company without losing financial momentum; pulling the tablecloth out from under while simultaneously resetting the table. It was a difficult thing to do, but we got lucky through the naivety of simply wanting to do what felt right and somehow finding a gap in the market and a place in the hearts of our clientele. Naturally this was a point of generational transition, but also a reflection of our times and a growing intolerance of the ordinary.

Ultimately we are in the business of narrative. It's essential that we tell stories that are interesting and that clearly demonstrate the rationale of our decision to realize the work of a chosen designer through an excellent result. The most successful products elicit an immediate visceral understanding from the audience and require no more than a sentence or two of explanation… perhaps biographical details about the designer, the intent of the undertaking, interesting facets of the design or manufacturing process and aspects of functionality. Adjectives hold very little place in our approach… they are subjective superlatives, and subjectivity should be left to the client and not imposed by the salesperson or the company. Our clients know what they like… our job is to create and explain.

REPRODUCING SCHOLTEN & BAIJINGS

Louise Schouwenberg

They are standing in strict ranks, as if part of an abstract composition. Because of this unusual arrangement, the photograph draws attention to the line play of the angular shapes of the *Paper Porcelain* crockery rather than its possible use. The viewer can imagine the experiments in paper that preceded the manufacture of the porcelain cups and saucers. In other photos the photographers Scheltens & Abbenes zoomed in on a detail or the colours of a design to the extent that only the texture is visible–the feel of the object, as it were, not the product itself. This is the case, for instance, in the picture of the *Art Parts* of *Colour One for MINI*, which shows only a window and a form that hints at a wheel. This is apparently all that is required to conjure up a sense of movement and depict Scholten & Baijings' highly individual take on cars

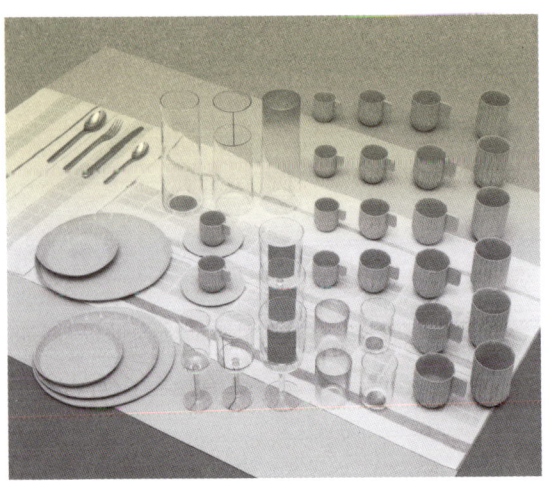

Paper Table 2009. Photography Scheltens & Abbenes

–in this case a design of a concept car for the future, commissioned by the BMW Group for MINI.

'There were instances where they would look at a shot and at first didn't even recognize parts of their own work!' says Maurice Scheltens who has photographed, together with his partner Liesbeth Abbenes, almost all works of Scholten & Baijings. 'It is definitely cool that Stefan and Carole see the value of our approach and embrace it warmly. That they are able to understand that someone else can have their own interpretation of the colours, the shapes, the feel of their designs. When we shoot something, the photo never depicts exactly what the product is. We don't provide a service in the traditional sense, but we create an autonomous image based on the ingredients a client provides us with. This means that we usually make a new composition in the studio with the materials they have worked with–the cardboard, the adhesive tape, the porcelain, the colours–but we also use non-physical elements such as the brief, the atmosphere they have created or the context in which the objects are placed. With every picture we try to capture the essence of the material and thus create a new perspective on the way in which they have worked with that same material.'

According to Stefan Scholten and Carole Baijings, this approach always yields beautiful abstract pictures, as well as a fresh view of their theme. For them, the photo almost always represents a point of reference, a moment of reflection–something that provokes new conclusions and often provides an impetus for their next phase of work.

The particular beauty of the colours and the exceptionally high quality of craftsmanship and detailing are the features most often referred to in any description of the designs of Scholten & Baijings. What is not immediately apparent, and therefore less often mentioned in articles about their work, is the quality of the underlying design and the continuous character of their design process. Each single material and colour test calls for a subsequent experiment, each prototype prompts a follow-up version, and each family of objects can be extended endlessly. The process has no end but encourages ongoing deepening and widening. Scheltens & Abbenes' photography plays a part in this process, whereby even a product presentation at Milan's Salone Internazionale del Mobile (International Furniture Fair) is considered a snapshot moment by the designers. Abbenes: 'The presentation in a photographic image will outlive the product itself. This requires an awareness that design is not just about products, but also about context. The whole. Stefan and Carole have this awareness.'

The importance of Scholten & Baijings' design process, which actually has no final stage but is mainly made up of reference points that invite following phases, is also what strikes graphic designer Joost Grootens: 'Every step in their research paves the way for a next step, but also contains the realization that this might be the finished product. When I first talked to them in their studio about the book we would make, I was surprised about their high level of design research. Of course I was familiar with the end products, but I had no idea about the huge amount of cardboard scale models, test swatches and colour sequences involved. Not only do these bear witness to the almost obsessive manner in which they investigate something, but each transitional object is so beautiful it seems as if it has reached its final stage. I think many designers would stop at the point where they simply continue.'

Cardboard models, Paper Porcelain 2009

Scholten & Baijings definitely don't rush into things. Each one of the industrially produced fabrics and furnishings, the handcrafted crockery and the unique handmade items show evidence of the intensive research that preceded them. Every investigation consists of experiments carried out in their own studio, as well as experiments conducted in close cooperation with specialist professionals. The design process dictates all their preliminary conclusions and generates a level of beauty and an almost un-Dutch elegance that could be called characteristic of the Scholten & Baijings label. There is beauty in the forms, pared down to their essence, in the surprising colour palette and colour gradations, in the visible traces of the production, in the compositions of lines and surfaces, the exquisite detailing, the perfect finish; and there is beauty in the way Scholten & Baijings are able to bridge the gap between contemporary industrial design and local, ancient crafts. There is beauty also in the sense of multilayering and the coherence of the different stages of their oeuvre, in the presentations and re-presentations of their work, which they design and elaborate down to the smallest detail.

Through their work, Scholten & Baijings have slowly but surely conquered a unique place in the design world over the past fourteen years. During this period they have worked for a variety of leading international companies and institutions, including Maharam, Thomas Eyck, Royal VKB, BMW Group/MINI, Established & Sons, HAY, the Zuiderzee Museum, the Textiel-Museum, Pastoe, 1616/Arita Japan, Karimoku New Standard, Georg Jensen, J. HILL's Standard, Luce di Carrara, IKEA, Moooi, and Moustache. They have won several awards and their works are part of prestigious collections, including those of the Museum Boijmans Van Beuningen in Rotterdam, the Stedelijk Museum Amsterdam, the Stedelijk Museum 's-Hertogenbosch, the TextielMuseum in Tilburg, the Zuiderzee Museum in Enkhuizen, the Centre National des Art Plastiques (CNAP) in Paris, the Fédération Nationale d'Achats des Cadres (Fnac), the Art Institute of Chicago, and the Cooper-Hewitt National Design Museum in New York.

Amsterdam Armoire in conjunction with the Zuiderzee Museum 2010. Photography inside Scheltens & Abbenes

STEFAN SCHOLTEN AND CAROLE BAIJINGS

'The key is the symbiosis between us. As individuals, we never would have been able to make these designs. It really is Scholten & Baijings,' agree Carole Baijings (born 1973) and Stefan Scholten (born 1972).

Baijings: 'I grew up with grandparents who owned a wholesale business in Persian rugs and collected Eastern European glassware. This meant that I developed an early affinity for unusual fabrics, unique colour combinations and exotic patterns. During my upbringing there was much attention to cultural education and creativity; my mother always had a great feeling for beauty. But I am definitely not from a designer family. I was not predestined to become a designer of contemporary products. After high school I looked into art. But after preliminary training at the Gerrit Rietveld Academie in Amsterdam, I went to work for a film director. As an assistant director I worked on several commercials and, since I was involved in the entire process, I soon became familiar with the power of images. How different elements can create synergies in one particular image. I have no idea what direction my career would have taken if I had not met Stefan in 1999. Luckily, we don't have to speculate about that. Our talents seem to complement each other exceptionally well. We

Colour Carpet 04 for HAY 2011

explore all aspects together, but you could say that, of the two of us, I'm the perfectionist. Stefan is a real designer, he's always making sketches everywhere. He devises plans and has the ability to implement them. It is because of him that our designs become real. He can draw beautifully, is technically savvy and extremely handy. Stefan can do anything!'

Scholten: 'Carole can read my drawings and translate them into the final finished design like no other. She has a great eye for detail, a special intuitive feeling for colour, and she keeps a watchful eye over the final outcome. She never stops. Whenever we're in a store or an exhibition in which our work is presented, she'll perfect the display by moving cups around, or pulling the bedspread just a bit tighter. You could say that, for me, it's down to the centimetre, but for Carole it's down to the millimetre.

'As a little boy I took everything apart, I wanted to know how things were put together. I think my fascination with making things was born then. In addition, I grew up with design. Good living. We had furniture by Memphis, chairs by Marcel Breuer and Mies van der Rohe, a cabinet by Aldo van den Nieuwelaar. My parents were not real collectors but we had tasteful items at home, and a lot of attention was paid to art. My father was on the board of the Groninger Museum for some time and on the board of Museum Arnhem before that. What also sparked my interest in design was probably our frequent moving because of my father's work. Once every three years we ended up in a different city in a new house that had to be furnished again. Soon I developed an eye for the furniture and the objects we surrounded ourselves with. So it wasn't

Strap Chair for Moustache 2014

surprising that I became a designer. When I looked into the available study options I also considered TU Delft (Delft University of Technology), but the focus there was mainly on a technical approach rather than design. After a visit to the Design Academy Eindhoven on Open Day, which at the time was called Akademie voor Industriële Vormgeving Eindhoven (Academy for Industrial Design), I fell in love with the design profession as it was taught there. We still apply many of the methods I learned during my studies. And, not unimportantly, I also learned what I didn't want. After my final exams in 1996, I worked with Bob Copray for five years. We mainly designed furniture and interiors under the name Copray & Scholten. Despite our success, I decided at some point to take a different course. From the moment I started working with Carole, it all came together.'

Scholten & Baijings was born in 2000, based on a clear ambition. The two designers wanted to design functional products, collaborate with the best professionals in the world and create a balance between industrially produced series and experimental projects.

DESIGN ACADEMY EINDHOVEN

Scholten tells how, at the beginning of his studies, he had expected that students would be working on design, functionality and industrial production as well as market mechanisms. But during his time at the academy, between 1991 and 1996, these values were hardly addressed as subjects in his department, 'Man and Living'. At the time, the department was led by designer Gijs Bakker, who in 1993 founded Droog, the platform for conceptual design. Bakker attached great importance to concept development. 'The department was extremely popular, despite–or precisely because of–that hostility to the market. If you wanted to mean anything as a designer, you had to either study with Gijs Bakker, or with Ulf Moritz ("Man and Identity" department), that much was clear.'

As Scholten reminisces, he recalls many inspiring assignments, such as putting dots on a sheet of paper with black ink and a dip pen. 'That was called an optical grammatical study, aimed at creating exciting compositions with attention to rest spaces.' Or the assignment to create a three-plane composition in paper and cardboard. 'Using those simple means, we had to suggest space. At the same time we learned not only how to cut out all those forms with precision, but also what materials, type of knife, glue or brand of tape were most suitable. In our studio we create all the models ourselves and are endlessly working on materials, shapes, colours. Perhaps that's an after-effect of the training.

'I can also remember a fantastic assignment by Mathieu Meijers: an apple-y apple–which is, of course, a delicious apple. Just try to express that in colour and form! We developed a close friendship afterwards and worked together when we both taught at the Design Academy Eindhoven's Kompas department "Atelier". The head of "Atelier", Bernardine Walrecht, has also been instrumental for our careers. Together with her and Mathieu, we sparred endlessly about the profession. Those were very inspiring times. Endless talks about the layering of colours. We were very evenly matched!'

Scholten also speaks with enthusiasm about his internships. When he worked for designer Piet Hein Eek he had to mainly sand old boards and remove nails. 'At one point I indicated that I wanted to design something myself, which he thought was fine. He put out a table especially for me and regularly came by and then said mockingly, "Well, monkey face, are you still designing?"

'I remember mostly the projects with Eek that took me through all the phases of a design; the entire process of an assignment. I still see that reflected in our current work. It doesn't stop with the prototype, not even with the product. As a designer, you're also responsible for the presentation. The whole picture.'

Since the training comprised a mix of conceptual thinking and modernist purism, this was where, according to Scholten, he really learned to justify the how and why of what he did. He also learned how to reduce forms to their bare essence. Simplicity. It was never enough and never finished. You were always supposed to go on. Moreover, a very strong competitive spirit prevailed. 'We had to work very hard in those days. There was a lot of pressure and I believe that's good. It was like that in all the departments but in "Living" and "Identity" it was the worst. Students were terrified during reviews – it was a real ordeal, every time. In fact, it was very much the way things are in actual practice.'

Baijings: 'That you have to work hard to achieve your goals also applies to the profession itself. Your idea of it is always more romantic than the reality. You hardly ever have a moment of rest. You have to keep studying. The last few years have been like top-level sport for us. We have designed many collections and have travelled to numerous countries, such as Japan, America and Denmark. Working sixty to seventy hours a week has been normal for us. Our work is our life, but now I realize why weekends exist!'

Colour Plaid 04 2005.
Photography Inga Powilleit

DUTCH DESIGN

In the early 1990s a group of Dutch designers won fame in the international design world, among them Hella Jongerius, Jurgen Bey, Marcel Wanders, Richard Hutten, Piet Hein Eek and Tejo Remy. Most of them had studied at Design Academy Eindhoven, a few years before Scholten. Their designs were widely praised for their conceptual sharpness, simple language and basic execution. Dutch Design became a well-known concept in the world, and for a long time it was synonymous with Conceptual Design. This did not necessarily make things easier for the generations that followed. The media were lurking, waiting to discover new Dutch talent, but how long could this success last? Most of the historical design movements had only lasted for a few years, and were soon followed by some other hype in some other place in the world. That was the mood when Scholten was studying. But it turned out well after all. In the late 1990s, Job Smeets, Bertjan Pot, Wieki Somers and Maarten Baas graduated, and just like the earlier generation, they soon gained fame in the international media and the exhibition circuit. Later still, Christien Meindertsma, Joris Laarman, Andrea Trimarchi and Simone Farresin (Formafantasma), and others would rise to fame. Design Academy Eindhoven has a long history of successful alumni. Scholten is definitely one of them.

Scholten finds it unfortunate that, in their early days, there were virtually no good alternatives to Droog Design as a subsidized platform for young designers. An exception is Dutch Individuals, the state-subsidized organization that was established in 1998 and consisted of a loose group of individual design firms. Significant for Scholten was their presentation of stacked containers on the private grounds of the Italian architect Alessandro Mendini in Milan, which took place during the Salone del Mobile, and their group exhibition in a warehouse right in the middle of trendy Brick Lane in London. Designers who presented works under the Dutch Individuals banner included Ineke Hans, Job Smeets, Hugo Timmermans, Richard Hutten, Hella Jongerius, Dum Office, Edward van Vliet, Jan Broekstra and Copray & Scholten.

Scholten: 'During my studies I felt I didn't really connect with the conceptual ideas Droog stood for. Although my teachers did appreciate my graduation project–a set design for a theatre play, as well as a sofa and an armchair that were later purchased by the Centraal Museum in Utrecht. We didn't seek to connect with the Dutch conceptual design that was doing so well in the international design world at the time. Many colleagues went off to do things for Droog Design. Carole and I followed our own course. We quickly learned that you have to struggle to get things done. What I have learned from conceptual design during my studies is awareness. You have to know what you want, realize what your own ideas are, be aware of the context for which you design something. I also learned that it works if you have a good strategy for presenting designs. Conceptual design became important because the designers were presented as a group, as a movement. Everything is relative. When Droog Design was first launched in Milan in 1993, Jasper Morrison gave a presentation at that very same fair. He had done something quite unique in collaboration with industry, but because of the hype surrounding Droog he was entirely ignored by the media. In retrospect you could conclude that Morrison's approach did yield great results in the long run. I find that very interesting because cooperation with industry is a key element for us as well '

Tilt Top Table in collaboration with Mathieu Meijers (Artwork) 2009

Baijings: 'In our work, the emphasis is not only on the conceptual statement. We do start from a concept, an idea, but we go a step further by engaging in collaborations with industry. We attach great importance to the quality of the execution. That quality lies in the attention to the detailing of the materials and the techniques we choose, the manner in which we make our compositions, the colours, the layering. These are qualities that do not shout at you, but rather whisper.'

Scholten: 'We knew from the start that because of this subtle approach it would take longer for our work to become recognized.'

Since then, Scholten & Baijings have more than earned that recognition. For many years now, both in the Netherlands and abroad, they have been known as a leading design label, separate from any overarching paradigm such as Dutch Design – which has indeed suffered from inflation. Too many designers of various levels have exploited this designation for marketing purposes, so that it has become quite meaningless today. Just like other great Dutch designers, Scholten & Baijings are appreciated in the international design world for their own qualities.

Although the catch-all classification has disappeared, it still remains remarkable that a small country like the Netherlands has produced such a large percentage of good designers, including an increasing number of foreign designers who had opted for Dutch design-training and never left. There is no longer a common style, no Dutch Design. At best, there is a (self-)conscious design approach, in which the conditions of both the profession and applied production techniques are continuously scrutinized, which is rather characteristic of Dutch designers. While in the 1990s the Netherlands mainly boasted a host of individual star designers, it has produced a remarkably large number of design duos since the beginning of this century.

CONTEMPORARY DESIGN AND CENTURIES-OLD TECHNIQUES

In recent decades, crafts have enjoyed a new level of popularity among the vanguards of the visual arts, fashion, design and architecture. Since the beginning of the twentieth century, ancient techniques and local traditions had declined into a moribund existence on the margins of the cultural landscape until they were dusted off and given new impetus. This relatively sudden revival of interest in crafts had a lot to do with the realization that globalization and industrial innovations have not only brought benefits. No one can deny that since the 1980s, mass consumption has been taking a heavy toll on the environment and has led, as a logical consequence, to an impoverishment of the relationships people have with their everyday objects. Typical of the throwaway society are short-lived fashions and the all-too-easy convenience of being able to prematurely discard well-functioning household objects. This development has now placed sustainability high on the agenda of most designers. While some of them focus primarily on better waste management, recycling, and sustainable materials and production methods, others aim for psychological durability. How can products, through their appearance, high level of quality and traces of conscientious production foster a closer relationship between user and object? Less than thirty years ago, visible marks of craft production were considered telltale signs of an outdated view of design, but now they represent a valid alternative to mass production and its harmful consequences.

Like any movement in design, this development has both good and bad consequences. All too often, for instance, nostalgic and allegedly authentic meanings are projected onto materials, techniques and local traditions, while contemporary innovations are naively ignored. Only the better designers manage to move beyond nostalgia and superficial associations to access multiple layers of meaning and create design products that do justice to both the past and the present. Scholten & Baijings undoubtedly belong to that group. Their body of work contains numerous significant examples that demonstrate how the two designers breathe new life into traditional craft techniques from different regions. Take, for instance, the three series of utensils and furniture they

DOT Chair for HAY 2013.
Photography Inga Powilleit

created in 2008 in close cooperation with the Zuiderzee Museum and the companies Thomas Eyck and Royal Leerdam Crystal: *Truly Dutch*, *Woven Willow* and *Table Glass*. For *Colour Wood* (2009), *Colour Porcelain* (2012) and *Tea with Georg* (2013) they worked together with the master craftsmen of 1616/ Arita Japan, Karimoku New Standard and Georg Jensen. Projects in which they have incorporated their fascination with handcrafted finishes in industrial products are *Bed Linen* (2011) for the Danish company HAY, and *Blocks & Grid* (2014) for the American company Maharam.

Butte Tree 2010

Scholten & Baijings' work includes numerous references to historical design movements such as Arts and Crafts, the Wiener Werkstätte, the Bauhaus, Modernism, even aspects of conceptual design. Their fascination with artisanal manufacture and decoration recalls the ideas of William Morris, who in the nineteenth century opposed the 'soullessness' of industrial products and became an advocate for artisanal craftsmanship. The talent to create intriguing relationships between colours and graphic patterns calls to mind the work of Bauhaus designers such as Johannes Itten and Josef Albers. The sober design language of functionalism and the pursuit to push the technical possibilities of materials beyond their known boundaries places them in a long tradition of industrial designers such as Charles and Ray Eames, and more recently Konstantin Grcic, Jasper Morrison and Naoto Fukasawa. They share with many other Dutch designers an awareness of the multiple layers of meaning embedded in products, and the realization that the context in which products are produced affects their value. Scholten & Baijings are author-designers who resist incorporating easy and clichéd references to craft production in their work. They combine the best of both worlds by linking a universal industrial design language to a pristine execution rooted in local artisanal techniques. They consciously play with various references, but always do so in a subtle and calm way, rather than through loud proclamations.

Each item in the ever-expanding family of products reveals a strong individual character, while collectively representing the typical Scholten & Baijings signature. The designers, according to trend forecaster Lidewij Edelkoort, do not only create beautiful functional products but also present an alluring lifestyle that in many ways connects with our present time. Edelkoort in *Blush – Design in Full Colour* (2011): 'Industry recognizes the power of thinking through making, asks for help and gives them *carte blanche* for cooperation. Manufacturers don't want a new design, but demand, as it were, a piece of the creators' existence, an intimate relationship with Carole and Stefan's lives. This makes their signature increasingly clearer and more prominent. The colour schemes become brighter and almost compulsive; the range of variations becomes ever larger. The result is a Scholten & Baijings collection produced by the best manufacturers in the world.'

INDUSTRY = CRAFT

Baijings: 'Nature spoils us with so many fascinating hues and tonal variations. That is something you want to translate into a product, a fabric, but then you inevitably run into the inherent restrictions of, for example, the yarn, the dye baths, the looms. Nature never lets you win. It makes you feel like a bumbler, time and again. But you have to keep trying. This means that as a designer you have to create your own colour alphabet, a personal colour palette. To us, colour is as important as form. For a long time it was not even addressed in design. At one point almost all interiors were virginal white, yet colour can add so much to the quality of life. We think in colour – it is definitely not a choice we make afterwards.'

To translate the variability of natural colours into, for instance, textiles, glass or porcelain enamel, the designers work with ranges that run from light to dark, from one hue to another, or they drape colour fields in juxtaposed layers into a clever web of graphic patterns. Bright fluorescent colours give their timeless designs an undeniably contemporary look. The use of colour and the intriguing play with colour tonalities recall the paintings of

Shift for Pastoe 2012

Mark Rothko and Barnett Newman. The geometric compositions with colours and lines are reminiscent of the paintings of Josef Albers and Frank Stella, while

37

the experiments with colours on solid forms evoke the sculptures of Donald Judd or the coloured spatial layerings of James Turrell.

For the producers of their colourful designs it is often a major challenge to translate the colour samples, which the designers create in their own studio, into an industrial production process. Scholten: 'This is only possible when you have a client who trusts you, who sees where your talents lie and who works with the best manufacturers. It starts with a good brief for the commission. For example, Michael Maharam didn't just ask us to simply design something, something he could just as easily have asked others to do. The company asked us to design an upholstery fabric with an accent on colours and geometric planes. When Michael Maharam saw our first design proposals, he knew right away which weaving mill to set us up with. And then the design process started all over again, so to speak. In close cooperation with the experts at the weaving mill, we tried to find the most beautiful colours, the best weaving solutions. Unlike the TextielMuseum, where we had conducted our first tests, this weaving mill has machines of which both the warp and the weft can be varied. That expanded our colour range and enabled us to create a richer layering. We then went to work on these first samples. This going back and forth between making tests and then reworking the design in our workshop is a long and intensive process through which we really get to know and take advantage of the technical competence of a producer.

In our studio we work with eight permanent employees, mainly designers, and a few interns. There is a close cooperation on all projects. The occasional studio projects that are not commissioned by a client, but that we initiate ourselves, give us the opportunity to invest in the autonomous creative process. This is when we give ourselves the freedom to unrestrictedly explore what we want to express with a given material, colour or shape. When you work in an intensive artisanal manner you have to accept the fact that with each project you are actually making a detour. In the early years this was an investment in the future, and now it is part of every project. Detours that lead away from your own studio, to various professionals and external workshops, such as the European Ceramic Workcentre in 's-Hertogenbosch or the TextielLab in Tilburg, are invaluable experiences.'

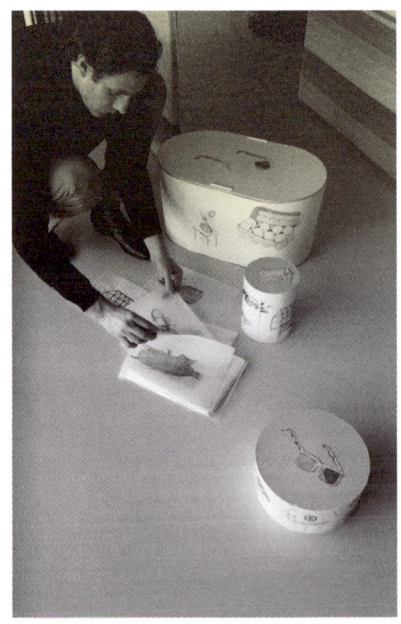

Stefan with the first cardboard prototypes of the Butte 2010. Photography Inga Powilleit

Baijings: 'Because we make numerous preliminary studies for each project, the models are quite often developed to the point where they look like finished products. They're just not ready for use yet. During the subsequent phase we are at times surprised by the new possibilities opening up. Things we could not achieve in our studio, but which a specialist company or a specialized craftsperson are perfectly able to realize. An amazing feeling!'

Scholten: 'In 2007, Thomas Eyck asked us to design a woven wicker collection. During our preliminary research we watched a film at the Nationaal Vlechtmuseum (National Wickerwork Museum) in Friesland, which showed a girl weaving wicker. A great craftswoman, who works in a very delicate and precise manner. She also restores dolls' furniture at the Rijksmuseum, using a particularly fine technique called *fijnscheenwerk*. We contacted her and proposed working together on the Thomas Eyck project. Sometimes we come across this kind of exceptional expertise entirely by chance, but usually it just naturally follows on from the kind of assignments we accept.'

Baijings: 'At the same time, because of our intensive working method, we not only enjoy the confidence of our clients but also of museum curators. They commission work, invite us to take part in exhibitions and press for our work to be included in important collections. It's cross-pollination. Through museum purchases and attention in the media we managed to gain the trust of manufacturers, which now enables us to serve a greater part of the market.'

Stefan Scholten and Carole Baijings call themselves industrial designers because they adhere to a number of values that are inextricably linked with industrial design, such as the primary requirement that the products they conceive must be functional and user-friendly. They also believe that large-volume production is one of the essential factors in the field. This requires professional expertise and the awareness that the realization of a design need not necessarily rely on handicraft.

Scholten: 'We are not leaning towards art. Even when we work on a non-commissioned project, such as the *Vegetables*, there is always in the back of our minds the thought of how we could translate certain solutions into an industrial product.'

Vegetables 2009. Photography Yves Krol

Baijings: 'As soon as we team up with a company, we start exploring the possibilities. The client's history and expertise become part of our design process. We visit the company, investigate the possibilities of their technical know-how, the capabilities of the machines, and the talents of the professionals with whom they work. We then present proposals that challenge the company to branch out and do something different from what they're accustomed to. As we strive for perfection, we only work with high-quality companies.'

Scholten: 'If, as a designer, you do not engage closely with a company's professionals, you'll lose during the process. By working together, you can safeguard your own standards. That's when you actually discuss every detail: what you want exactly and why, and how the machines can be used in the most optimal way.'

Baijings: 'For us, working for industry is a pleasure, not a necessary evil. The changes that have to be made to accommodate the production process never feel like concessions. With every transition to another level of scale you are confronted with new challenges. Companies have their own professionals: specialists who know exactly what the machines can do and how materials behave under certain conditions. We want to use their expertise to the maximum. For us it is always a challenge to choose, together with a manufacturer, the scope of the products. Sometimes you work for a small exclusive market, sometimes for a large one.'

Scholten: 'I find it strange that so few Dutch designers have connections with industry. Within the Dutch design landscape, we can be situated among designers–such as Alexander van Slobbe, Claudy Jongstra, Hella Jongerius and Studio Job–who, like us, collaborate with industry and work on self-initiated projects.'

Close cooperation with professionals within the industrial context also provides a new insight into the relationship between trade and industry, whose definition, according to Scholten, needs revising. 'It is always being assumed that craft production is expensive. But it's really all about output and efficiency. The process is the same in China. But there, they have eighty people at the ready to do a job, whereas here you'd only have one. Obviously, on the other side of the world you have to be wary of unacceptable working conditions. But you can also learn from their greater level of efficiency. They've been accustomed to this for a much longer time. Whether something is expensive has everything to do with the artisanal manufacturing method. Besides, what is craft? The boundary between industrial and craft production is not clear. Even in a company such as BMW, much is made by hand. You could even say that industry is essentially artisanal. When traditional techniques are applied efficiently you create products with a luxurious appearance that are accessible to many people. When Li Edelkoort talks about the lifestyle our products represent, she refers to the attention we have for the everyday world of user objects, our attention to colours, decorative patterns, the traces of an attentive production process. That lifestyle can be described as "luxury" because of the labour-intensive and thus relatively costly aspect of the products. But it is not that simple. The idea that traditionally produced products are expensive and therefore only accessible to the happy few is entirely outdated. Think of something as simple as the tea towels with special colours that we designed for HAY.'

The companies with whom the designers work are located around the world, which obviously involves extra efforts when it comes to exploring possibilities. Baijings: 'We are starting to understand the signals abroad better and better. Sometimes totally different words are being used to communicate something, and sometimes the same words mean something very different than they do to us. If you work on the other side of the ocean, you must not only master different languages, but also the codes used to express something. We both have a lot of experience with foreign countries. I was born in Jakarta and have lived in various world cities, including Paris, Milan, London and Tokyo. My family travelled a great deal and I was exposed to many cultures. That goes for Stefan as well. I think this is something that shapes you for life. Working with clients on the other side of the world has become very natural to us.'

Tea Towels Big Dots 2014

Scholten: 'The fact that our parents were entrepreneurs has also helped us. They know exactly how to tackle things. We have regular meetings with them. It feels good that we can still rely on their expertise.'

INVESTIGATIVE DESIGNING

The Scholten & Baijings signature lies in the multilayered production process. Every project starts with a 'studio approach', as the designers call it. In their studio, they endlessly develop new materials, colours, colour gradations, variations on patterns; together with their staff they are busy with spools of thread, markers, glue, knives, paper and cardboard. Then they put together books full of 'recipes' that accurately describe the ingredients and techniques they have used. Their cabinets and drawers are overflowing with scale models, swatches and colour samples.

Unlike many contemporary designers, they are not seduced by the quick results of intelligent computer programmes. Scholten: 'It would mean working solely on a visual level. When you make models in paper and cardboard you get more information right away because you can actually hold the cup and feel the roundness, the size, the proportions. That's quite different from a 3D computer image. Our method is traditional at every level. We don't just invent forms and then find the right materials and the right producer. First, we dive into the process ourselves. This means that we remain open to the surprises that can occur while we're experimenting with materials. One experiment logically leads to another, and often there are unexpected bonuses along the way that you could not have envisaged beforehand.'

Still Life made with cardboard models.
Photography Scheltens & Abbenes 2010

Baijings: 'For us, design is not a cerebral process. Many ideas emerge through the process of working with materials. We call it "thinking through making".'

What Baijings calls 'thinking through making' is a topic that has come to be widely recognized since the publication of Richard Sennett's book *The Craftsman* (2008). Sennett's idea that making and thinking come together in the craft process has captured the imagination of both artists and designers. It goes against the persistent misconception that a good idea is all that is needed to realize a good design or a work of art – a remnant of the popular canon of conceptual art. In many creative courses, for instance, students still postpone the execution of their projects until the last weeks, while experts and professionals know all too well that virtually any material – and certainly difficult materials such as porcelain and textiles – only reveals its secrets after having been worked with exhaustively. Whatever the cerebral design approach fails to achieve turns out to be well within the scope of the 'dirty hands' method: exploring the possibilities and limits of materials and techniques through trial and error.

A good illustration of Scholten & Baijings' approach is the *Paper Porcelain* collection, which initially was to consist of round shapes. Because the designers made scale models in cardboard, they were forced to come up with solutions for making the curves, which they did by cutting through the cardboard and then bending it. The result was a series of polygonal shapes that turned out to be particularly appealing. Baijings: 'This sort of thing can't be worked out mentally in advance; it emerges while you experiment with materials and shapes. We thought those angular shapes were finished and decided to translate them into porcelain cups.' Scholten: 'So we had to find the right professionals who were able to execute this. It sounds easier than it is: from cardboard model to porcelain cup, which also has to be suitable for use. Carole makes sure that the final outcome is never anything less than the basic idea. A Chinese factory got the cardboard colour wrong and produced B-grade pottery. This would never get past Carole. Helen van Ruiten, owner of Galerie Binnen, Amsterdam, once characterized her

42

quite well: "For Carole, everything goes, but not every thing goes." So it was goodbye China and hello Japan.'

At first glance the fragile ceramic objects of *Paper Porcelain* still exude the delicacy of the cardboard models, a quality that Scheltens & Abbenes managed to capture perfectly in their photos. This particular quality of the model is important, for each model naturally holds a promise. It's a characteristic that architects usually exploit to the full in their work. A scale model has to fire the imagination, reveal something about its future expression and the use of the real building. Moreover, the model can make various problems visible and similarly hint at logical solutions. For the designers, there is another phase that takes place between the scale model and the final product: the prototype stage, which, like the scale model, primarily expresses a promise that appeals to the imagination. But what is impossible in architecture is possible in design: in the prototype stage, the final product can be fully tested before it is put into production.

What sets Scholten & Baijings apart from many of their colleagues is the way in which they investigate, and are able to appreciate, both the potential of the material experiments and the first scale models, as well as the potential of the prototype. Before making the models they experiment with shapes, colours and materials. Between the model and the prototype stages they continue to experiment, adding the requirements regarding construction and production to the list of constraints for which they need to find solutions. Even at the working prototype stage, the design research continues. Between the prototype and the final product they rework the design, now in close collaboration with the professionals in the various client companies. The designers turn their attention to even the most minute detail. At the same time, and quite uncommonly so, they give the professionals with whom they work a great deal of freedom. The Japanese ceramist, the American producer, the Frisian wicker-weaver, the photographers – all the people with whom they work add their own voice. Apparently the duo possesses the ability to both control the process and let it go at exactly the right moment. And they also possess the talent to infuse all the different stages of their design process with the preliminary promise of their initial

The Dinner Party, True-to-Life Design in Victoria & Albert Museum London 2013. Photography Inga Powilleit

model, the preliminary promise that the process could go on indefinitely. This also applies to their presentations at the Salone del Mobile, as well as to the museum display *The Dinner Party, True-to-Life Design*, which they realized at London's Victoria & Albert Museum in 2013. These settings present ideal images of the world of Scholten & Baijings, frozen moments in time, embedded in memory as abstract images.

THE FUTURE OF DESIGN

Currently, in the wake of the global economic crisis, many young designers and design students have come to question the necessity of their field. Why design a new chair when there are already so many well-functioning ones? Scholten & Baijings do not believe that the field has reached the final stage and they point to the importance of testing innovative manufacturing processes that are more efficient and more sustainable, or of exploring hitherto little-known areas such as nanotechnology. They are also convinced that every era develops its own specific visions of beauty, challenging designers to capture the spirit of their time. That spirit, according to the duo, currently calls for a particularization of the functional objects with which people surround themselves daily, a particularization that is unthinkable without zooming in on the colours, the details, the traces of the production process.

In order to fully explore the challenges of their profession, Scholten & Baijings consciously work across the spectrum of the design field and create designs that are both mass produced and made as limited editions. They consider the designs that they have realized for the Danish label HAY as being their most democratic ones. At the other end of the spectrum is their studio project *Veg-*

Clock for IKEA PS 2014

etables. Between these two extremes, they design smaller and larger editions for artisanal and industrial clients. Among them are remarkably few Dutch companies. Scholten: 'Regrettably, Dutch industry is doing very little with Dutch design. Many companies are doing poorly because of the crisis. That is one of the reasons why they don't want to take risks. But it's also a question of mentality. They are waiting until the crisis is over, even though waiting will get them nowhere. In Denmark, for instance, things are quite different. The Danish are much more open to suggestions, and the companies have a level of precision that is unheard of in the Netherlands. At all levels, they know exactly how to get something off the ground. At Georg Jensen, for instance, even long before a collection is launched, they already have their whole communication strategy worked out. It's the same in Japan. The crisis has struck there as well, but they have a different attitude than the Dutch. Maybe it all started with the disaster that took place there. They are more open, share their skills with the world.'

What is the greater ambition of Scholten & Baijings? Scholten: 'I don't know if it should be described as "greater". Our ambitions are in line with what we're doing already. The concept car for MINI still holds many developmental opportunities. And we recently designed a chair for HAY and another one for the French company Moustache. Both designs will be launched soon. In the future, we want to focus more intensively on furniture design. We see enlarging the scale of our work and expanding into other disciplines as a challenge. Think of architecture, fashion, accessories and consumer electronics. We also intend to do more work in the United States. The contacts are in place and we want to develop them. Italian design is generally considered the pinnacle of industrial design. But this view ignores the importance of American design of the mid-twentieth century. Consider the products of Buckminster Fuller, Nelson, Girard and, of course, the innovative products of Charles and Ray Eames. For years there seemed to be no development in the USA, but recently a great deal has been happening there. I see opportunities for us.' Baijings: 'When we talk about future plans we must also mention the Saga project. 2016 will see the celebration of the 400-year history of Japanese Arita porcelain. In the seventeenth century this porcelain was transported to Europe by the ships of the Dutch East India Company. The Netherlands has had a long relationship with Japanese craft businesses! Together with Teruhiro Yanagihara, artistic director of 1616/Arita Japan, we will be the project's art directors. The idea–inspired by the founding of Arita in 1616–is to link 16 European designers to 16 artisanal porcelain companies in Japan.

'Another future plan is to just quietly work somewhere. Over the past fourteen years our studio has expanded; we fly all over the world to meet with clients who give us the most diverse commissions. I think it is good to take time out at some point for prolonged reflection. What are our next steps in design? Where do we find inspiration? What other disciplines do we want to involve in our work? All these aspirations are of course subordinate to our parenting and educating of our son Rem, our biggest challenge yet!'

SCHOLTEN & BAIJINGS – THE BOOK
In the words of graphic designer Joost Grootens, who designed this book at the request of Michael Maharam: 'A book has to be didactically interesting. It should contain something you could call knowledge production, or knowledge development. Of course, a book about the oeuvre of Scholten & Baijings must give a clear picture of their works. But one goal alone is not interesting. You have to, as it were, transcend the subject and provide information that reaches beyond the obvious. Their design process offers plenty of scope for this.'

That Grootens was chosen to make a book about product designers was, according to him, not that obvious. 'I'm not object oriented; my work is oriented towards architecture and graphic design. You can call me a modernist. I'm not interested in aesthetics as such, but in a systematic rational approach, through which I open up a subject by mapping out all its components. Scholten & Baijings, however, are interested in aesthetics. They operate in another province of the design profession. That does not mean I don't have great respect for their work and their way of working. When I immersed myself in that process, I was impressed by the high standard of their design research. That concept is popular nowadays, but I see very few designers who actually dive deeply into the matter they deal with. With Scholten & Baijings, every step of the research leads to a next step. At the same time, there is the understanding that every stage of the experimentation process with materials might yield a final product. They are not just muddling along. Just look at the endless series of cardboard models. That's an example of what design research can be: a synergy between intuitive and systematic research. That investigation expands, becomes more layered. A project is not only about the beauty of the individual product, but about the family of objects in which it is embedded. The totality. The seven projects we highlight here show the multilayered nature and consistency of the designs, which actually permeate Scholten & Baijings' entire oeuvre. The colours, the simplicity of the design language, the manner in which they approach a client's commission, their courage to break boundaries as, for example, in the *Colour Porcelain* tableware series. In my view, that project in itself shows the entire scope of their talent. The *MINI* makes clear that they can also handle bigger assignments, larger scales. If a client's assignment is too limiting, it fails to do them justice.'

As a reflection of the work of Scholten & Baijings, this book is primarily a visual record of their working method. How many steps do they take between the stages, from idea to experiment, to prototype, to product and to presentation?

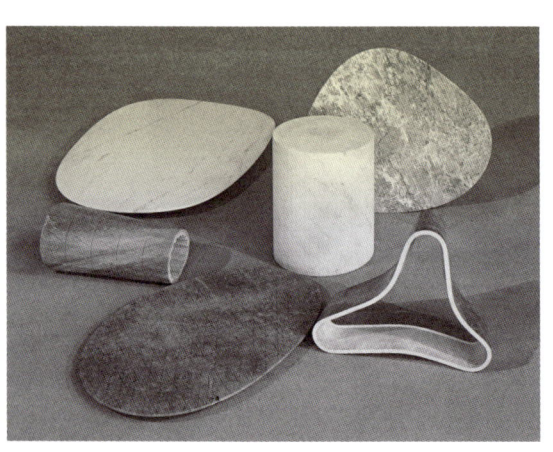

Solid Patterns for Luce di Carrara 2014.
Photography Scheltens & Abbenes

How many more process stages follow, and what are these processes like? The design process includes several pivotal moments, temporary final stages. This is evident in the often abstract images created by Scheltens & Abbenes, and in the overviews of the presentations. As Grootens explains: 'The book does not follow the design process chronologically. It does not work towards a final image. With Scholten & Baijings, there are no final images. The process never stops. I emphasize this through a variety of interventions in the book, by means of, for example, perforations in the pages. I try to stay close to the designers and translate their language into the language of the book. Significant for me is also the alternation between aesthetic images and almost ugly, meaningless images. This accentuates the beautiful pictures, but it also relates to scale. You can create a beautiful composition with uninteresting pictures or a beautiful book with boring pages. In the work of Scholten & Baijings I see an obsession with beauty on every level of scale, which at times can be very pleasant yet at others almost oppressive: an elegant ensemble consisting of beautiful items in beautiful colours with beautiful details made in a perfect way. Insignificant pictures help create a nice sort of tension between all these parts.

'Stefan and Carole apologized in advance for the fact that later, at the end of the process, they might react rather strongly. They are, after all, perfectionists. Colour freaks. But that turned out to be OK. Throughout the entire collaboration they have been very open to my input. I suspect that a large part of their success is due to the ease and respect with which they interact with clients, producers, professionals, photographers, curators. That, also, is part of the design process. Everything is connected.'

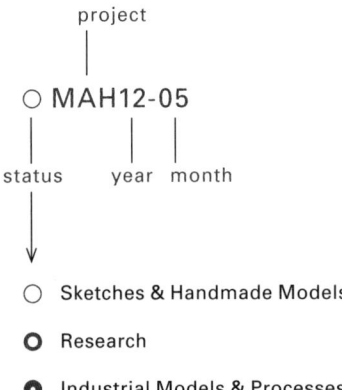

project

○ MAH12-05

status   year month

○ Sketches & Handmade Models

◉ Research

⬤ Industrial Models & Processes

● Finished Works & Presentations

WOVEN WILLOW

WOVEN WILLOW (2008)

Artisanal Product

Limited and unlimited editions. The set includes a decanter, bowls, damask
   tablecloth with napkins, and napkin rings

Materials/Techniques: Willow branches, glass, papier-mâché, plastic, textile,
   paint/ *fijnscheenwerk* (fine wicker-weave)

Colours: Various

Client/Producer: Thomas Eyck, t.e. (the Netherlands)

Centrepieces have been used for centuries to liven up a table. The centrally placed object was usually displayed as a decorative element, but could just as well have been a semi-functional object such as a candlestick, a vase or a fruit bowl. The centrepiece was also referred to as a conversation piece: as well as creating an overarching theme, it provided a topic of conversation, inviting guests to talk about its design, the special materials it was made of and the artful manner in which it was produced.

The Woven Willow objects allude to this old custom, while also breathing new life into another tradition – that of the ancient craft of wicker-weaving. In the past, this technique was mainly used to make everyday items such as baskets. Today, the craft is in danger of becoming extinct because it is hardly being taught any longer. Scholten & Baijings not only decided to revive this ancient craft, but also to enhance its status through the creation of showpieces.

According to ancient custom, willow rods have to be dried for at least a year before they can be split. After they have been split, the willow strips are shaved to precisely the size required. Before the willow strips are woven they have to be moistened with a few drops of water. By combining the willow with other materials, such as plastics or papier-mâché, and by adding colour, a pleasing balance can be created between old and new.

To make the Grand Bernard jug, willow strips were used to create a mould into which liquid glass was blown. After cooling, the crystal glass object revealed the wicker-weave pattern imprinted on its surface. The colourful jug, with a unique lip and handle, takes its name from Bernard Heesen, the renowned glassblower who made the jug. While wicker-weaving has been used, directly or indirectly, in almost all the elements of the series, this does not apply to Tape Bowl, whose design came about virtually by chance. Scholten: 'While experimenting with materials you often get surprising results, other than those you had in mind. To produce a round mould for a willow bowl, we experimented with tape on a balloon. This produced such an amazing surface that we wanted to translate it into glass.'

The design of Woven Willow was commissioned by Thomas Eyck, initiator and distributor of distinctive, exclusive design products, usually produced in small limited editions. Eyck pays great attention to combining the right craft with the right designer. For the Woven Willow project, the designers themselves found a suitable artisan, a woman who is one of the few experts in the Netherlands still capable of making the traditional willow wicker-weave, called *fijnscheenwerk*.

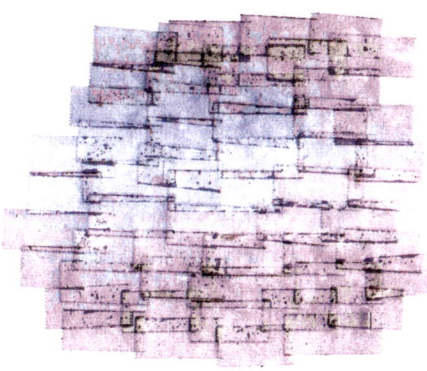

Scholten & Baijings firmly believe that the design process is not just a thought process, but also a work in progress, enabling them to learn from 'making', and from using one's hands.
— Lidewij Edelkoort, Trend Forecaster

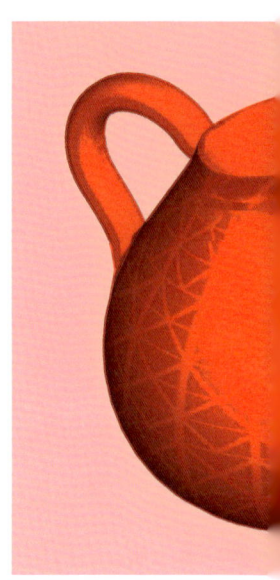

We really do design with our hands by making the models, scale models and prototypes. Because we don't have the result set out in advance, we come up with designs and techniques while working that wouldn't have been discovered otherwise.
— Carole Baijings

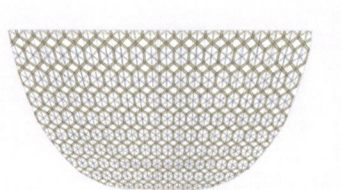

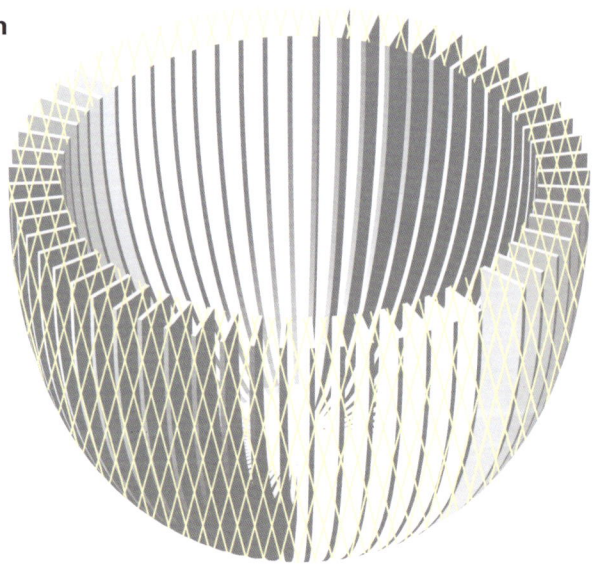

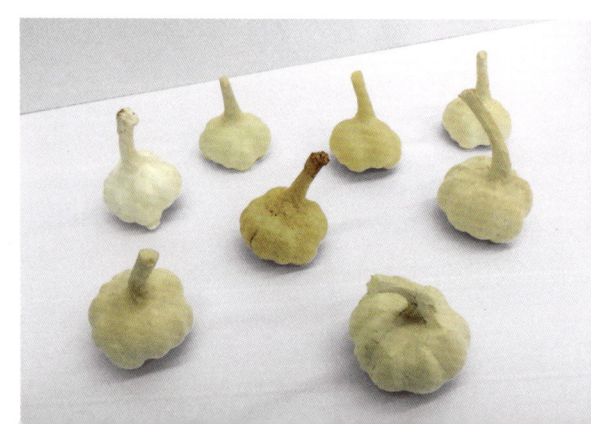

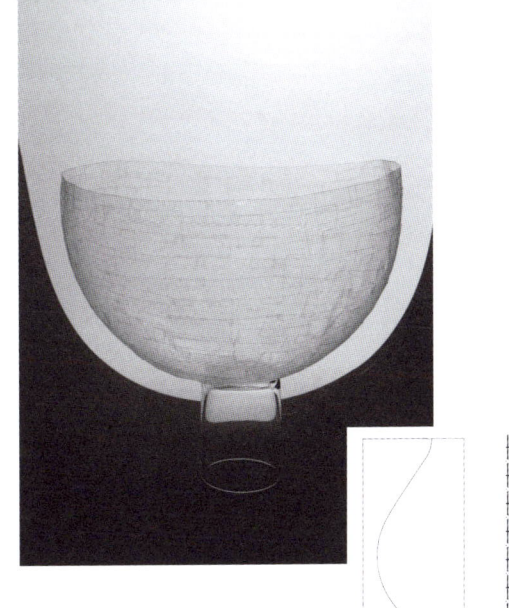

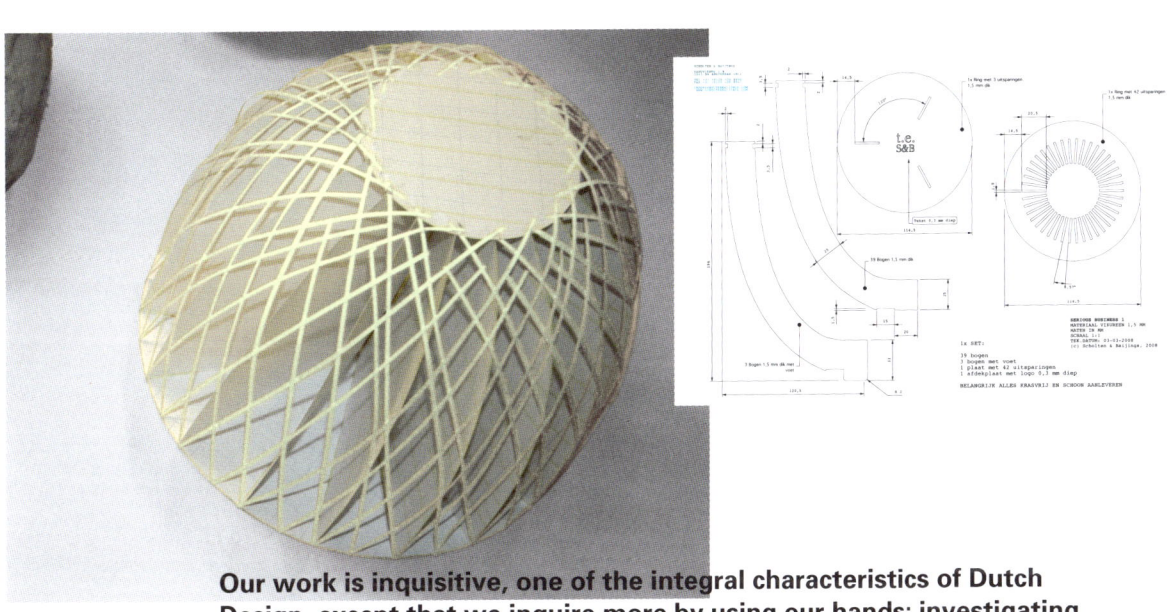

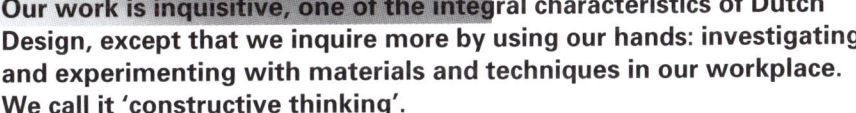

Our work is inquisitive, one of the integral characteristics of Dutch Design, except that we inquire more by using our hands: investigating and experimenting with materials and techniques in our workplace. We call it 'constructive thinking'.
— Stefan Scholten

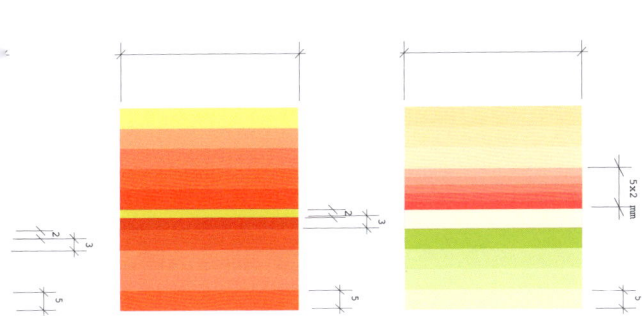

Willow is a naturally oily material that repels paint. We wouldn't have been able to colour it in the past, but today's new paints made it possible.
— Carole Baijings

They are uniquely aware of the fact that the study of material and colour comes before form and function.
— Lidewij Edelkoort, Trend Forecaster

We're not concerned with a glorified notion of 'handicraft', but rather with the surprising results that can only emerge during the process of making the object.
— Stefan Scholten

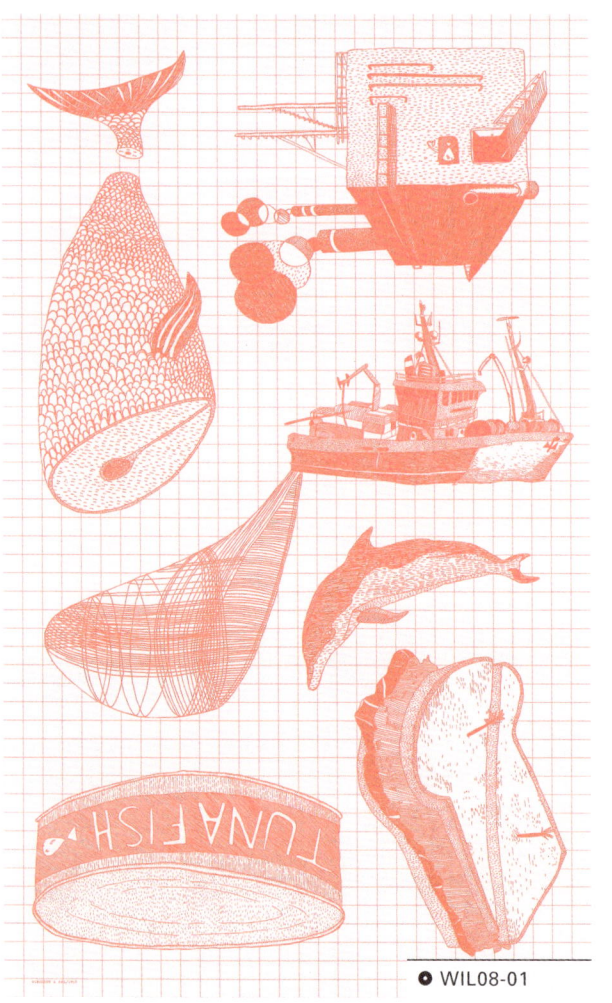

● WIL12-11

● WIL08-01

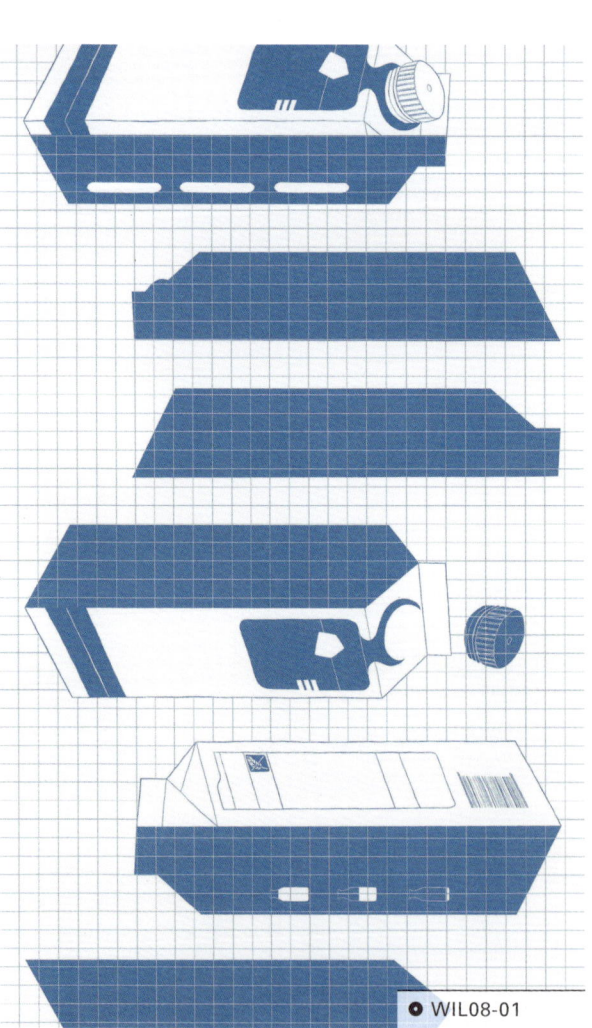

● WIL08-01

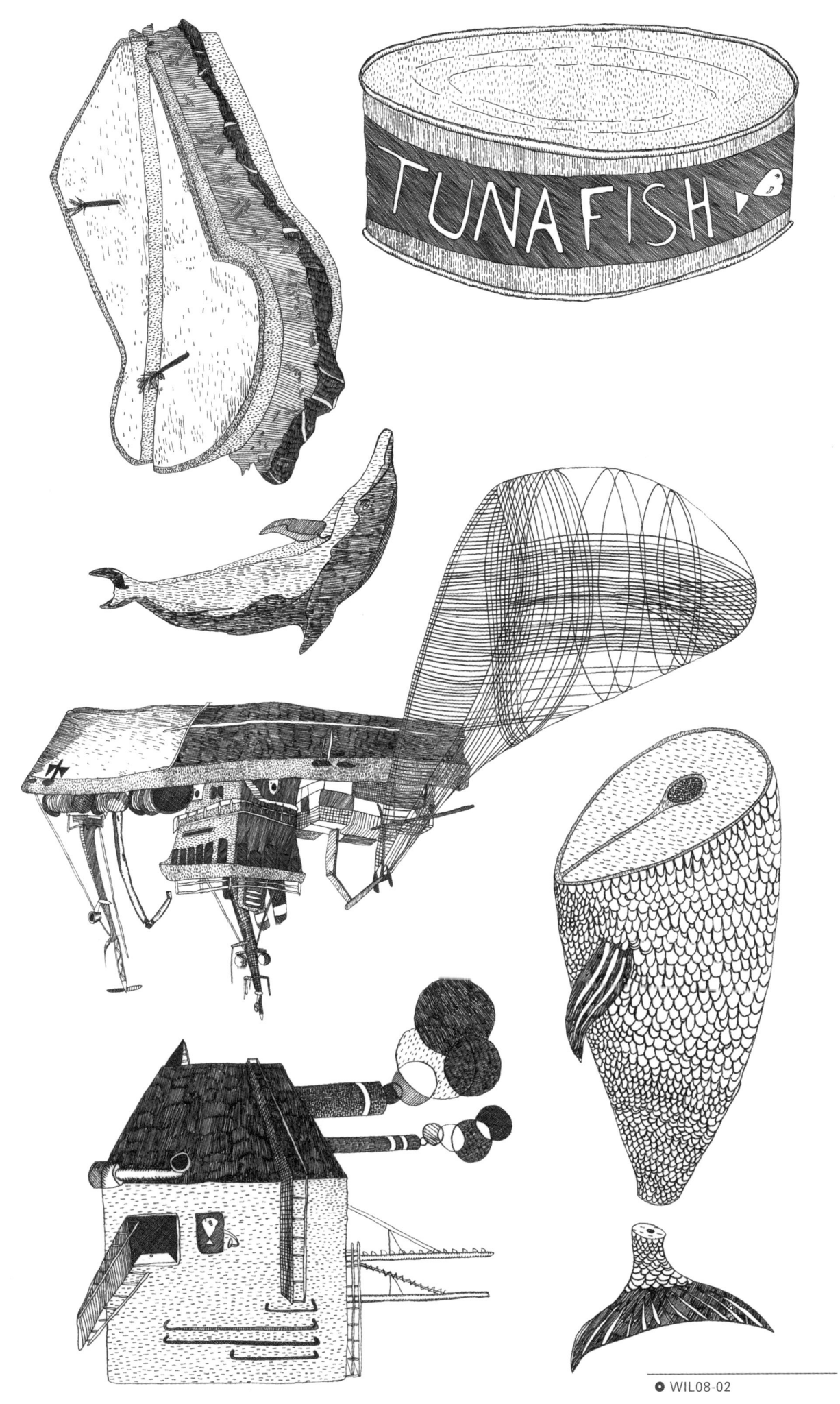

TUNAFISH

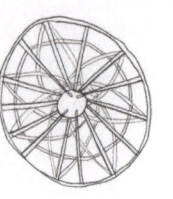

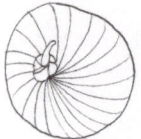

○ WIL08-03

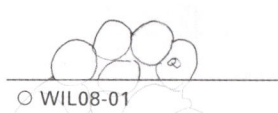

○ WIL08-01

○ WIL08-01

○ WIL08-01

○ WIL08-03

60

○ WIL08-01

● WIL08-04

WIL08-02

WIL08-02

WIL07-12

WIL08-01

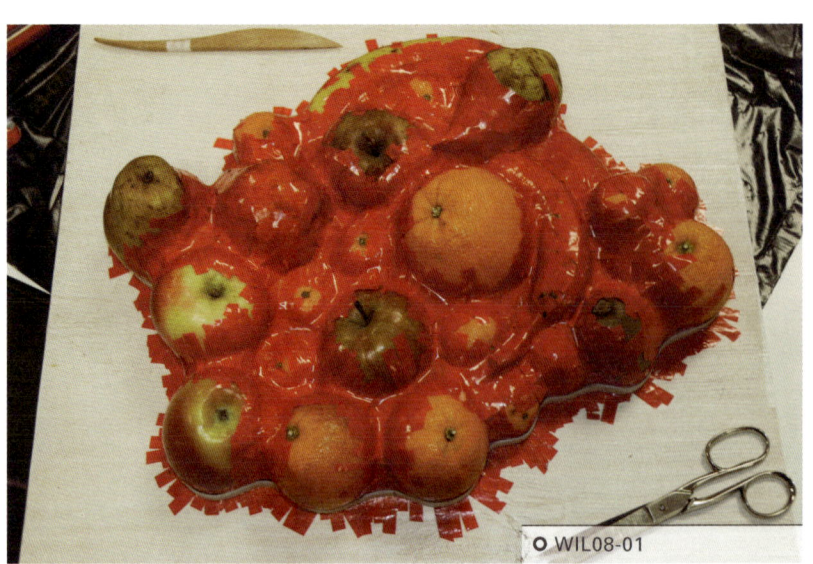

WIL08-01

● WIL08-02

● WIL08-04

● WIL08-02

63

The Fox Carnation
t.c. kan met ribben
Punch Bowl

I look through transparant things
and I feel ok.
Jujiya & Miyagi nr.5   Sucking punch

SdB '08

○ WIL08-01

● WIL08-04

● WIL08-02

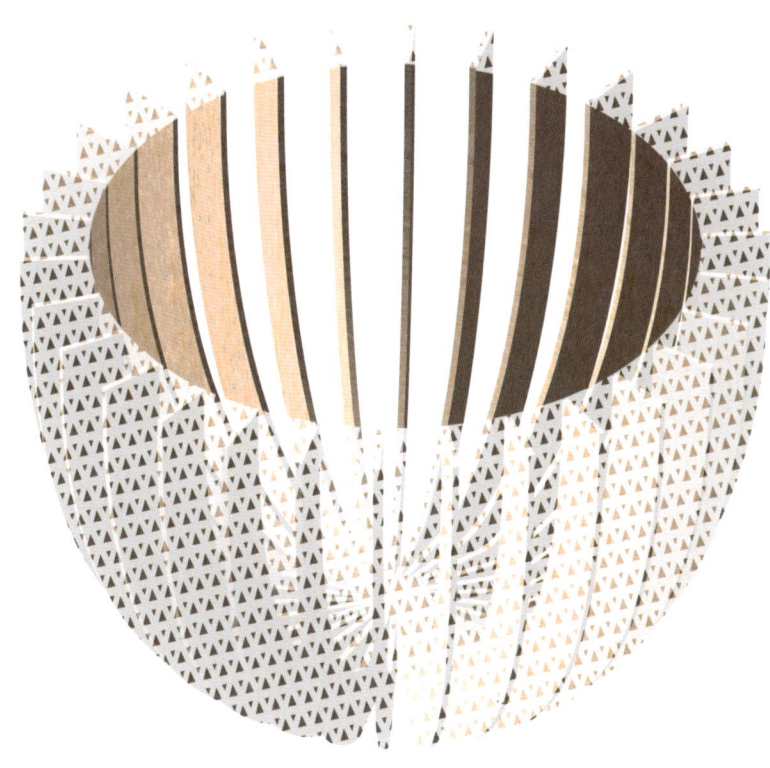

● WIL08-02

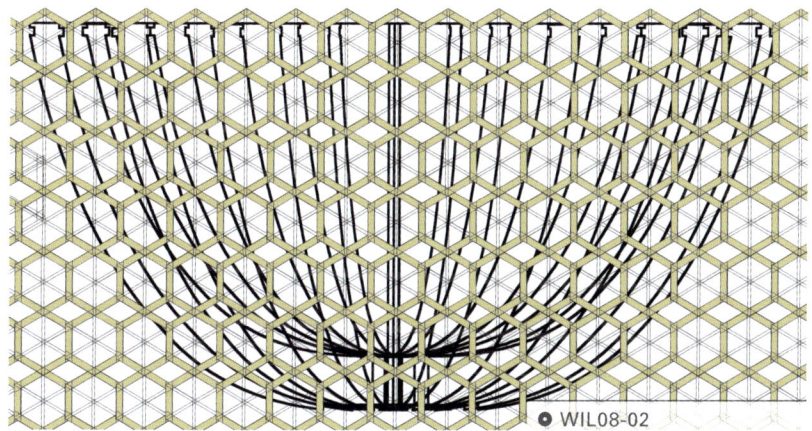

● WIL08-02

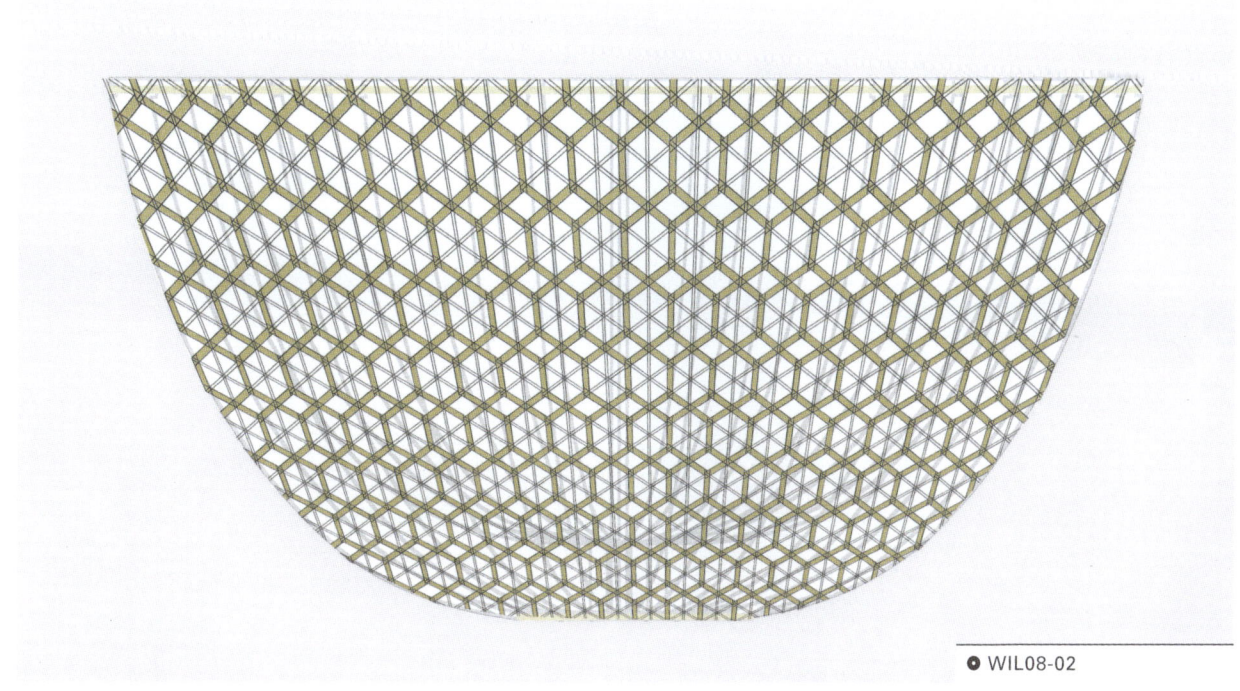

● WIL08-02

● WIL10-09

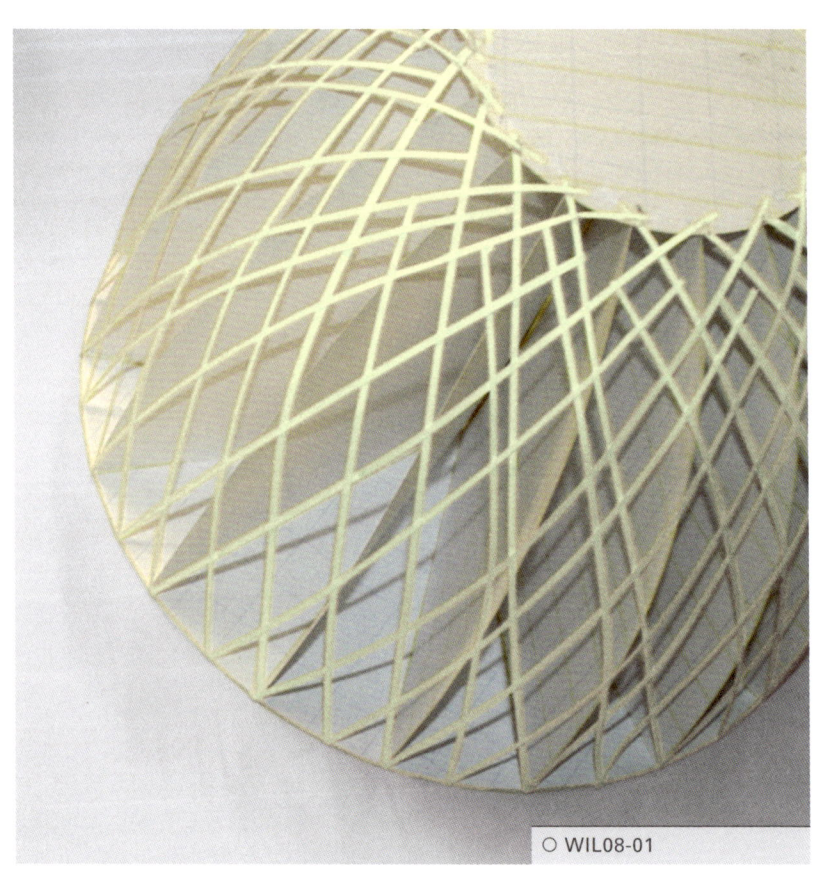

○ WIL08-01

○ WIL08-01

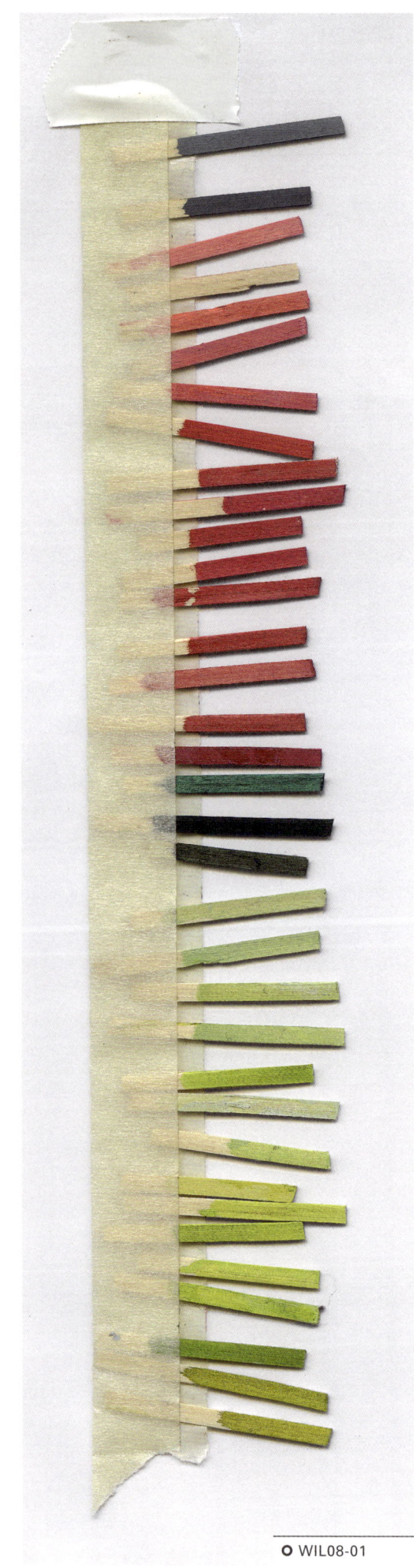

○ WIL08-01

○ WIL08-01

○ WIL08-02

68

WIL08-04

● WIL08-03

Base Green is 6:1 (25g yellow : 4g soft green)

Base pink is (25g white : 5g magenta, 2g Ye.

Base yellow is 25g yellow 5g white

Base orange 25g white 10g orange 2g yellow

} with Acrylic flourescent top coat.

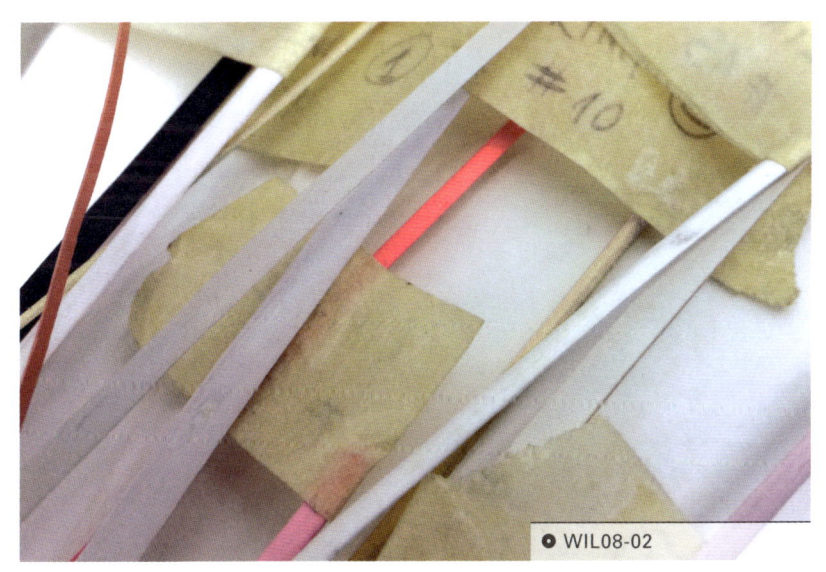

WIL08-02

● WIL08-02

● WIL08-04

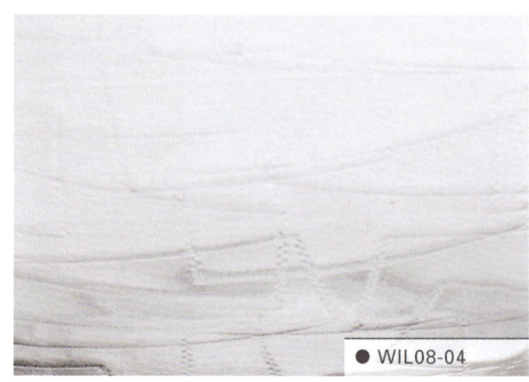
● WIL08-04

● WIL08-04

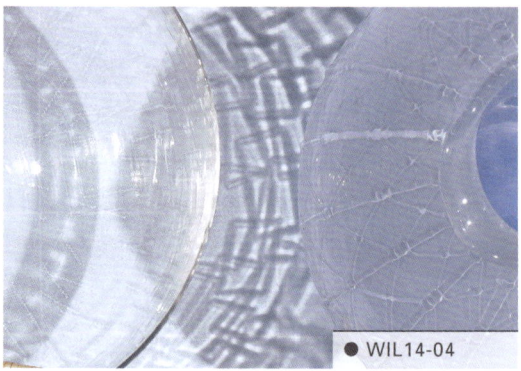
● WIL14-04

● WIL08-02

○ WIL08-01

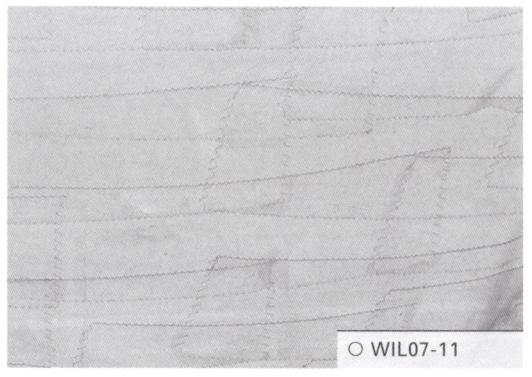
○ WIL07-11

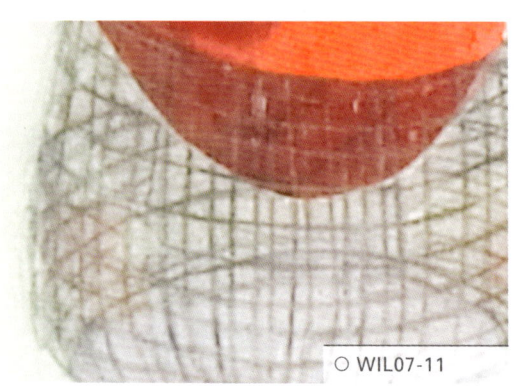
○ WIL07-11

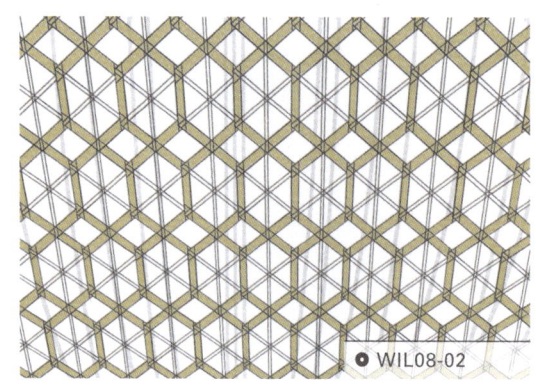
● WIL08-02

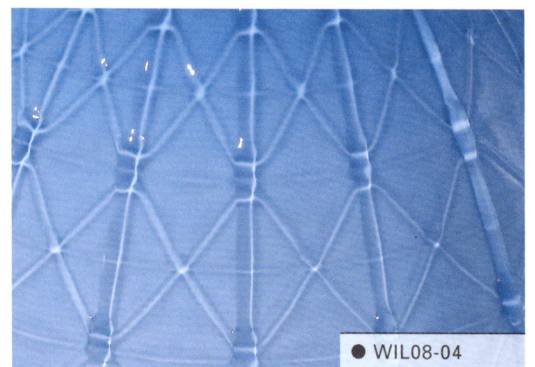
● WIL08-04

● WIL08-01

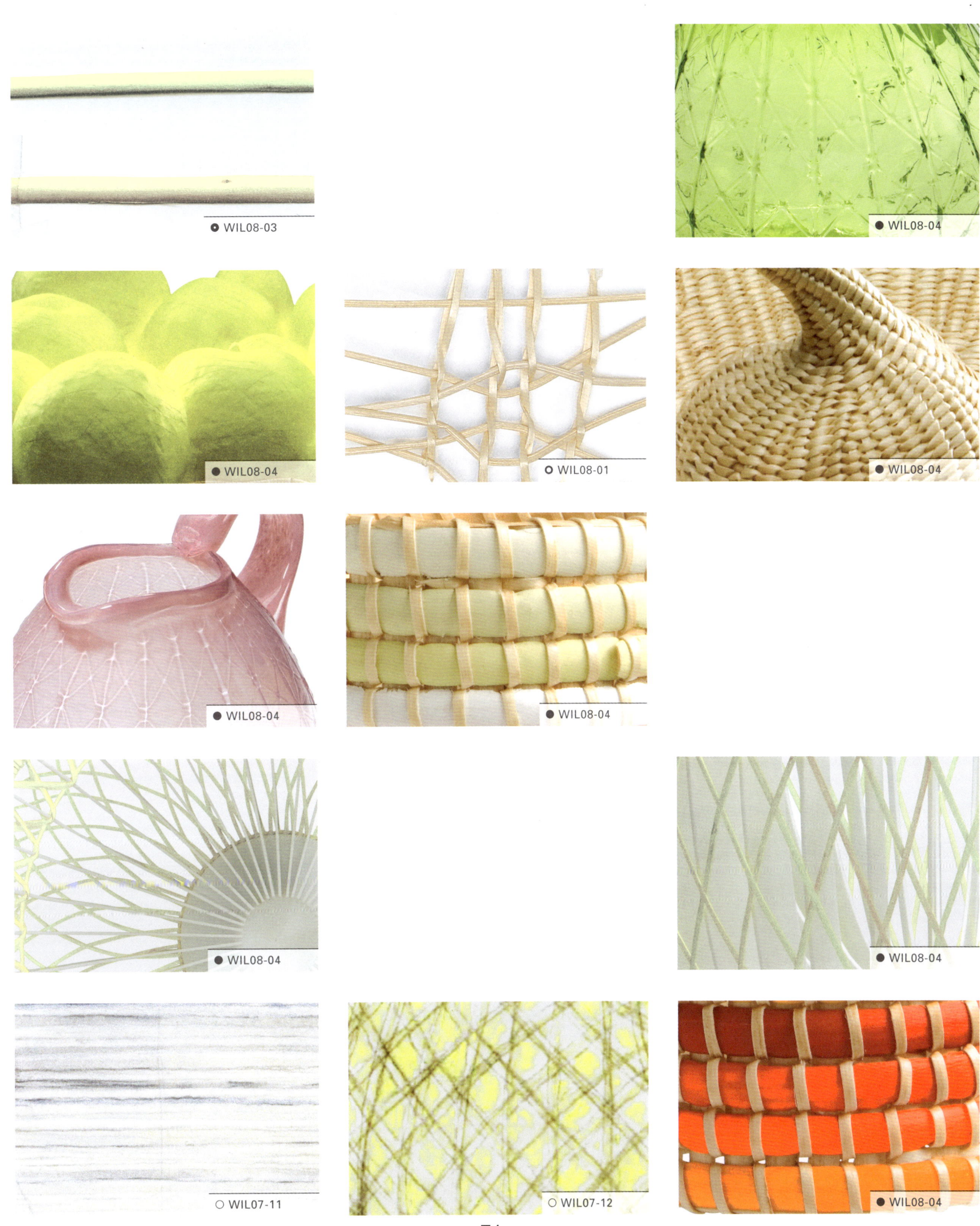

● WIL08-03

● WIL08-04

● WIL08-04

○ WIL08-01

● WIL08-04

● WIL08-04

● WIL08-04

● WIL08-04

● WIL08-04

○ WIL07-11

○ WIL07-12

● WIL08-04

● WIL08-04

● WIL08-04

● WIL08-04

● WIL08-04

● WIL08-04

● WIL08-04

● WIL08-04

● WIL08-04

● WIL08-04

● WIL08-04

● WIL08-04

● WIL08-04

● WIL08-04

● WIL08-04

● WIL08-04

● WIL08-04

● WIL08-01

● WIL08-01

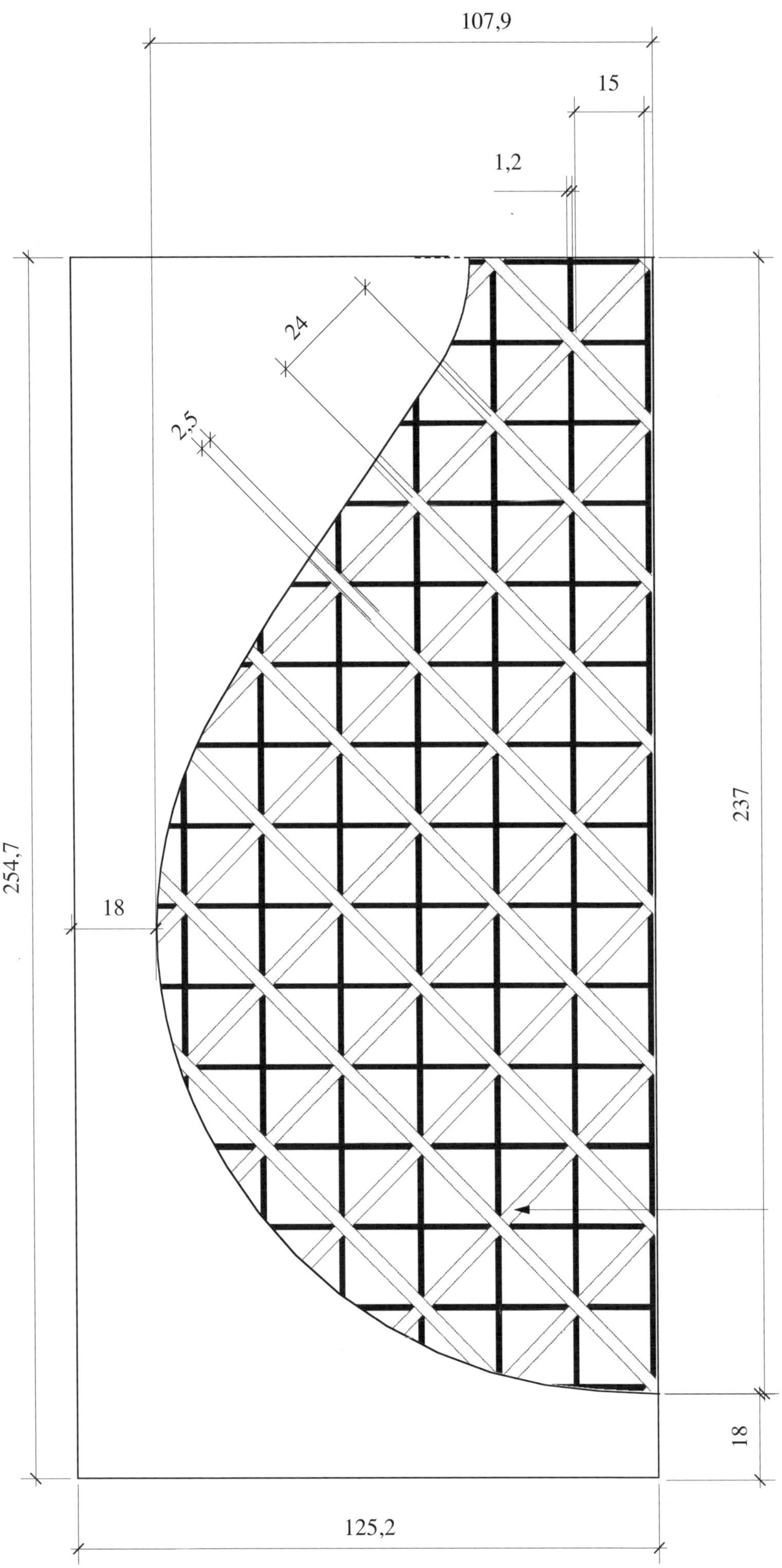

107,9

15

1,2

24

2,5

254,7

237

18

18

125,2

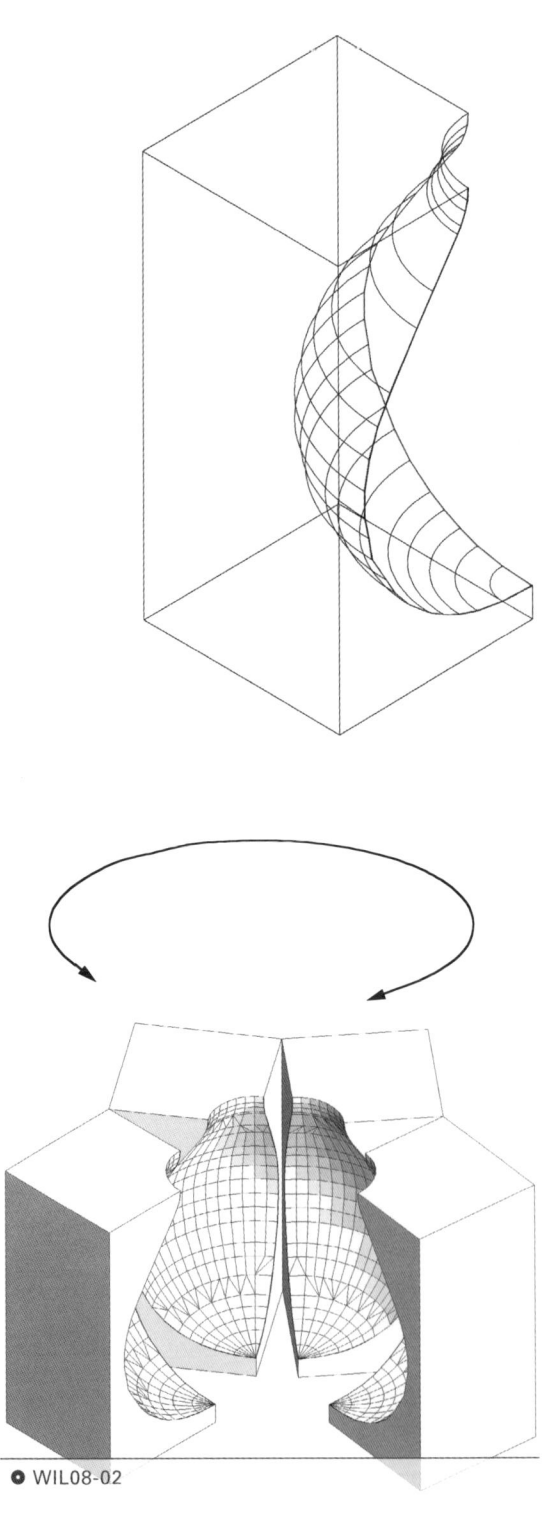

● WIL08-02

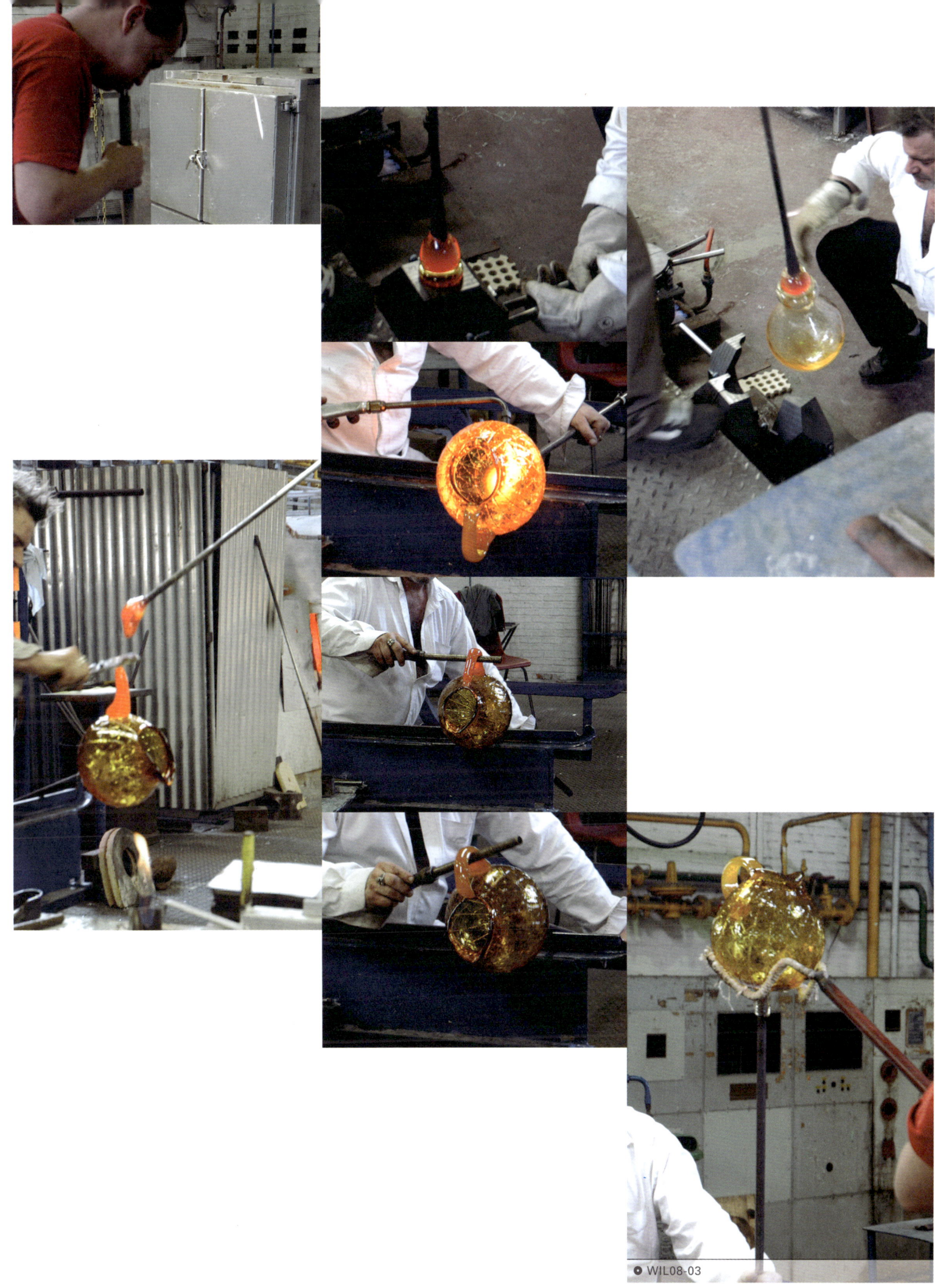

WIL08-03

● WIL08-03

○ WIL08-03

○ WIL08-01

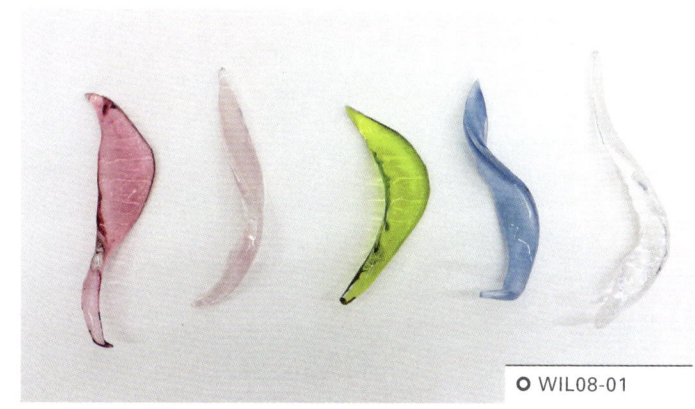

○ WIL08-01

● WIL08-04

○ WIL08-04

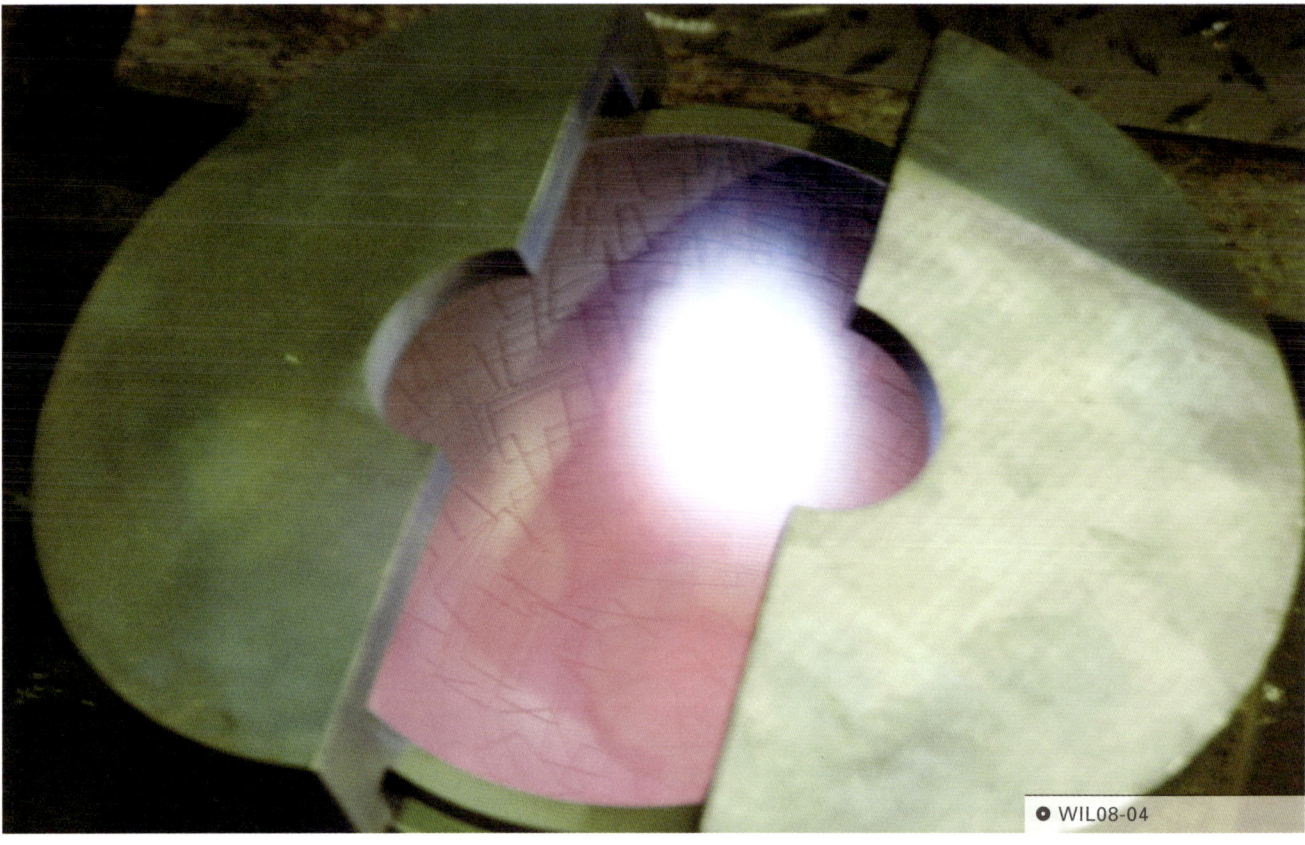

● WIL08-04

● WIL08-04

t.c. plakhandschaal + lepel

SdB 60

○ WIL08-01

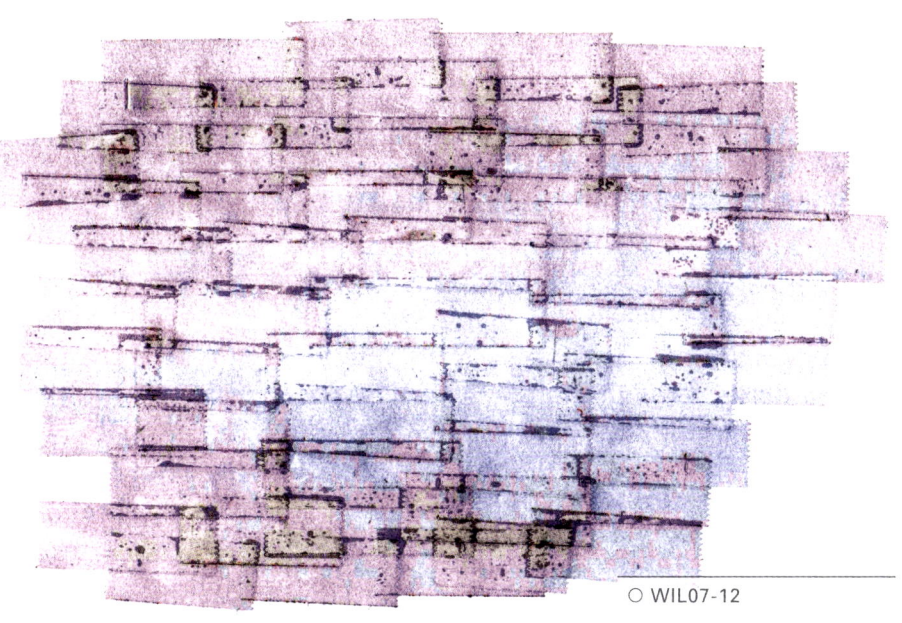

○ WIL07-12

● WIL08-04

○ WIL07-11

● WIL12-11
Detail of Damask 'The Life of a Tuna Fish' tablecloth set, woven at the TextielMuseum, Tilburg, in grey linen with cream-coloured cotton
November 2012

◑ WIL08-01
Design of the Damask 'The Life of a Tuna Fish' collection, commissioned by TextielMuseum, Tilburg
January 2008

◑ WIL08-01
Design of the Damask 'Milk Carton' collection, commissioned by TextielMuseum, Tilburg
January 2008

● WIL08-02
1:1 drawings for Damask 'The Life of a Tuna Fish'
February 2008

● WIL08-03
Definitive form and size of garlic bulb, cast in hard plastic for 'Garlic Queen'
March 2008

○ WIL08-01
First cast garlic bulb was too upright
January 2008

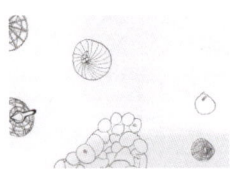

○ WIL08-01
Sketch of the Woven Willow collection
January 2008

○ WIL08-01
Real garlic bulb on plate
January 2008

● WIL08-03
Various garlic bulbs cast in different kinds of plastic, varying in hardness and size
March 2008

○ WIL08-01
First prototype of 'Garlic Queen', porcelain plate with a real garlic bulb fastened with paper tape
January 2008

● WIL08-04
Detail of braided 'Garlic Queen' made of willow rods, shaved precisely to the millimetre
April 2008

○ WIL07-12
Sketch of different components of the Woven Willow collection
December 2007

○ WIL08-02
The polyurethane orange is part of the ultimate composition cast for the 'Fruit Party' model
February 2008

◑ WIL08-02
Polyurethane pear
February 2008

○ WIL08-01
Fruit composition for the 'Fruit Party' fruit bowl
January 2008

○ WIL08-01
Fruit composition with tape; in retrospect, unfortunately not usable for making the 'Fruit Party' model
January 2008

◑ WIL08-02
Detail of silicone mould with fluorescent-yellow papier-mâché
February 2008

● WIL08-04
'Fruit Party' for Thomas Eyck (t.e.)
April 2008

◑ WIL08-02
Silicone mould for papier-mâché 'Fruit Party'
February 2008

○ WIL08-01
Page from sketchbook. Sketch for 'Serious Business', construction in plastic
January 2008

● WIL08-04
'Serious Business' Natural for Thomas Eyck
April 2008

◑ WIL08-02
3D rendering of the inside ribs for 'Serious Business'
February 2008

◑ WIL08-02
Rendering of the ribs with braidwork for 'Serious Business'
February 2008

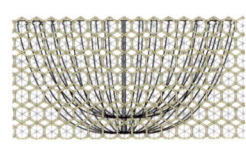

◑ WIL08-02
Rib construction for 'Serious Business' Natural with braidwork design
February 2008

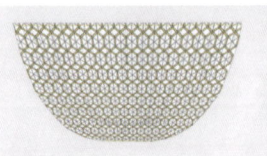

◑ WIL08-02
Design drawing of grid braidwork for 'Serious Business' Natural
February 2008

● WIL10 09
Scholten & Baijings presentation at Woonbeurs Pin 2010 during Woonbeurs Amsterdam
September 2010

○ WIL08-01
First paper model of 'Serious Business' Yellow with fluorescent-yellow printed paper, handmade in the studio
January 2008

○ WIL08-01
Paper prototype of 'Serious Business' for the professional weaver who specializes in fine skeined willow work
January 2008

● WIL10-01
'Serious Business' Yellow with paper model and hand-painted willow rods, photographed by Merel van Beukering for *Frame*, Issue 73 (March/April 2010)
January 2010

○ WIL08-01
Colour samples for willow rod
January 2008

○ WIL08-01
Design for 'Colour Rings'
serviette rings
January 2008

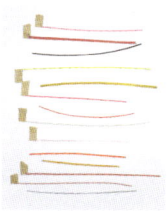

○ WIL08-02
Colour samples on willow
rods for Woven Willow
collection
February 2008

○ WIL08-03
Braided examples for
determining the right
size of 'Colour Rings'
March 2008

● WIL08-04
Different 'Colour Rings'
April 2008

● WIL08-02
Recipes of dyes for willow rod
February 2008

● WIL08-02
Hand-painted willow
rods with colour coding
February 2008

● WIL08-04
Detail of 'Colour Ring' t.e. 048
April 2008

● WIL08-04
Detail of 'Tape Bowl'
April 2008

● WIL08-04
Detail of 'Serious Business'
Red
April 2008

● WIL14-04
Detail of 'Tape Bowl' and
'Grand Bernard' Blue,
photographed by
Scheltens & Abbenes
April 2014

● WIL08-02
Colour samples
on willow rods
February 2008

○ WIL08-01
Detail of 'Garlic Queen'
prototype
January 2008

○ WIL07-11
Detail of 'Tape Bowl'
prototype made from
pieces of tape
November 2007

○ WIL07-11
Detail of sketch for
Woven Willow collection
November 2007

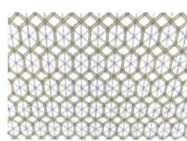

● WIL08-02
Detail design drawing
of grid braidwork for
'Serious Business' Natural
February 2008

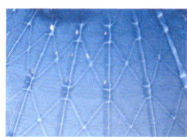

● WIL08-04
Detail of 'Grand Bernard' Blue
April 2008

● WIL08-01
Detail of Damask 'Milk Carton'
January 2008

● WIL08-03
Detail of willow rods
painted in fluorescent yellow
March 2008

● WIL08-04
Detail of 'Fruit Party'
April 2008

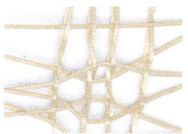

○ WIL08-01
Sample of braidwork
January 2008

● WIL08-04
Detail of 'Garlic Queen'
April 2008

● WIL08-04
Detail of spout and handle
of 'Grand Bernard' Pink
April 2008

● WIL08-04
Detail of 'Colour Ring' t.e. 052
April 2008

● WIL08-04
Detail of 'Serious Business'
Yellow, top view
April 2008

● WIL08-04
Detail of 'Serious Business'
Yellow
April 2008

○ WIL07-11
Detail of sketch for
'Tape Bowl'
November 2007

○ WIL07-12
Detail sketch of
'Grand Bernard'
December 2007

● WIL08-04
Detail of 'Colour Ring' t.e. 051
April 2008

● WIL08-04
'Serious Business' Yellow
April 2008

● WIL08-04
'Serious Business' Red
April 2008

● WIL08-04
'Colour Ring' t.e. 051
April 2008

● WIL08-04
'Colour Ring' t.e. 052
April 2008

● WIL08-04
'Colour Ring' t.e. 048
April 2008

● WIL08-04
'Colour Ring' t.e. 049
April 2008

● WIL08-04
'Colour Ring' t.e. 050
April 2008

● WIL08-04
'Colour Ring' t.e. 053
April 2008

● WIL08-04
'Grand Bernard' Transparent
April 2008

● WIL08-04
'Grand Bernard' Pink
April 2008

● WIL08-04
'Grand Bernard' Green
April 2008

● WIL08-04
'Grand Bernard' Blue
April 2008

● WIL08-04
'Garlic Queen'
April 2008

● WIL08-04
'Tape Bowl'
April 2008

● WIL08-04
'Fruit Party'
April 2008

● WIL08-01
Damask 'The Life
of a Tuna Fish'
January 2008

● WIL08-01
Damask 'Milk Carton'
January 2008

● WIL08-07
Presentation on the occasion
of the purchase of the Woven
Willow collection
by Zuiderzee Museum,
photographed by Inga Powilleit
July 2008

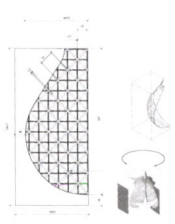

◉ WIL08-02
Technical drawing and 3D
rendering of grid in
'Grand Bernard' model
February 2008

◉ WIL08-03
Production process of
'Grand Bernard' with
unique spout and handle
March 2008

● WIL08-03
'Grand Bernard' Pink
March 2008

○ WIL07-12
Sketch of 'Grand Bernard'
December 2007

◉ WIL08-03
'Grand Bernard' with colour
samples serving as examples
for the production process at
Leerdam factory
March 2008

○ WIL08-01
Page from sketchbook.
Sketches for the production
process of the 'Grand Bernard'
model
January 2008

◉ WIL08-01
Colour samples
for 'Grand Bernard'
January 2008

● WIL08-04
Overview of the colours
selected for the production
of 'Grand Bernard'
April 2008

◉ WIL08-04
Production process
of 'Tape Bowl'
April 2008

◉ WIL08-04
Red hot model for
handblowing the 'Tape Bowl'
April 2008

◉ WIL08-04
Handblown 'Tape Bowl'
before being annealed
April 2008

○ WIL08-01
Page from sketchbook.
Drawings for the production
process of the 'Tape Bowl'
and glass spoon
January 2008

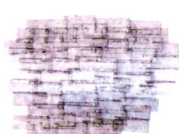

○ WIL07-12
Structure of small
pieces of tape fastened
on top of each other
December 2007

○ WIL07-11
Prototype of 'Tape Bowl'
made from small pieces
of tape
November 2007

● WIL14-04
Woven Willow collection,
excluding 'Fruit Party' and
Damask 'The Life of a Tuna
Fish', photographed by
Scheltens & Abbenes
April 2014

VEGETABLES

VEGETABLES (2009)

Studio Project/Artisanal Product
Numbered edition. The set consists of three rhubarb stalks, two lemons,
    a cut and a whole red cabbage, an artichoke, and two lettuce leaves
Materials/Techniques: Textile, yarn, foam, felt, metal/painting, stitching,
    embroidery, sewing, gluing
Colours: Various
Client/Producer: Studio project, available from Scholten & Baijings
    (the Netherlands)

Why a rhubarb stalk, an artichoke, a red cabbage, a lemon and a lettuce leaf? From a distance they look deceptively real, and the only question they prompt is: 'Why are they presented in a setting of design objects?'

Up close the textile fabric becomes visible, suggesting the texture of a living natural leaf, the embroidery threads bring veins to life, and stitching makes the fabric of the cabbage crinkle into dozens of curls. The Vegetables series is a feast for the eyes. The viewer marvels at the hyper-realistic, ingenious translations of reality into suggestion, and admires the huge range of techniques, used optimally to create illusory effects.

The creation of beauty seems to be the prime function of Vegetables. At the same time, the objects invite us to look for qualities in everyday life that we would otherwise hardly notice. The imagination triumphs in these fine examples of craftsmanship, through which Scholten & Baijings also make evident the extent of both their talents, while hinting at their larger ambition as designers: the particularization of everyday life. Red cabbage, lettuce leaves – they lie ready for use on the kitchen counter, we process them when making our meals, but how much time do we spend contemplating the beauty of their details? Do we take time to examine the layers of the cabbage, the curves and contours of the artichoke, the subtle range and colour gradation on the rhubarb stalk, the strange bulges of the lemon skin, the speckles strewn across its surface?

We look, but we don't see. At least, not as accurately as Scholten & Baijings. Through their handmade objects they encourage us to look with new eyes at something as simple as the visual richness of the vegetables displayed at the greengrocer's.

Once you start unpeeling nature, you see how refined the colours are.
— Carole Baijings

We started thinking about how a vegetable actually grows. Essentially, what we did was to rebuild a piece of nature.
— Stefan Scholten

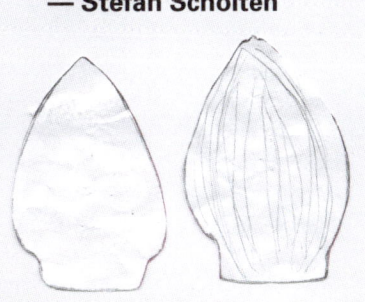

You can give colour to textile materials by dyeing them. But what happens when you change their texture? A shiny surface casts a different reflection than a rough one.
— Stefan Scholten

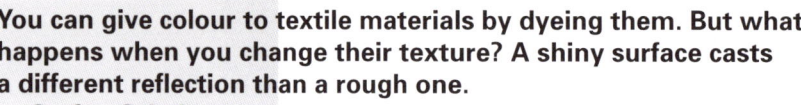

This work is something of a finger exercise for items that are being developed in collaboration with industry. Vegetables is a clear example of this: a textile series of deceptively 'real' vegetables.
— Carole Baijings

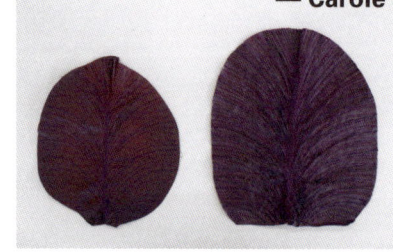

The red stem that becomes a paler and paler pink as it reaches the leaf, except for the darker veins. The leaf that curls whimsically and slowly spreads from tips of green to become soft yellow and, finally, pastel pink. It's only when the half-round, slightly trompe l'oeil stalks are right under your nose that the woven texture and the stitching become visible.
— Jeroen Junte, Journalist

We may be showing work in museums, but it is not art.
— Stefan Scholten

○ VEG09-10

○ VEG09-09

○ VEG09-09

92

● VEG09-10

● VEG09-10

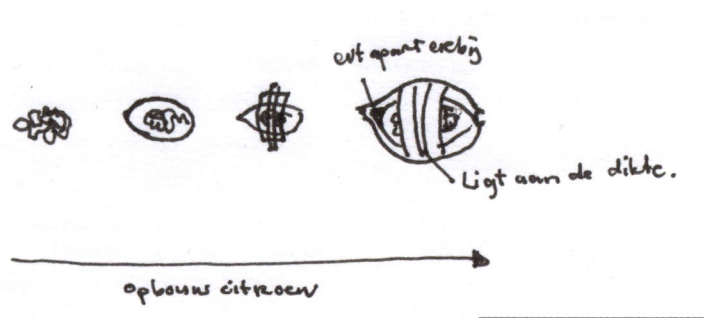

evt apart erbij

Ligt aan de dikte.

opbouw citroen

● VEG10-06

○ VEG09-09

stitched fabric
cream white

100% cotton

stitched fabric
colored by hand

100% cotton

● VEG10-06

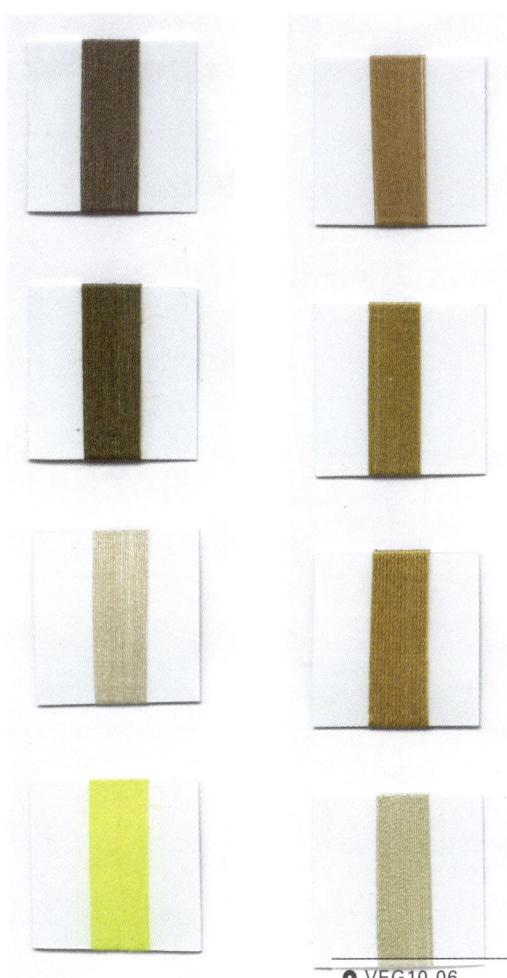

● VEG10-06

● VEG09-11

VEG09-10

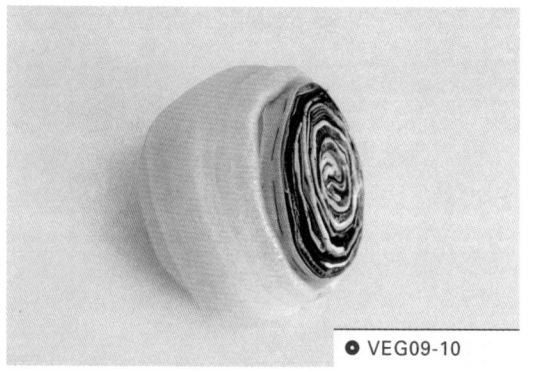

VEG09-10

VEG09-10

VEG09-10

● VEG09-11

● VEG09-11

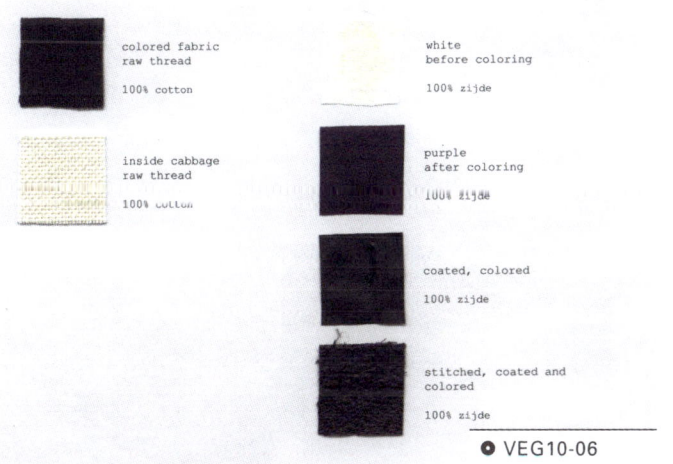

colored fabric
raw thread

100% cotton

inside cabbage
raw thread

100% cotton

white
before coloring

100% zijde

purple
after coloring

100% zijde

coated, colored

100% zijde

stitched, coated and
colored

100% zijde

● VEG10-06

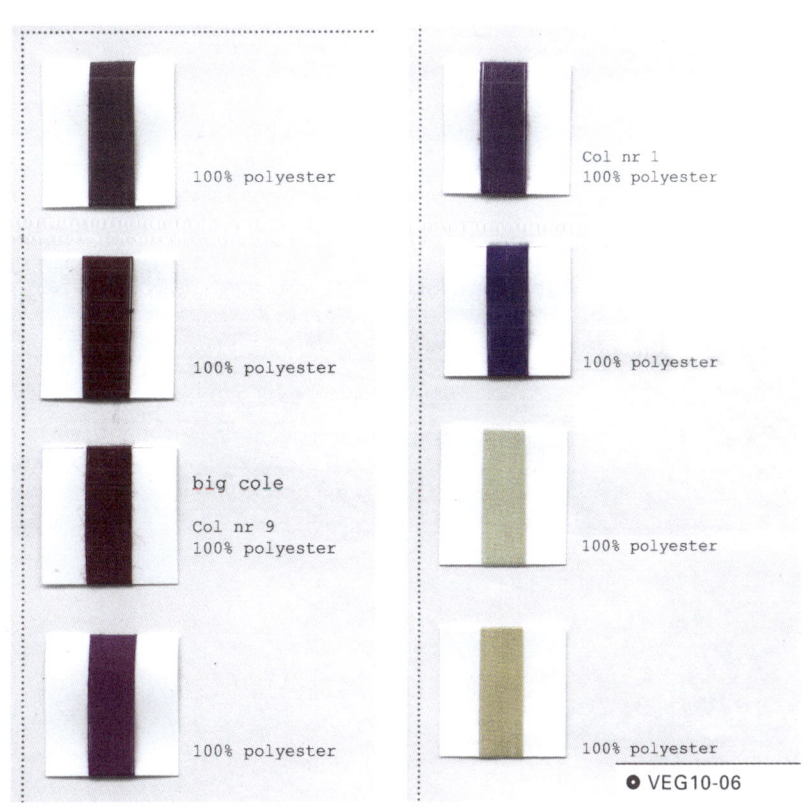

100% polyester

100% polyester

big cole

Col nr 9
100% polyester

100% polyester

Col nr 1
100% polyester

100% polyester

100% polyester

100% polyester

● VEG10-06

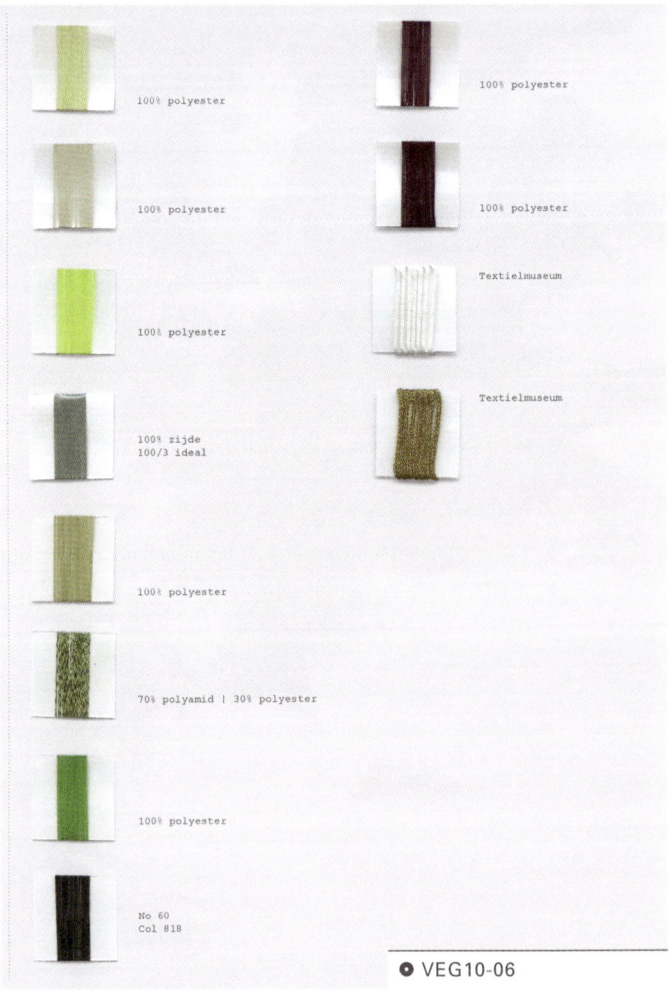

● VEG09-11

	100% polyester		100% polyester
	100% polyester		100% polyester
	100% polyester		Textielmuseum
	100% zijde 100/3 ideal		Textielmuseum
	100% polyester		
	70% polyamid | 30% polyester		
	100% polyester		
	No 60 Col 818		

● VEG10-06

● VEG09-11

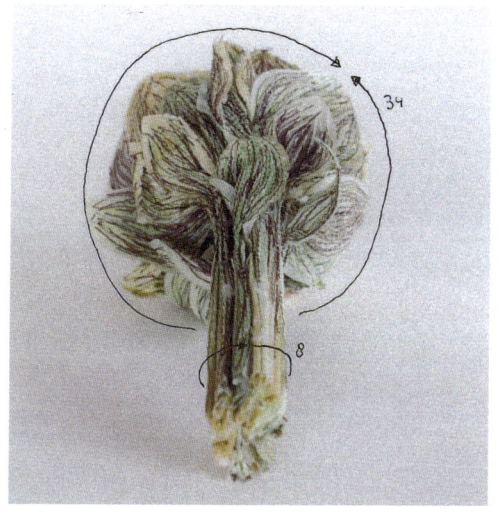

34

8

18

31   13

● VEG10-06

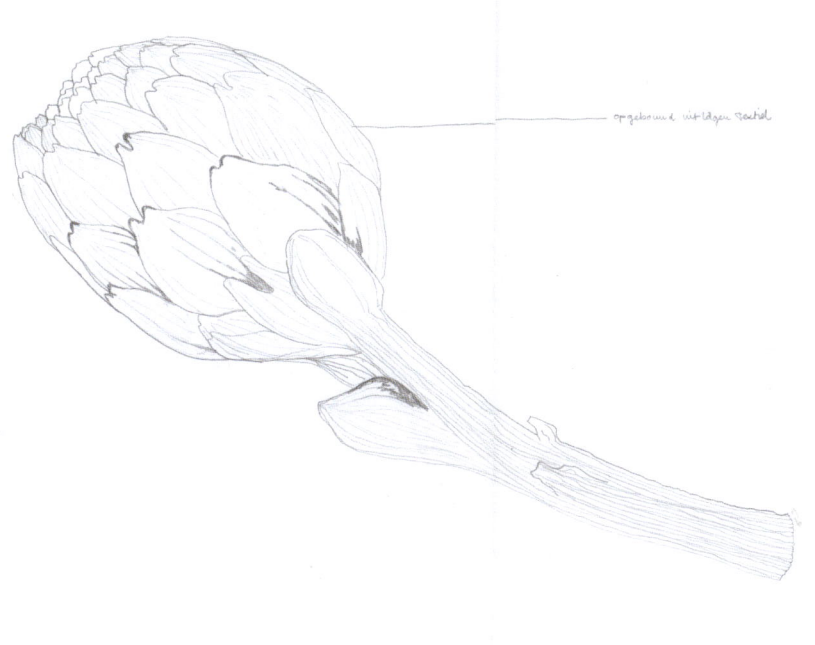

opgebomme ribridger Zachal

○ VEG09-09

VEG09-09

col

sil

col
sti

sil

VEG09-09

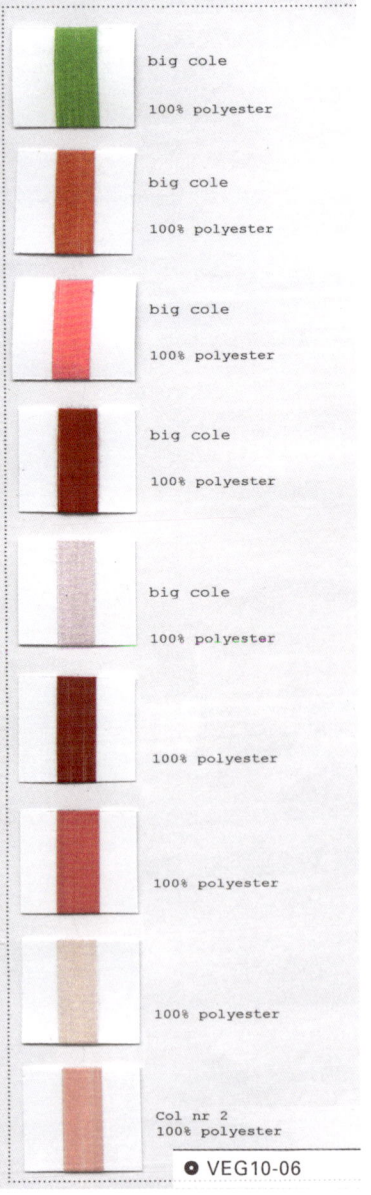

big cole

100% polyester

big cole

100% polyester

big cole

100% polyester

big cole

100% polyester

big cole

100% polyester

100% polyester

100% polyester

100% polyester

Col nr 2
100% polyester

VEG10-06

VEG09-10

100

● VEG09-11

● VEG09-10

● VEG09-10
Silk fabrics dyed in different shades of green for the inside and outside of the lettuce leaves
October 2009

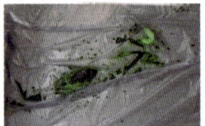

○ VEG09-09
Custom-mixed green dye to colour the silk fabrics used for the lettuce leaves
September 2009

○ VEG09-09
Embroidery tests on a variety of different fabrics for creating the structure of the lettuce leaves
September 2009

● VEG10-01
Lettuce leaf from the Vegetables series, photographed by Merel van Beukering (MB) for *Frame*, Issue 73 (March/April 2010)
January 2010

● VEG09-10
Outside of lemon No. 2, made in the studio
October 2009

● VEG09-10
Outside of lemon No. 1, made in the studio
October 2009

○ VEG09-09
Test for lemon skin No. 2, dyed, embroidered an sewn
September 2009

● VEG10-06
Sketch showing the layers of the lemon's interior that gives it the right firmness
June 2010

● VEG10-06
Hand-dyed cotton for lemon No. 2
June 2010

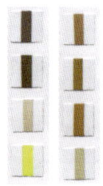

● VEG10-06
Some of the yarns used for the skin and the protruding end of lemon No. 2
June 2010

● VEG09-11
Lemon No. 1 and lemon No. 2 from the Vegetables series, photographed by Yves Krol
November 2009

● VEG09-10
Red cabbage leaf, dyed in-house by hand, coated, embroidered with different colour yarns and cut into shape
October 2009

● VEG09-10
The cut red cabbage consists of various coloured layers of fabric, modelled into shape and embedded in foam
October 2009

● VEG09-10
The robust shape is surrounded by handmade leaves
October 2009

● VEG09-10
All of the different leaves are attached to each other in their appropriate places
October 2009

● VEG09-11
Cut red cabbage and red cabbage from the Vegetables series (YK)
November 2009

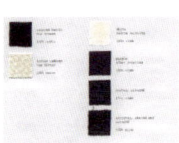

● VEG10-06
All of the fabrics used for the whole red cabbage
June 2010

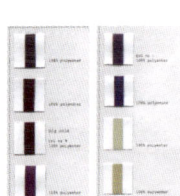

● VEG10-06
All of the different yarns used for the cut red cabbage
June 2010

● VEG09-11
Artichoke from the Vegetables series (YK)
November 2009

● VEG09-11
Detail of the embroidered leaves
November 2009

● VEG10-06
Different yarns used for the leaves of the artichoke
June 2010

● VEG10-06
Dimensions of artichoke
June 2010

○ VEG09-09
Sketch showing the build-up of the textile layers of the artichoke leaves
September 2009

● VEG09-09
Dyed and embroidered silk for the rhubarb leaf
September 2009

● VEG09-09
Dyed colour gradients on silk and translucent plastic for the rhubarb stalks
September 2009

● VEG09-10
Assembly of the rhubarb stalk, including the green leaf (MB)
October 2009

● VEG10-06
Yarns used for the underside of the rhubarb stalks
June 2010

● VEG09-11
Rhubarbs from the Vegetables series (YK)
November 2009

○ VEG09-10
'The making of' the rhubarbs (MB)
October 2009

● VEG14-04
Vegetables, photographed by Scheltens & Abbenes
April 2014

COLOUR WOOD

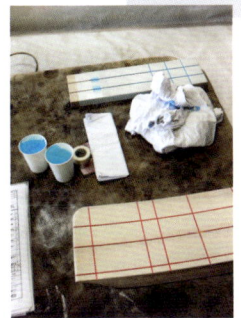

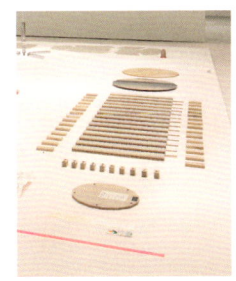

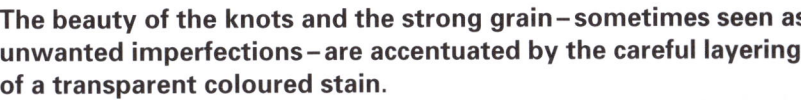

The beauty of the knots and the strong grain – sometimes seen as unwanted imperfections – are accentuated by the careful layering of a transparent coloured stain.
— Stefan Scholten

Subtle. Sensitive. Strong.
— Jeanne Tan, Journalist

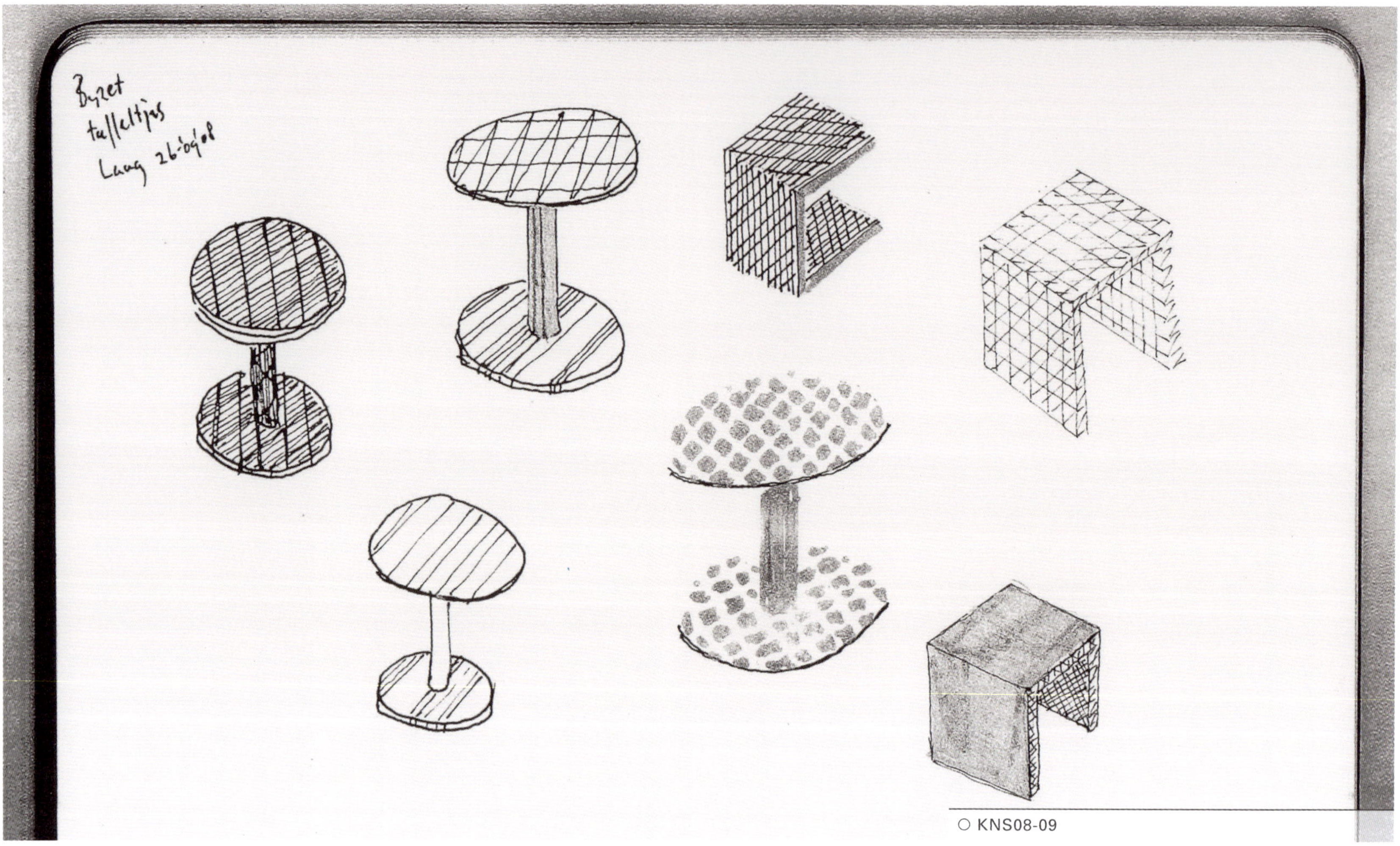

Byret
talleltjes
Laug 26·09·08

○ KNS08-09

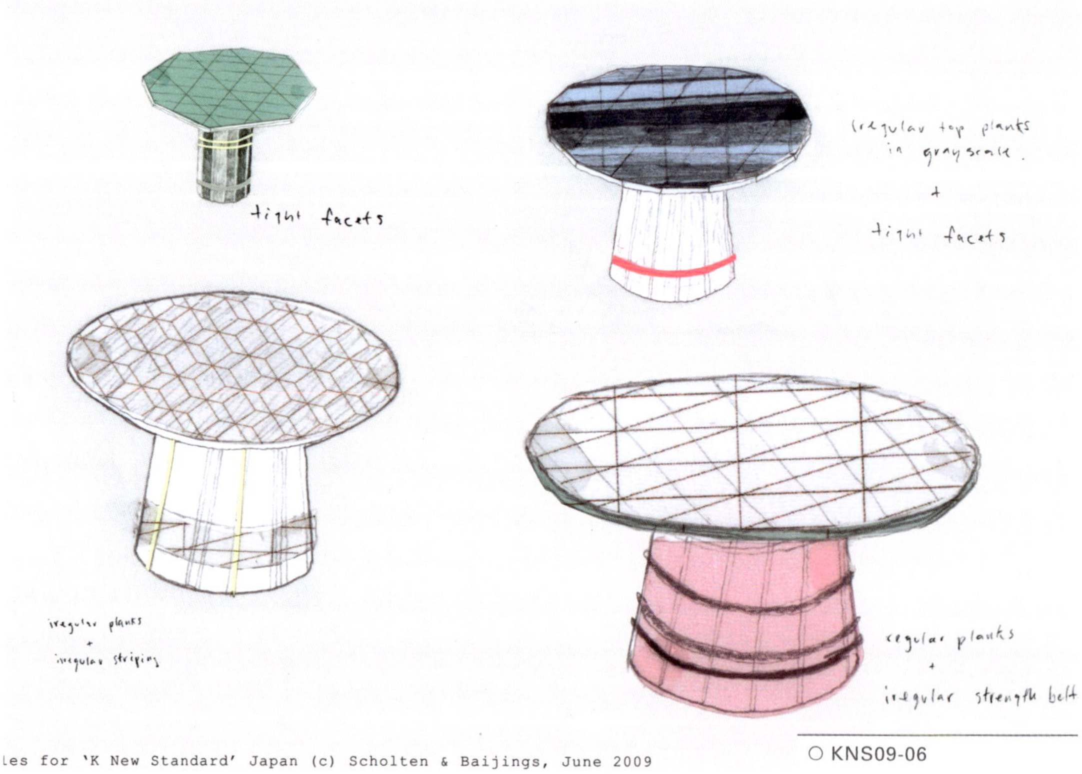

tight facets

iregular top planks
in grayscale.
+
tight facets

iregular planks
+
iregular striping

regular planks
+
iregular strength belt

les for 'K New Standard' Japan (c) Scholten & Baijings, June 2009

○ KNS09-06

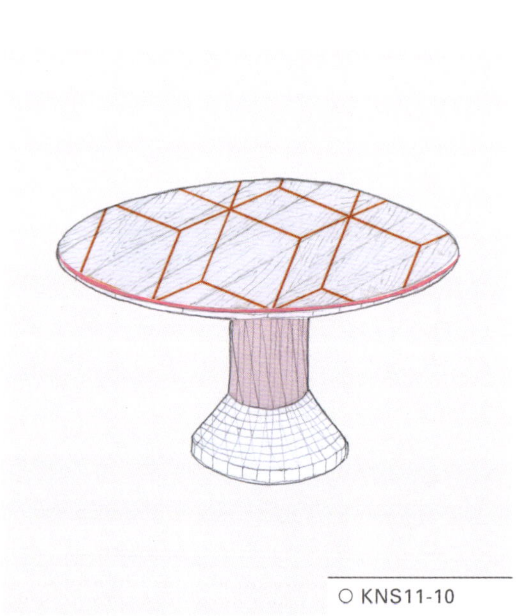

○ KNS11-10

○ KNS08-10

○ KNS08-10

○ KNS11-11

○ KNS09-07

○ KNS08-10

○ KNS09-07

○ KNS08-10

○ KNS08-10

○ KNS09-07

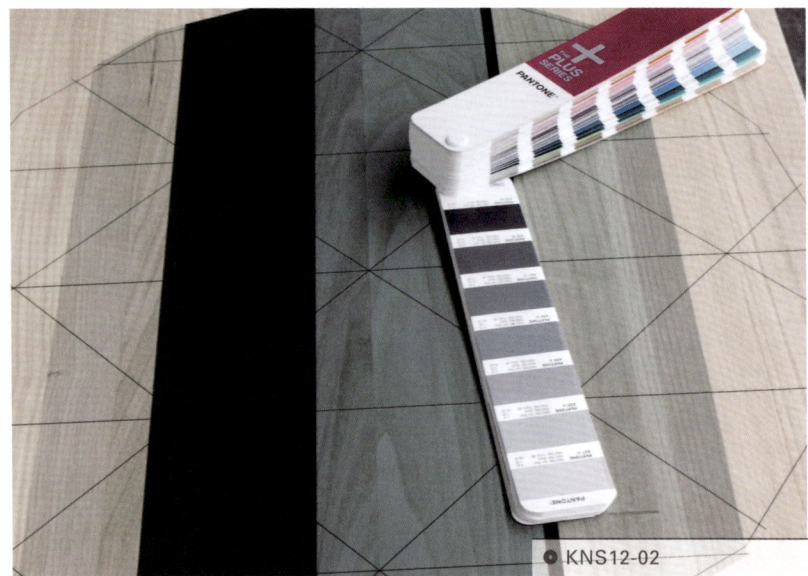

KNS12-02

KNS12-02

KNS09-10

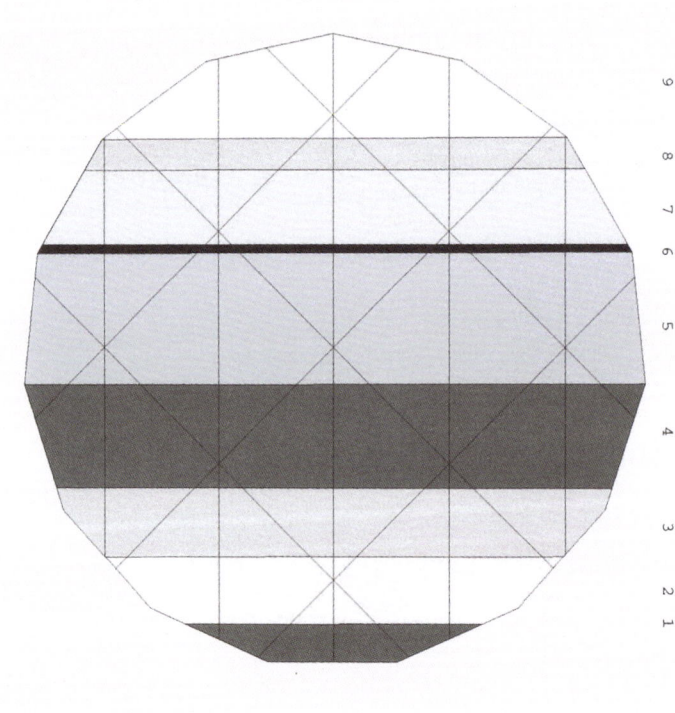

KNS09-09

● KNS09-10

○ KNS09-09

○ KNS09-09

○ KNS09-09

● KNS12-04

KNS09-10

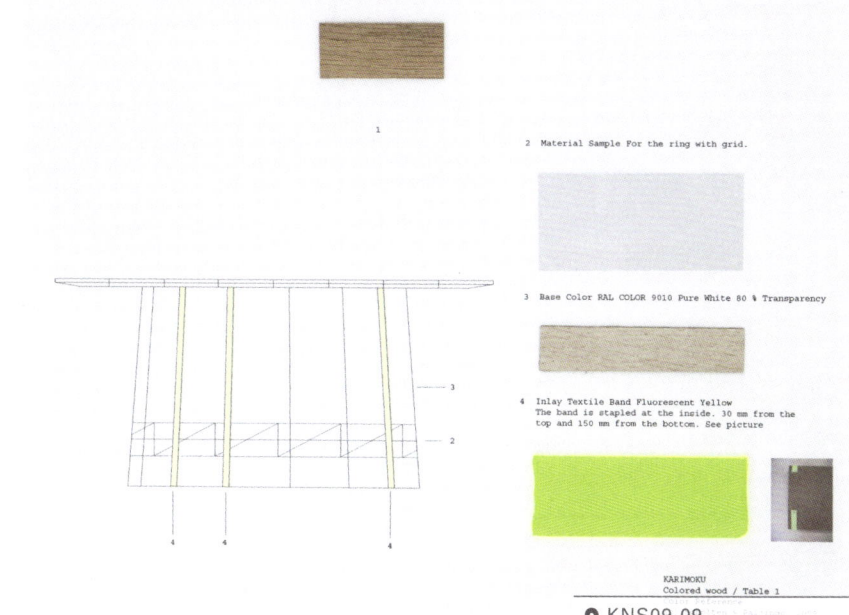

1

2 Material Sample For the ring with grid.

3 Base Color RAL COLOR 9010 Pure White 80 % Transparency

4 Inlay Textile Band Fluorescent Yellow
   The band is stapled at the inside. 30 mm from the
   top and 150 mm from the bottom. See picture

KARIMOKU
Colored wood / Table 1

KNS09-09

KNS09-10

KNS09-10

KNS09-10

● KNS12-02

● KNS11-09

● KNS12-02

● KNS09-10

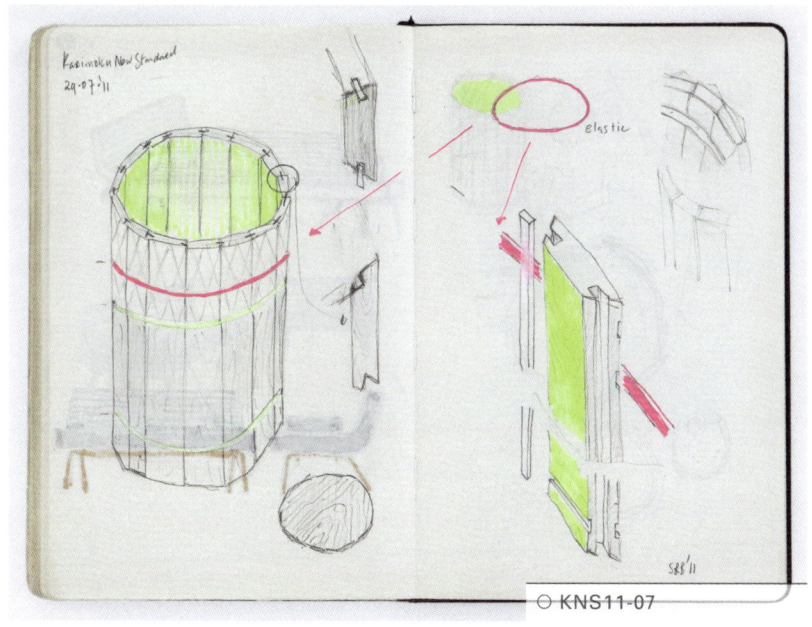

○ KNS11-07

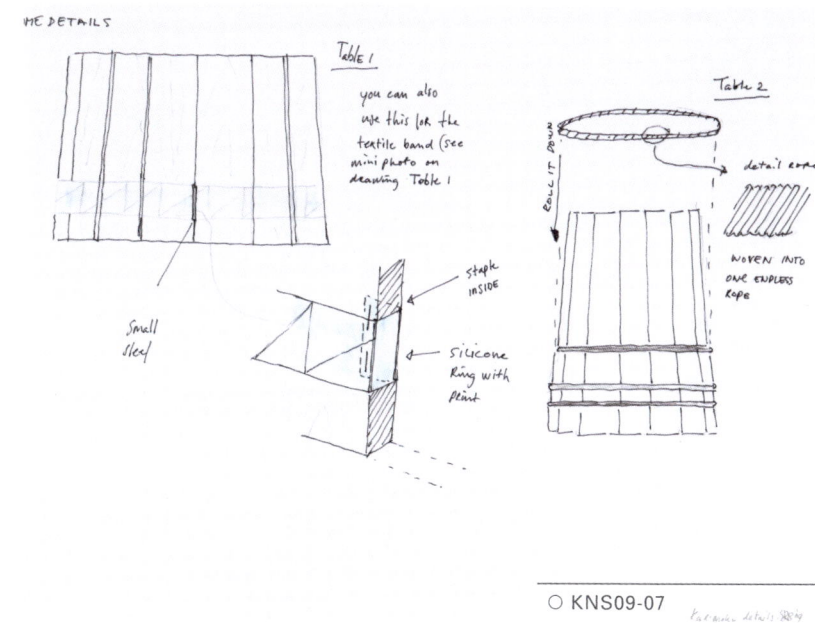

THE DETAILS

Table 1

you can also use this for the textile band (see mini photo on drawing Table 1)

Small steel

staple inside

silicone Ring with plant

Table 2

ROLL IT PRIN

detail rope

WOVEN INTO ONE ENDLESS ROPE

○ KNS09-07

Katumu details S&M

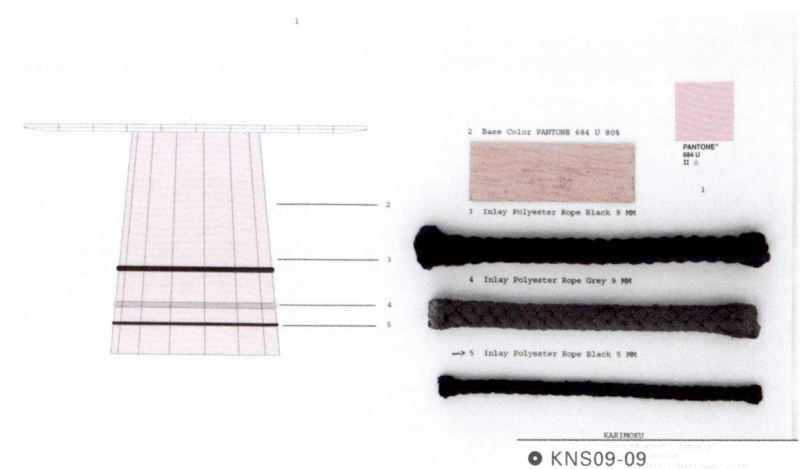

2 Base Color PANTONE 684 U 80%

PANTONE 684 U II

3 Inlay Polyester Rope Black 9 MM

4 Inlay Polyester Rope Grey 9 MM

→ 5 Inlay Polyester Rope Black 5 MM

KARIMOKU

● KNS09-09

● KNS12-02

KNS12-02

KNS11-07

120

○ KNS10-09

○ KNS10-09

○ KNS10-11

○ KNS11-03

KNS11-03

KNS11-03

KNS10-05

KNS12-02

KNS12-02

KNS12-02

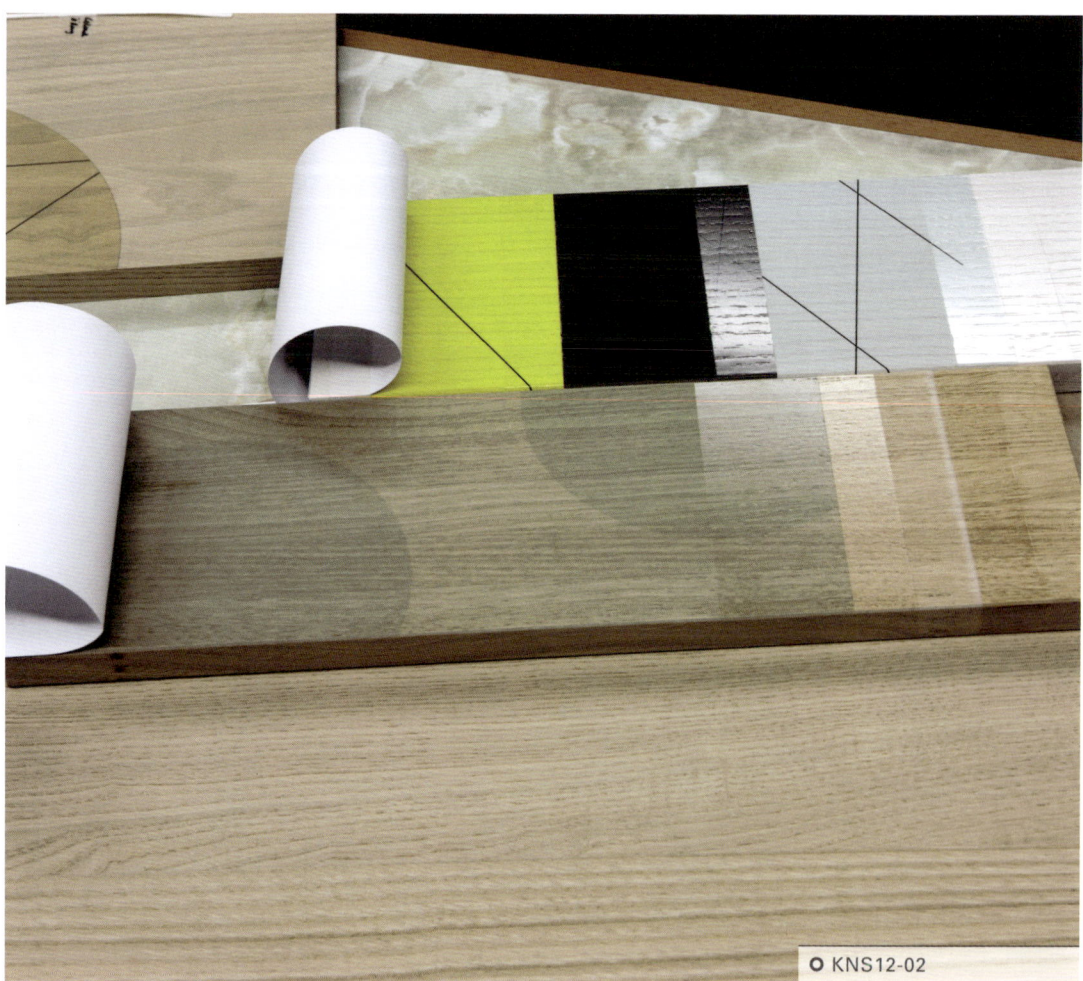

○ KNS12-02

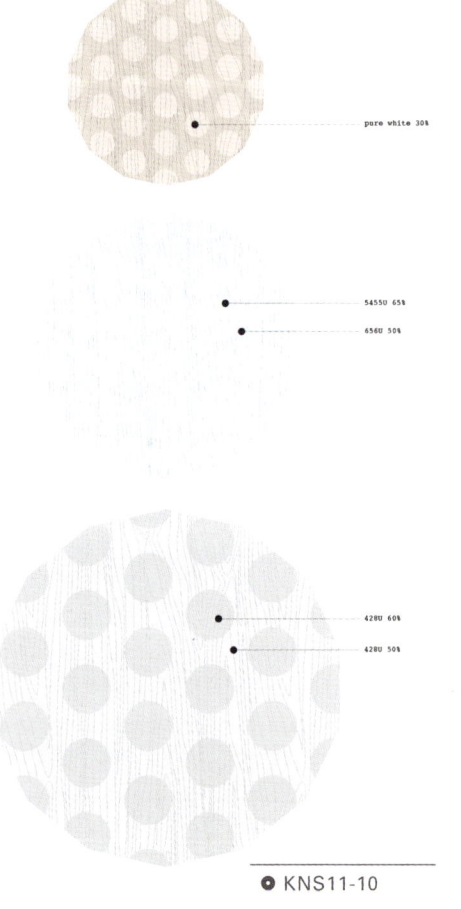

pure white 30%

5455U 65%
656U 50%

428U 60%
428U 50%

○ KNS11-10

○ KNS12-02

KNS12-02

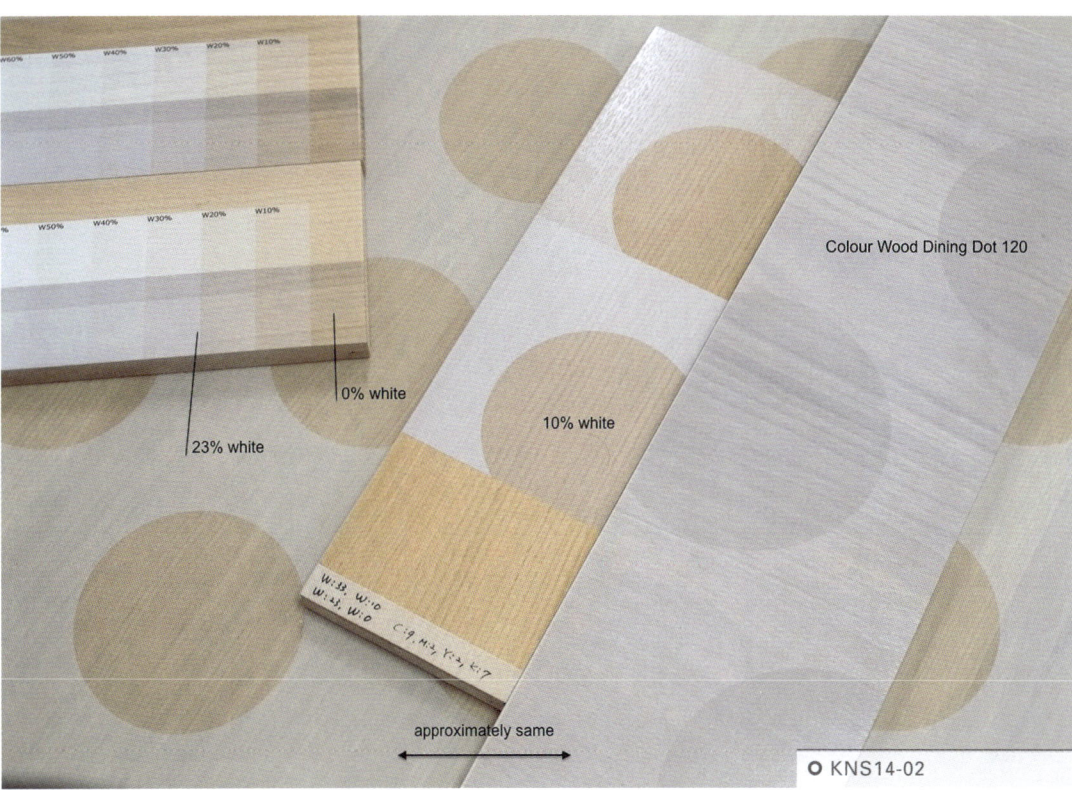

Colour Wood Dining Dot 120

23% white

0% white

10% white

approximately same

KNS14-02

KNS14-02

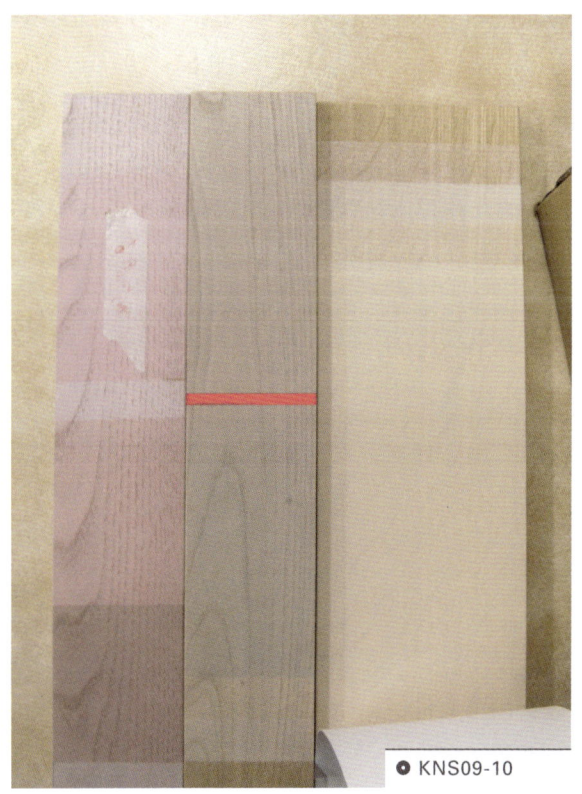

KNS09-10

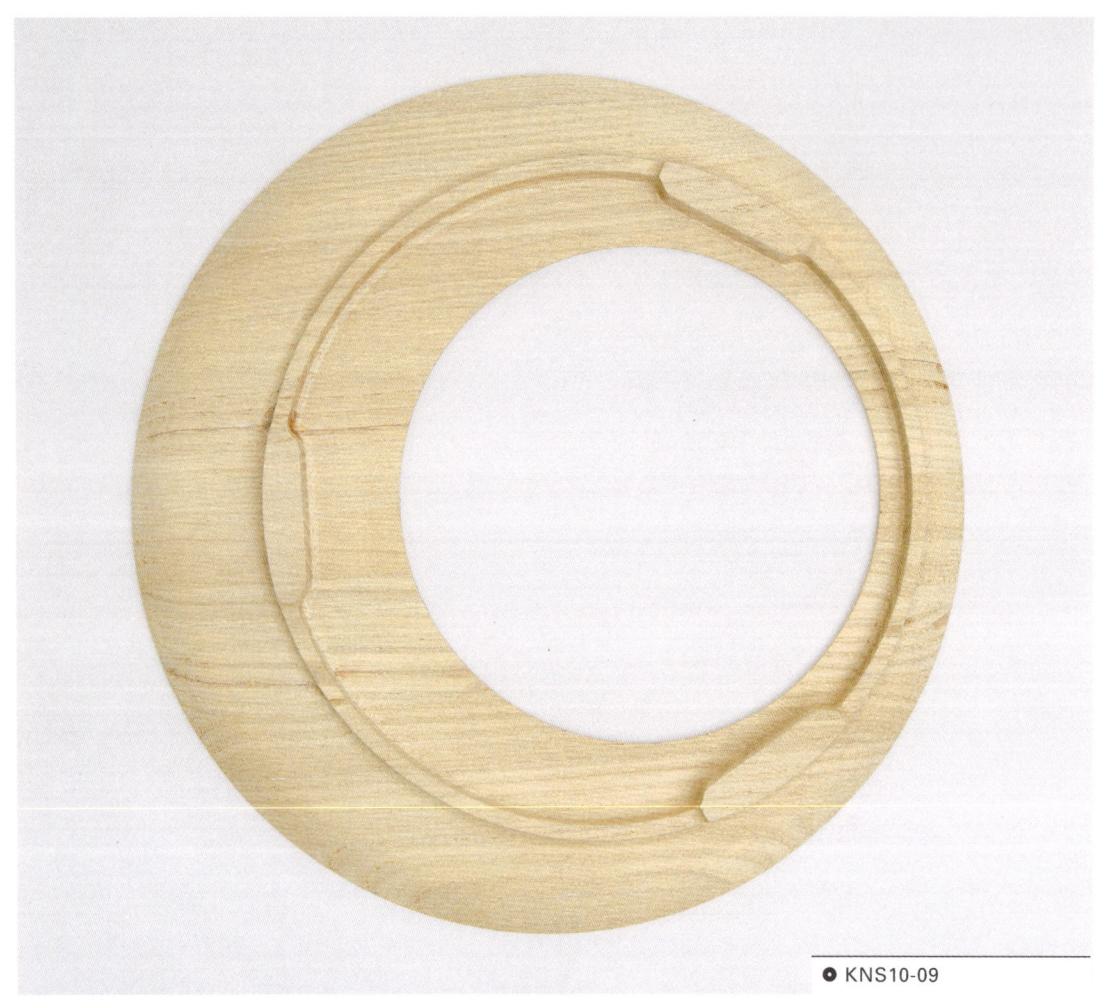

● KNS10-09

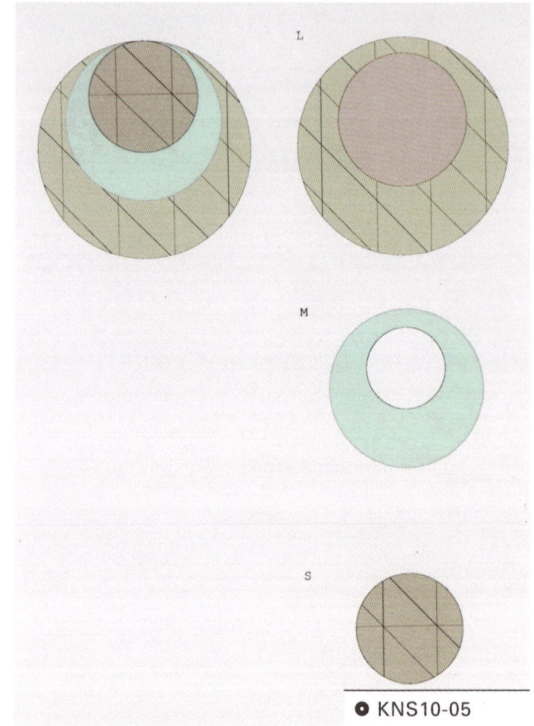

L

M

S

● KNS10-05

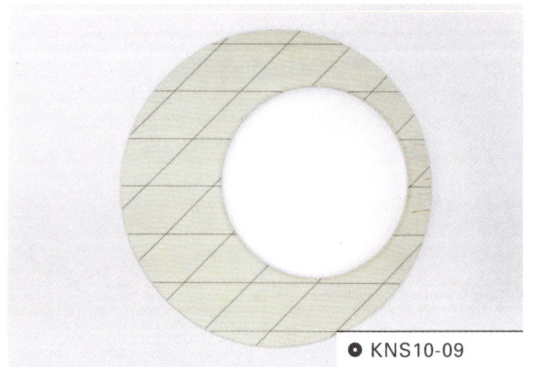

● KNS10-09

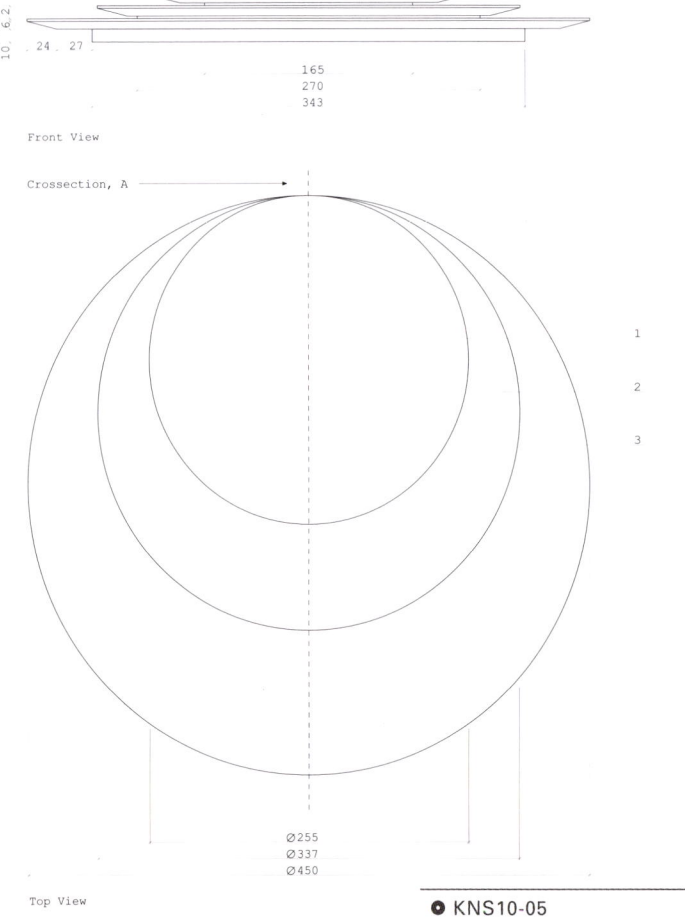

38
28
18.2
16.2
10 24 27

165
270
343

Front View

Crossection, A

1

2

3

Ø255
Ø337
Ø450

Top View

● KNS10-05

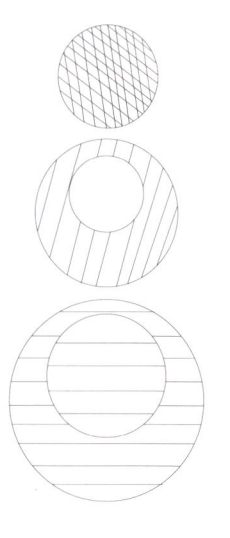

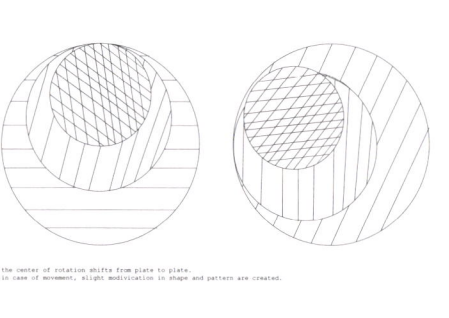

the center of rotation shifts from plate to plate.
In case of movement, slight modivication in shape and pattern are created.

● KNS10-05

注意！
筐体内に手を入れないで下さい。

■ Opening the front cover while printing is in progress causes an emergency stop.
To pause printing for any other reason than an emergency stop, press the [PAUSE] key.
■ 印刷过程中如打开前盖，机器将会紧急停止。
如需暂时停止，请按[PAUSE]键。
■ 印刷中にフロントカバーを開けると緊急停止します。
緊急停止以外の一時停止は、[PAUSE]キーを押してください。

● KNS12-02

● KNS12-02

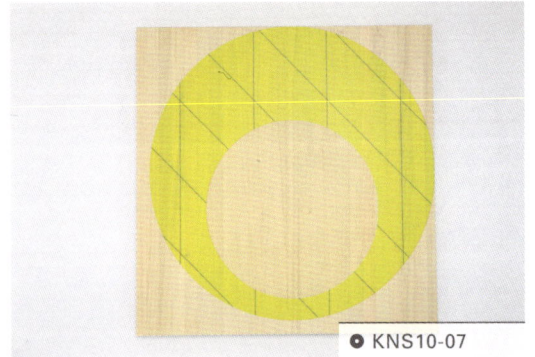

● KNS10-07

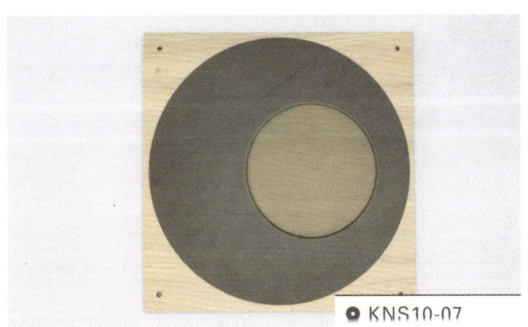

● KNS10-07

● KNS10-07

● KNS12-02

132

● KNS11-09

● KNS11-09

Serie 1

Plate 1
Plate 2
Plate 3
○ KNS10-06

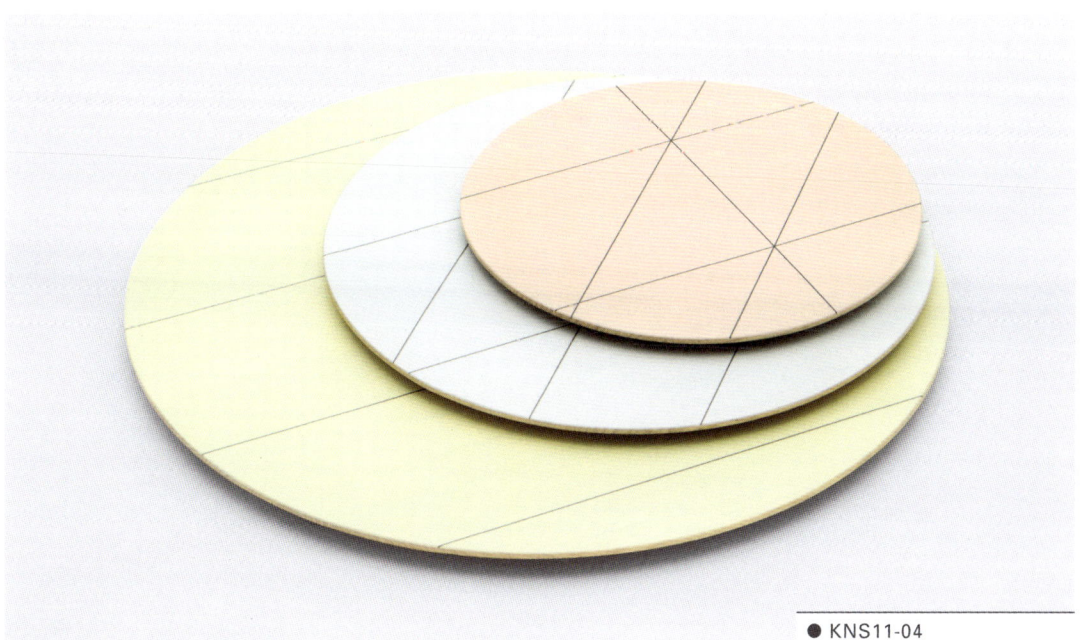
● KNS11-04

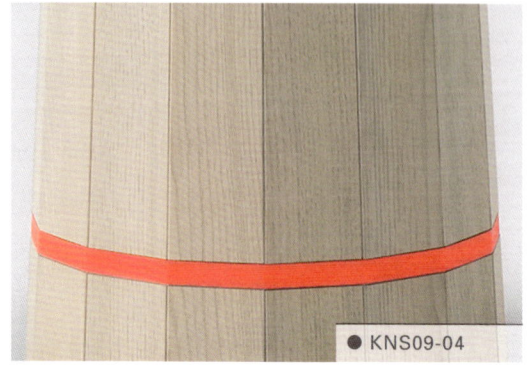

● KNS09-04

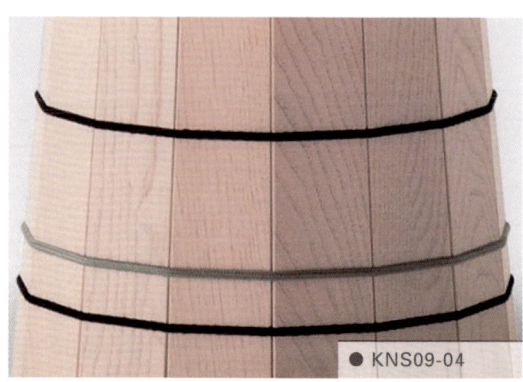

● KNS09-04

● KNS12-04

● KNS09-10

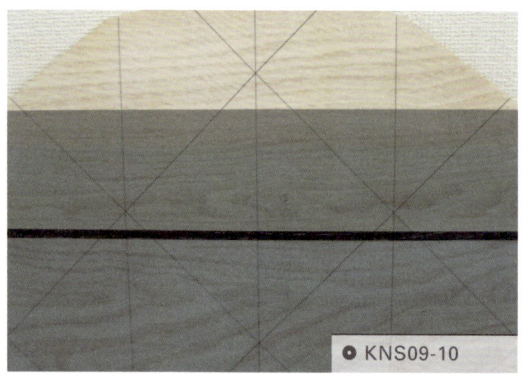

● KNS09-10

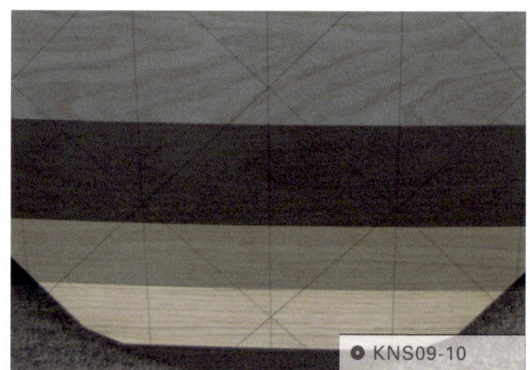

● KNS09-10

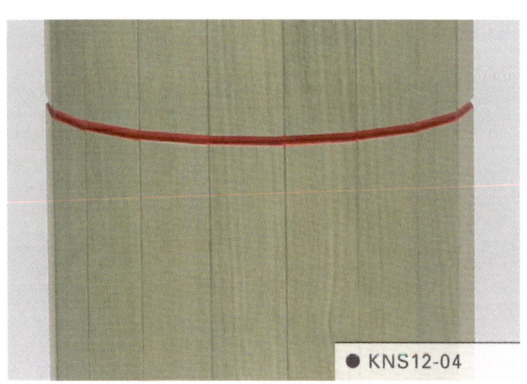

● KNS12-04

● KNS09-10

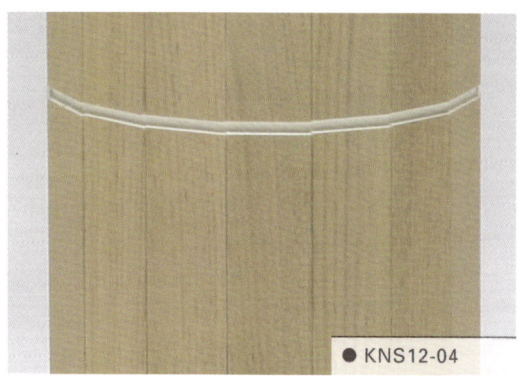

● KNS12-04

● KNS14-02

● KNS09-04

● KNS13-04

● KNS11-04

● KNS11-04

● KNS11-04

● KNS11-04

● KNS11-04

● KNS11-04

● KNS12-04

● KNS11-04

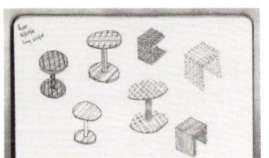

○ KNS08-09
Sketch of side tables
September 2008

○ KNS11-10
Sketch of Colour Wood Dining
October 2011

○ KNS09-06
Sketch of Colour Wood
June 2009

○ KNS08-10
Handmade scale model of
Colour Grid with additional
colour options for tabletop
October 2008

○ KNS08-10
Paper model of Table High
October 2008

○ KNS11-11
White paper scale model
of Colour Wood Dining
November 2011

○ KNS09-07
Scale model of Dark Grid
July 2009

○ KNS08-10
Paper model of Table High
October 2008

○ KNS09-07
Colour Bin Large
with Dark Grid top
July 2009

○ KNS08-10
Scale model of Table
Low with wooden base
October 2008

○ KNS08-10
Paper model of Table High
October 2008

○ KNS09-07
Scale model of Plain Grid
July 2009

◉ KNS12-02
Matching up colours for
Colour Grid tabletop,
photographed by Inga
Powilleit (IP)
February 2012

◉ KNS12-02
Colour Grid pattern on
wooden tabletop at the
Karimoku factory (IP)
February 2012

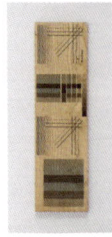

◉ KNS09-10
Wooden sample with printed
colours and varying line widths
October 2009

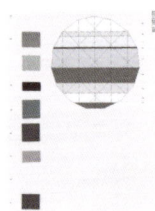

◉ KNS09-09
Design drawing of Colour Grid
tabletop with hand-painted
wooden colour samples
September 2009

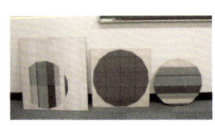

◉ KNS09-10
Colour samples for Colour
Grid and Dark Grid tabletops,
and separate Colour Grid
tabletop at the Karimoku
factory
October 2009

○ KNS09-09
Handmade wooden colour
samples for Colour Wood
September 2009

● KNS12-04
Erastudio Apartment Gallery
presents Karimoku New
Standard collection during
Salone del Mobile in Milan 2012,
photography Takumi Ota (TO)
April 2012

● KNS09-04
Dark Grid (TO)
April 2009

◉ KNS09-10
First prototype of Plain
Grid and Colour Stool
in the Karimoku factory
October 2009

◉ KNS09-09
Colour references for Plain
Grid with hand-painted colour
samples and textile ribbon
September 2009

◉ KNS09-10
Construction of Plain Grid
in the Karimoku factory
October 2009

◉ KNS09-10
Bottom of Plain Grid
in the Karimoku factory
October 2009

◉ KNS09-10
Discussing the prototype
of Plain Grid in Japan
October 2009

◉ KNS12-02
Measuring the prototype of
Colour Bin Medium at the
Karimoku factory in Japan (IP)
February 2012

○ KNS11-09
Fluorescent colour sample
for Colour Bin Small
September 2011

◉ KNS12-02
Construction of Colour Bin
Large and wooden colour
samples
February 2012

◉ KNS09-10
Discussing the construction
of the first design of Colour
Stool at Karimoku
October 2009

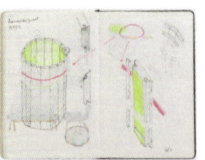

○ KNS11-07
Pages from sketchbook.
Sketch of the Colour Bin's
construction
July 2011

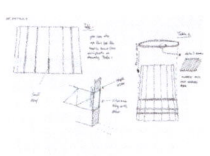

○ KNS09-07
Sketch depicting the assembly
of the textile inlays and braided
cord for Colour Wood
July 2009

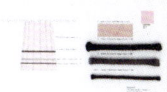

◉ KNS09-09
Colour references for Dark
Grid with hand-painted colour
sample and braided cord
September 2009

◉ KNS12-02
Production of Colour Bins
at Karimoku in Japan (IP)
February 2012

○ KNS11-07
Pages from sketchbook.
Sketches of Colour Bins
July 2011

● KNS12-04
Colour Bins (TO)
April 2012

● KNS14-04
Colour Wood for
Karimoku New Standard,
photographed by
Scheltens & Abbenes
April 2014

◉ KNS10-09
Different finishes for the bottom
of the Colour Stool legs
September 2010

◉ KNS10-09
Cross section of Colour Stool
seat
September 2010

◉ KNS10-11
Various finishes for bottom
part of Colour Stool legs
November 2010

◉ KNS11-03
CNC-cut seat of Colour Stool
at the Karimoku factory
March 2011

◉ KNS11-03
Seat of Colour Stool before
it is cut out
March 2011

◉ KNS11-03
Seat of Colour Stool painted
at the Karimoku factory
March 2011

○ KNS10-05
Cardboard model of Colour
Stool, made in-house and
by hand
May 2010

◉ KNS12-02
Spray-painting the coloured grid
on the Colour Stool seat (IP)
February 2012

◉ KNS12-02
Colour samples and paint for
spray-painting Colour Stool
Blue and Pink (IP)
February 2012

◉ KNS12-02
Sanding the surface of
Colour Stool seat (IP)
February 2012

● KNS11-04
Colour Stool Blue (TO)
April 2011

○ KNS12-02
Wooden colour sample with
printed colours for Colour
Wood Dining Gray Dot (IP)
February 2012

◉ KNS11-10
Designs of dot patterns for
the tabletop of Colour Wood
Dining Gray Dot
October 2011

◉ KNS12-02
Wooden printed colour
samples for Colour Wood
Dining Gray Dot and Colour
Platters (IP)
February 2012

◉ KNS12-02
Production at the Karimoku
factory in Japan (IP)
February 2012

○ KNS14-02
Transparent colour samples
on wood for Colour Wood
Dining Gray Dot
February 2014

◉ KNS14-02
First prototype of Colour
Wood Dining Gray Dot
at the Karimoku factory
February 2014

◉ KNS09-10
Various colour samples of
transparent wood-stain
gradations for Colour Wood
October 2009

◉ KNS10-09
Bottom of Colour Platter
Large
September 2010

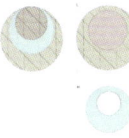

◉ KNS10-05
Design of Colour Platter Sand
May 2010

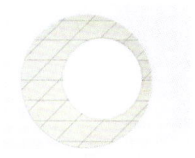

◉ KNS10-09
Colour Platter Sun Large
September 2010

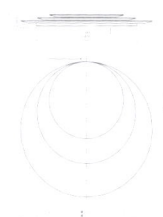

◉ KNS10-05
Dimensional drawing
of Colour Platters
May 2010

○ KNS10-05
Patterns of Colour Platters
May 2010

◉ KNS12-02
Inspecting the printed Colour
Platter Sun Large (IP)
February 2012

○ KNS12-02
Printing of Colour Platter
Sun Small (IP)
February 2012

○ KNS12-02
Printing machine at the
Karimoku factory in Japan (IP)
February 2012

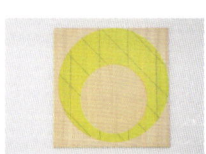

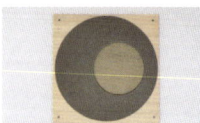

○ KNS10-07
Wooden colour samples
of Colour Platters
July 2010

○ KNS12-02
Drying the various printed
wood components for the
Colour Platters (IP)
February 2012

○ KNS11-09
Detail of Colour Platter Sun
Large
September 2011

○ KNS11-09
Prototype of Colour Platter
Design 03
September 2011

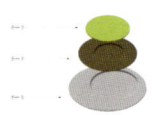

○ KNS10-06
Design drawing of Colour
Platter Sun
June 2010

● KNS11-04
Colour Platter Sand (TO)
April 2011

● KNS09-04
Detail of Colour Grid (TO)
April 2009

● KNS09-04
Detail of Dark Grid (TO)
April 2009

● KNS12-04
Detail of Colour Wood Dining
Gray Dot (TO)
April 2012

○ KNS09-10
Detail of Plain Grid
October 2009

○ KNS09-10
Detail of Colour Grid
October 2009

○ KNS09-10
Detail of Colour Grid
October 2009

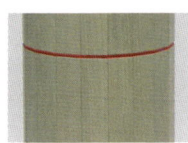

● KNS12-04
Detail of Colour Bin Large (TO)
April 2012

○ KNS09-10
Detail of Dark Grid
October 2009

● KNS12-04
Detail of Colour Bin Medium
(TO)
April 2012

○ KNS14-02
Detail of Colour Wood Dining
Gray Dot
February 2014

● KNS09-04
Detail of Plain Grid (TO)
April 2009

● KNS13-04
Detail of Colour Wood Dining
(TO)
April 2013

● KNS11-04
Detail of Colour Stool Blue
(TO)
April 2011

● KNS11-04
Detail of Colour Stool Pink
(TO)
April 2011

● KNS11-04
Detail of Colour
Platter Sand Small (TO)
April 2011

● KNS11-04
Detail of Colour
Platter Sun Medium (TO)
April 2011

● KNS11-04
Detail of Colour
Platter Sun Large (TO)
April 2011

● KNS11-04
Detail of Colour
Platter Sun Small (TO)
April 2011

● KNS12-04
Detail of Colour Wood
Dining Gray Dot (TO)
April 2012

● KNS11-04
Detail of Colour
Platter Sand Large (TO)
April 2011

● KNS13-04
'Kitchen Library' by Arabeschi
di Latte presented Karimoku
New Standard collection during
Salone del Mobile in Milan
2013 (TO)
April 2013

COLOUR PORCELAIN

COLOUR PORCELAIN (2012)

Artisanal Product
Unlimited edition. The series consists of 53 items, including bowls, plates,
  cups and vases
Materials/Techniques: Porcelain, various glazes/injection moulding in
  plaster moulds, hand painting
Colours: Greyish-white (porcelain colour), in combination with typical
  Japanese colours such as watercolour blue, light green, orange, yellow
  ochre and others
Client/Manufacturer: 1616/Arita Japan (Japan)

The name '1616/Arita Japan' refers to the long history of artisanal porcelain manufacturers in the Arita region. According to legend, this is where in 1616 a Korean craftsman discovered kaolin, a white clay that produces a superior kind of porcelain. Arita would soon become one of the most important regions in the field of high-quality porcelain. Everyone in Japan is familiar with the name, and Europeans have known Arita porcelain from as early as the seventeenth century, when the vessels of the Dutch VOC (Verenigde Oostindische Compagnie – United East India Company) transported shiploads of porcelain objects from Japan to Europe.

Noriyuki Momota, director of 1616/Arita Japan, believes that high-quality porcelain deserves a contemporary interpretation, so he appointed Japanese designer Teruhiro Yanagihara as creative director. He in turn asked Scholten & Baijings to bring together ancient Japanese ceramic tradition, contemporary European design, and the Scholten & Baijings signature.

In cooperation with the company's specialists, the duo explored the possibilities of creating a refined contemporary set of tableware that would be suitable for everyday use. Baijings: 'As soon as we team up with a company, we start exploring the possibilities. The client's history and specialty become part of our design process. We visit the company, investigate the potential of their technical know-how, the capabilities of the machines, and the talents of the professionals with whom they work. We then present proposals that challenge the company to branch out and do something different from what they're accustomed to. As we strive for perfection, we work only with high-quality companies. 1616/Arita Japan definitely belongs in this category. The company is known for their craftsmen's unparalleled skill and mastery of the material and the ancient traditions they preserve.' Scholten: 'They combine traditional craft techniques – such as the manual application of glazes – with high-tech techniques, which enable them to inject the porcelain into moulds. As a result, the production process can achieve a high level of efficiency.'

The designers did not want to create something suitable only for the Japanese market. The first models, realized in foam in the Netherlands, were brought to Japan, where, together with the company's directors, the designers conducted an in-depth analysis to establish which forms would be most appropriate for the various rituals and customs of each market. For instance, the Japanese use a bowl for drinking sake, while Europeans would use it for drinking tea. The set of fifty-three items clearly forms a family, yet each individual item has a distinct shape, texture and colour, and therefore its own particular character.

The Colour Porcelain objects exemplify both the visual signature of Scholten & Baijings – sober design, a high level of refinement and a subtle colour palette – and the typical characteristics of the wafer-thin Arita porcelain. Some parts reveal the greyish-white colour of the unfinished porcelain, while others are glazed in different shades, soft gradations from light to dark. The colours used by Scholten & Baijings – watercolour blue, light green, orange and yellow ochre – are derived from the traditional colour range of Arita masterpieces. Baijings: 'We pulled, as it were, the traditional colours apart, used them to create new compositions, and also devised variations with matt and glossy finishes – for example, by playing with matt underglaze instead of using the traditional high-gloss glazes. The traditional decorations were mostly landscape scenes. The colour gradations, which we have applied by hand, create unique abstractions of landscapes that are reminiscent of the original depictions on Japanese pottery.'

As a tribute to the labour-intensive production process, the names of the three series – Minimal, Colourful, Extraordinary – indicate to what extent colour and detail have been applied.

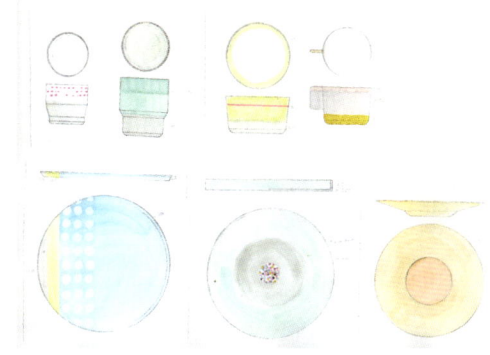

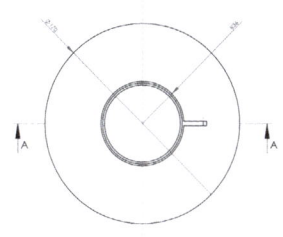

Getting to know a culture from the inside is one of the most rewarding aspects of our job.
— Carole Baijings

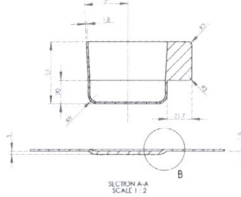

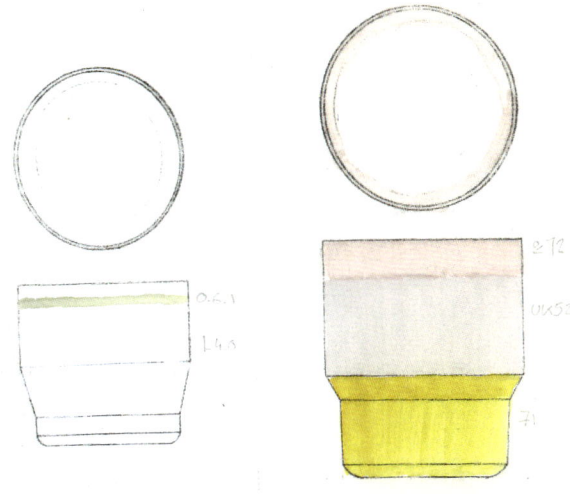

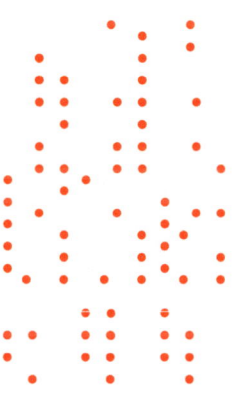

The tableware has a beautiful formal language. Surprising choices have been made with respect to the forms, imbuing them with a kind of naturalness.
— Selection Committee, Dutch Design Awards – Winner 2012 (Best Consumer Product)

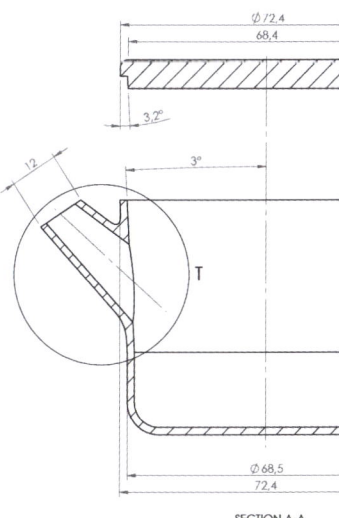

145

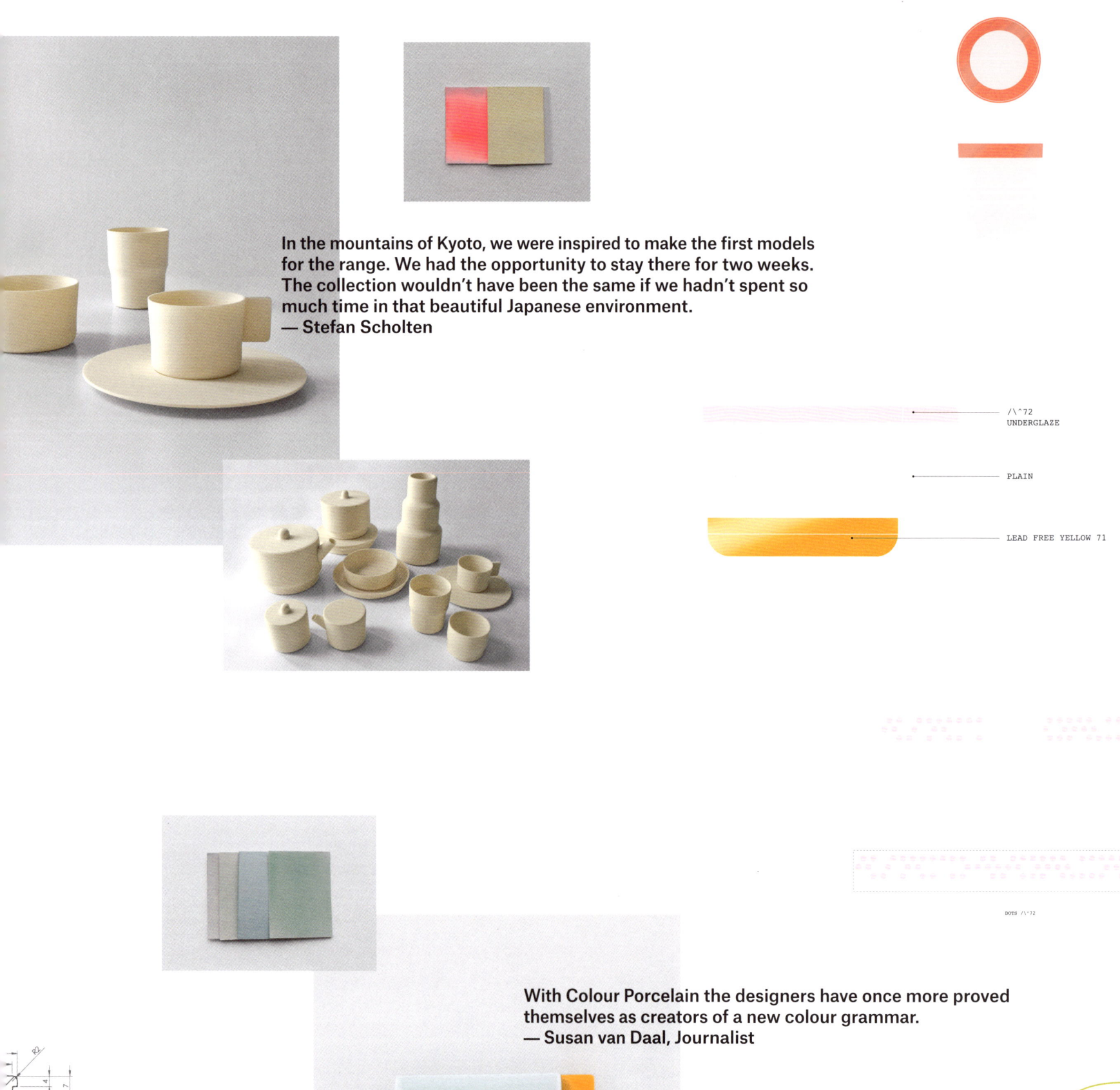

In the mountains of Kyoto, we were inspired to make the first models for the range. We had the opportunity to stay there for two weeks. The collection wouldn't have been the same if we hadn't spent so much time in that beautiful Japanese environment.
— Stefan Scholten

/\^72
UNDERGLAZE

PLAIN

LEAD FREE YELLOW 71

DOTS /\^72

With Colour Porcelain the designers have once more proved themselves as creators of a new colour grammar.
— Susan van Daal, Journalist

It had this beautiful light-grey hue. We immediately saw the potential of combining this pure, high-quality material with carefully selected colours.
— Carole Baijings

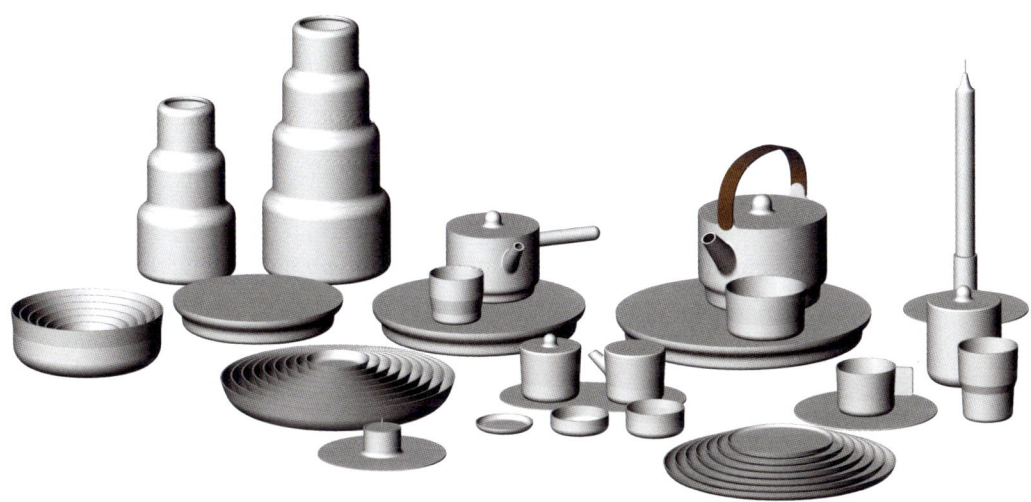

We selected the colours from centuries-old Japanese settings–ranging from soft-yellow to deep-red, from pastels to gold.
— Stefan Scholten

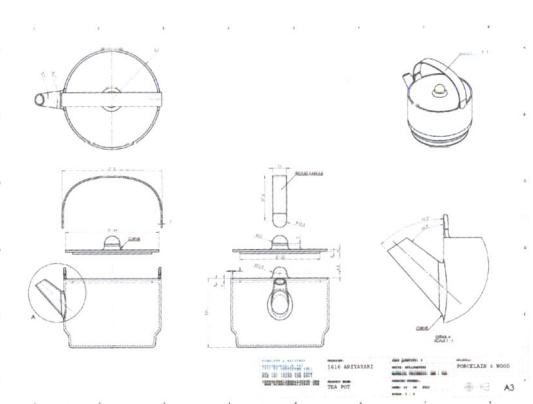

This collection couldn't have been made anywhere else. If we had asked a craftsman in Europe to make the foot of the candleholder this thin, he would have told us to redesign it. At Arita, a craftsman looks at it carefully, says it will be very difficult to realize, but finds a way to make it possible.
— Stefan Scholten

Coloured tableware is highly unusual in Japan, but it worked beautifully with the colours of Japanese food.
— Carole Baijings

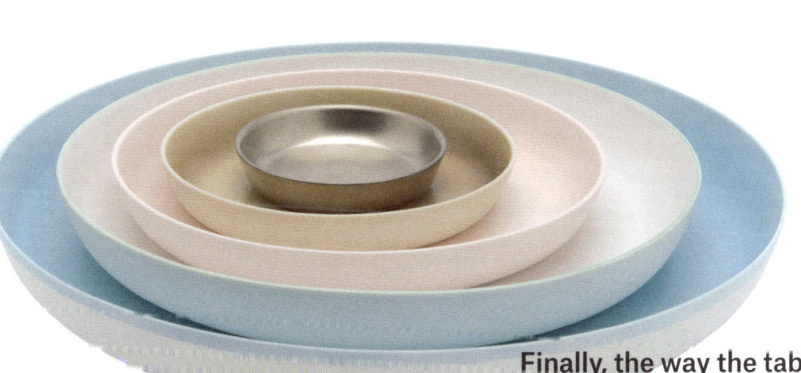

Finally, the way the tableware is used varies according to the cultural context, with the designs effortlessly supporting interchangeable functions. In Japan, the sugar & creamer set is used for soy sauce and ginger, while sake is drunk from the little cups.
— Susan van Daal, Journalist

149

○ ARI11-07

○ ARI11-07

○ ARI11-07

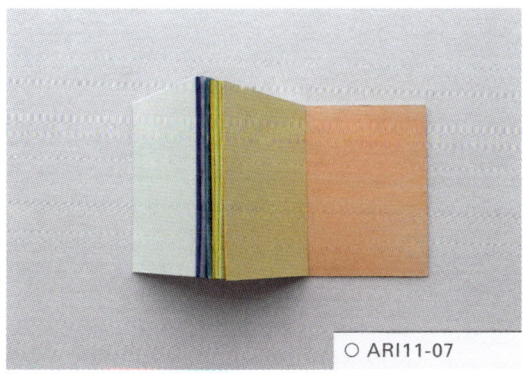
○ ARI11-07

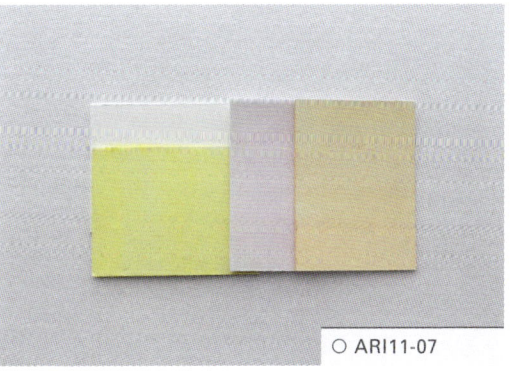
○ ARI11-07

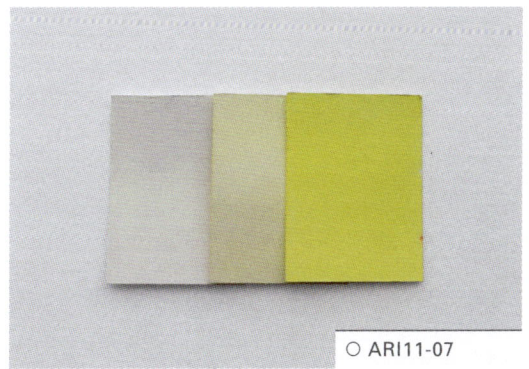
○ ARI11-07

● ARI11-10

● ARI11-08

○ ARI11-06

● ARI11-08

ARI11-09

● ARI12-04

● ARI12-04

● ARI12-04

● ARI12-04

● ARI12-04

● ARI12-04

● ARI12-04

● ARI12-04

● ARI12-04

● ARI12-04

● ARI12-04

● ARI12-04

● ARI12-04

● ARI12-04

● ARI12-04

● ARI12-04

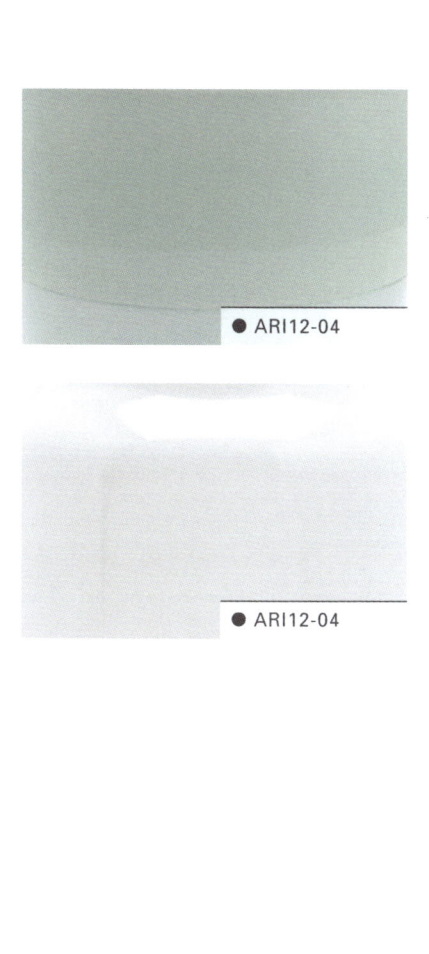
● ARI12-04

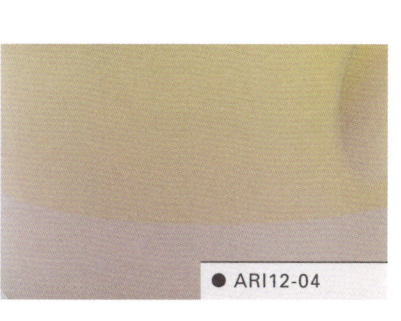
● ARI12-04

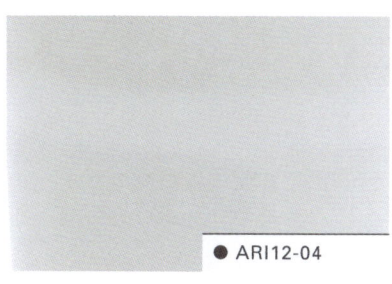
● ARI12-04

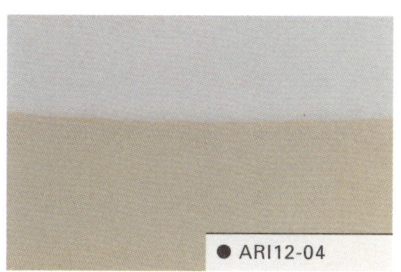
● ARI12-04

● ARI12-04

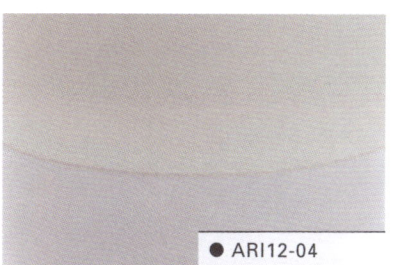
● ARI12-04

● ARI12-04

● ARI12-04

● ARI12-04

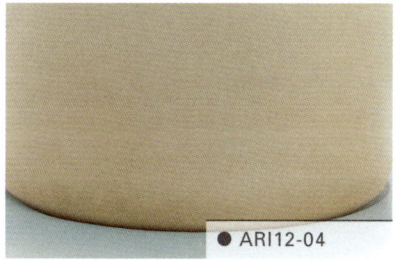
● ARI12-04

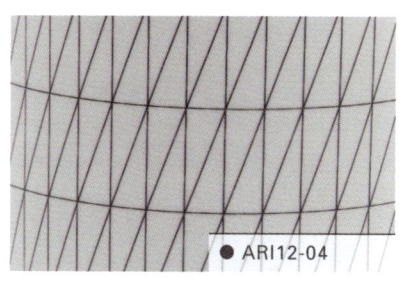
● ARI12-04

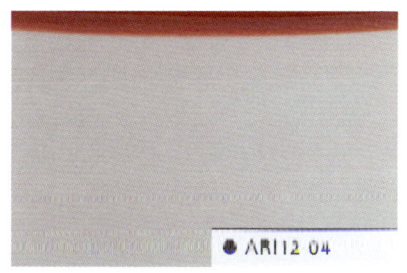
● ARI12-04

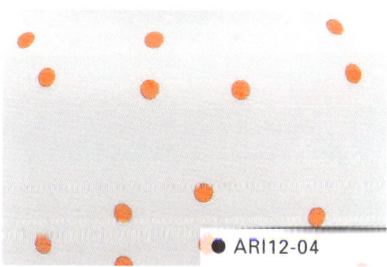
● ARI12-04

● ARI12-04

● ARI12-04

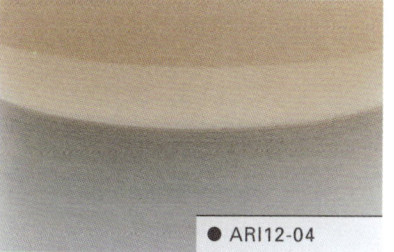
● ARI12-04

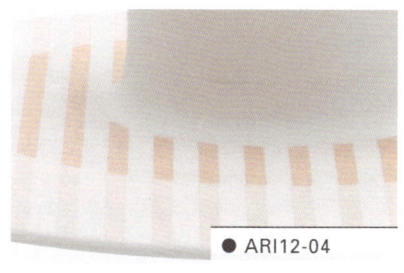
● ARI12-04

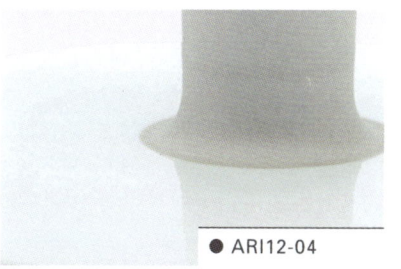
● ARI12-04

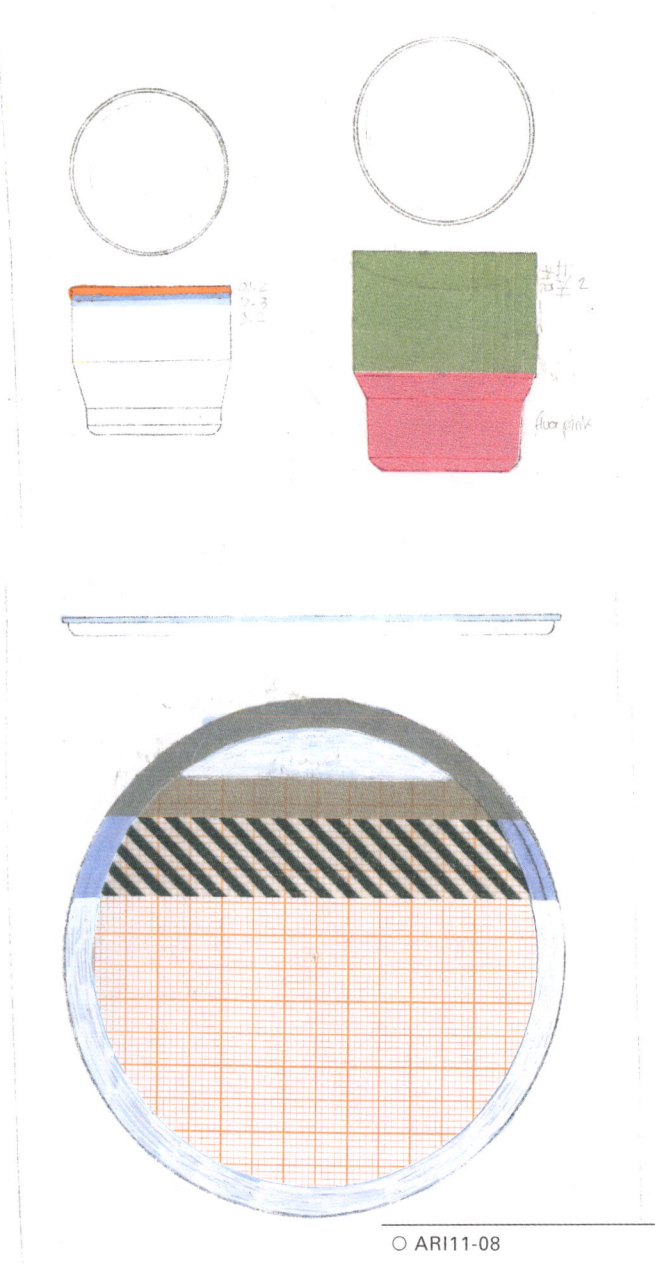

○ ARI11-08

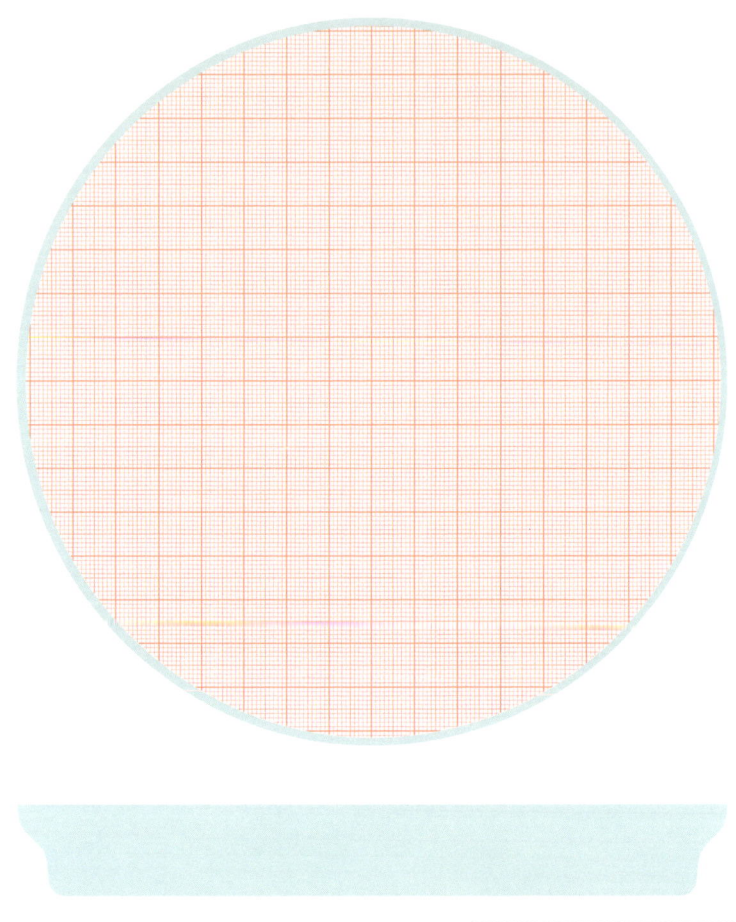

● ARI11-10

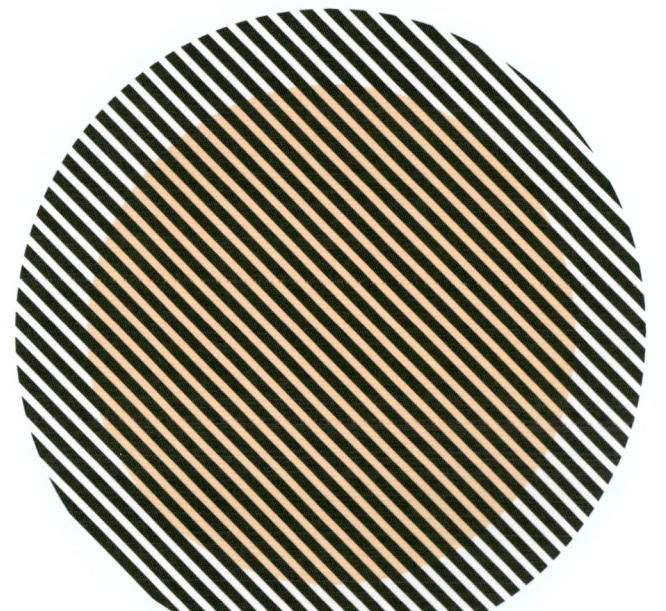

● ARI12-04

● ARI11-10

● ARI11-10

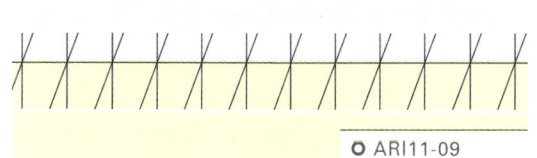

○ ARI11-09

● ARI12-04

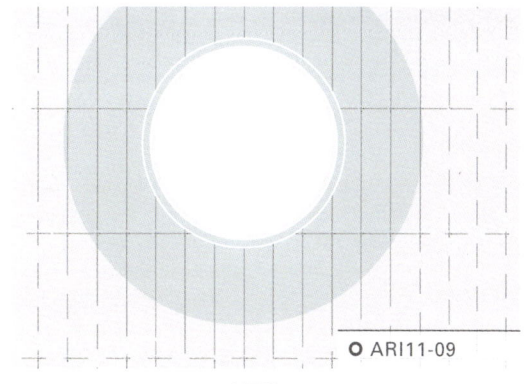

○ ARI11-09

○ ARI11-09

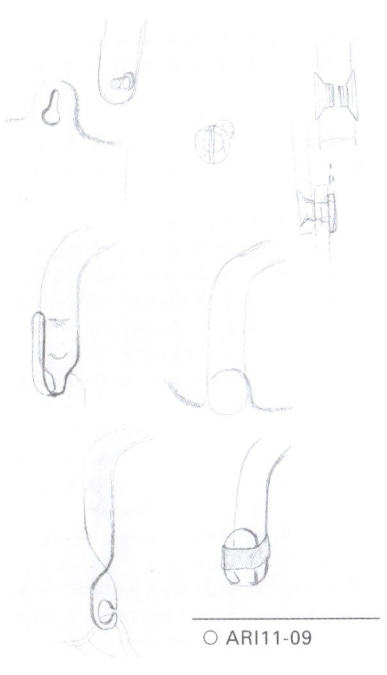

○ ARI11-09

○ ARI11-09

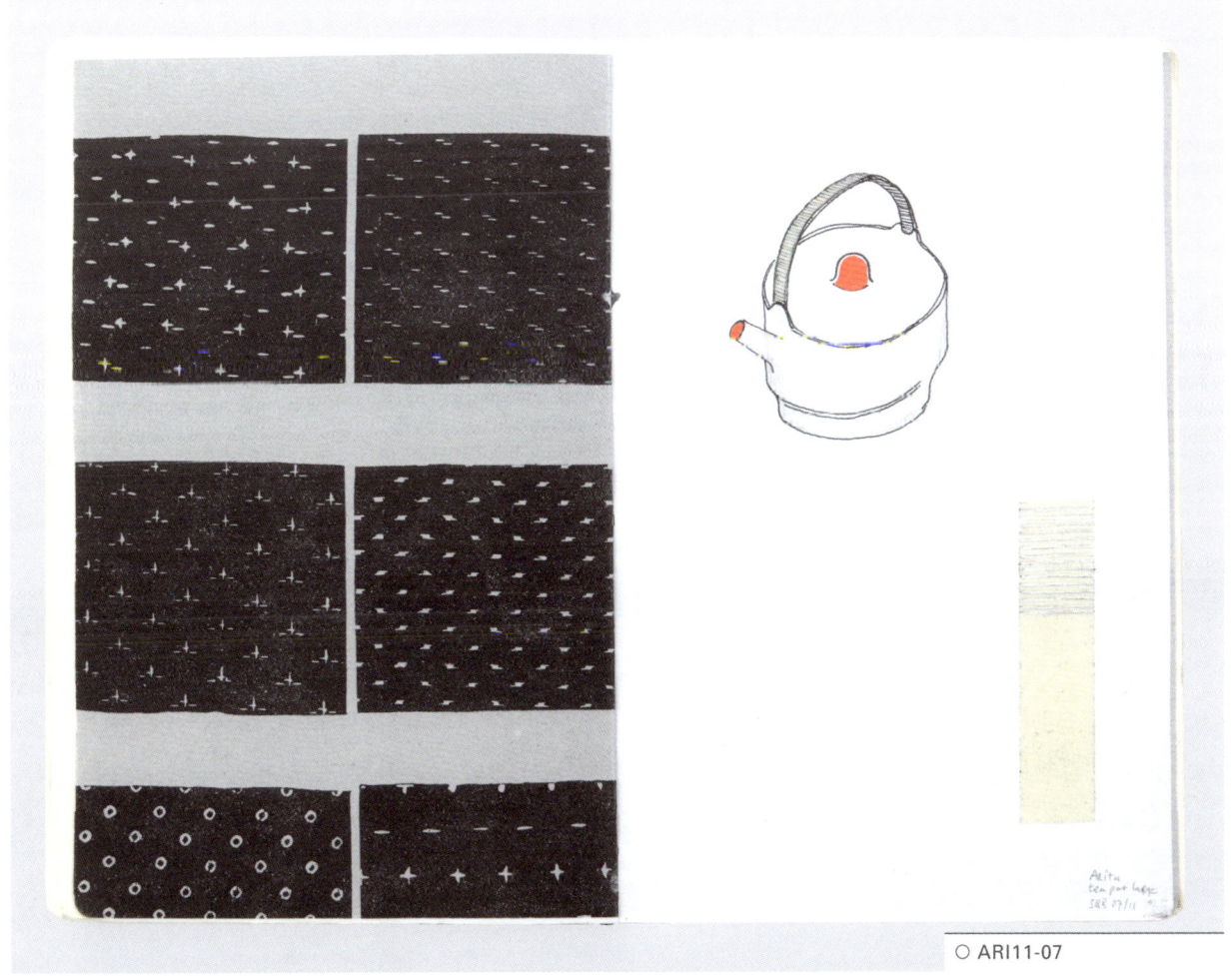

○ ARI11-07

○ ARI11-07

○ ARI11-07

○ ARI11-09

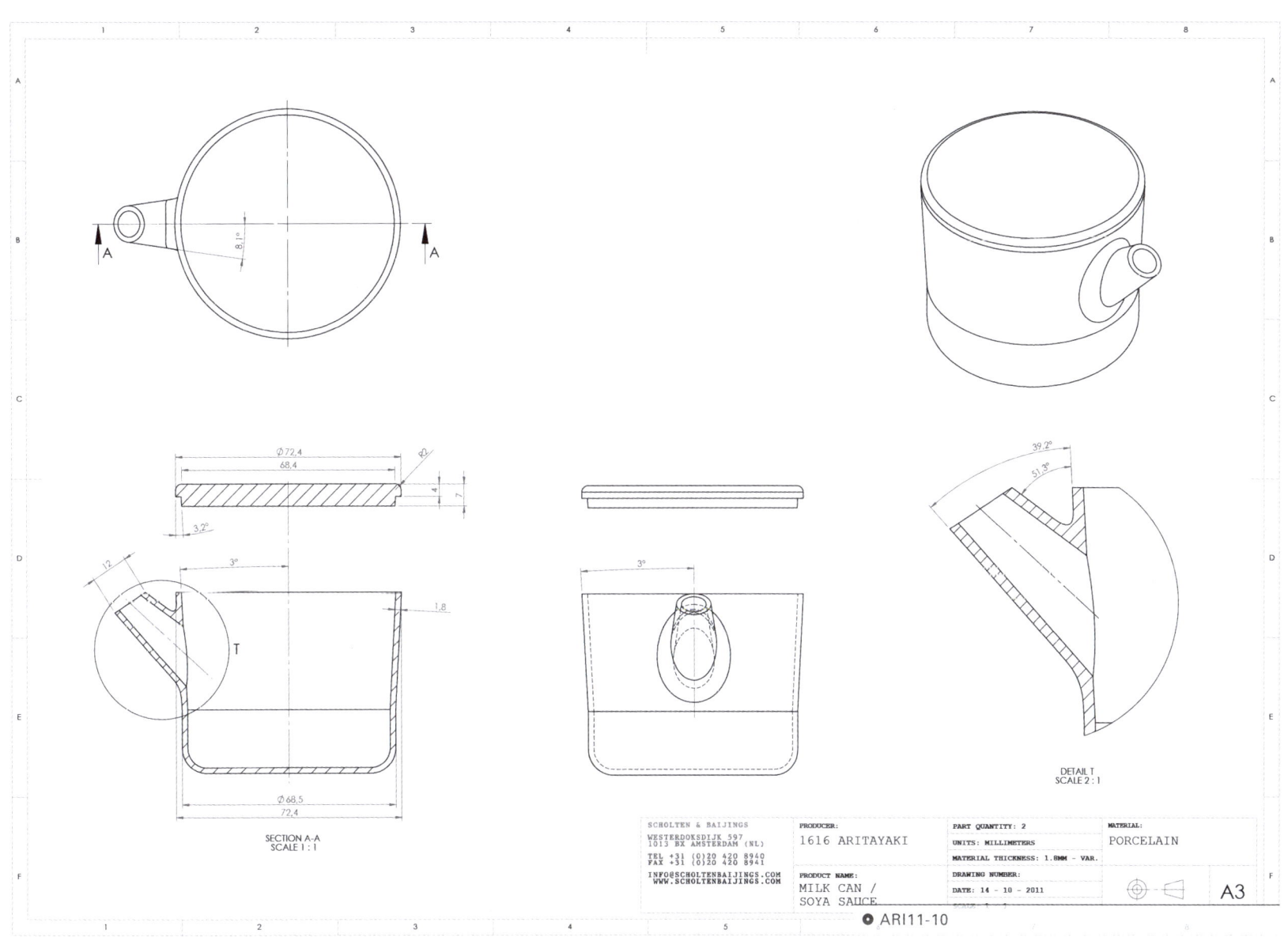

SECTION A-A
SCALE 1 : 1

DETAIL T
SCALE 2 : 1

SCHOLTEN & BAIJINGS
WESTERDOKSDIJK 597
1013 BX AMSTERDAM (NL)

TEL +31 (0)20 420 8940
FAX +31 (0)20 420 8941

INFO@SCHOLTENBAIJINGS.COM
WWW.SCHOLTENBAIJINGS.COM

PRODUCER:	PART QUANTITY: 2	MATERIAL:
1616 ARITAYAKI	UNITS: MILLIMETERS	PORCELAIN
	MATERIAL THICKNESS: 1.8MM - VAR.	

PRODUCT NAME:	DRAWING NUMBER:		
MILK CAN /	DATE: 14 - 10 - 2011	⊕ ⊲	A3
SOYA SAUCE			

ARI11-10

O ARI11-07

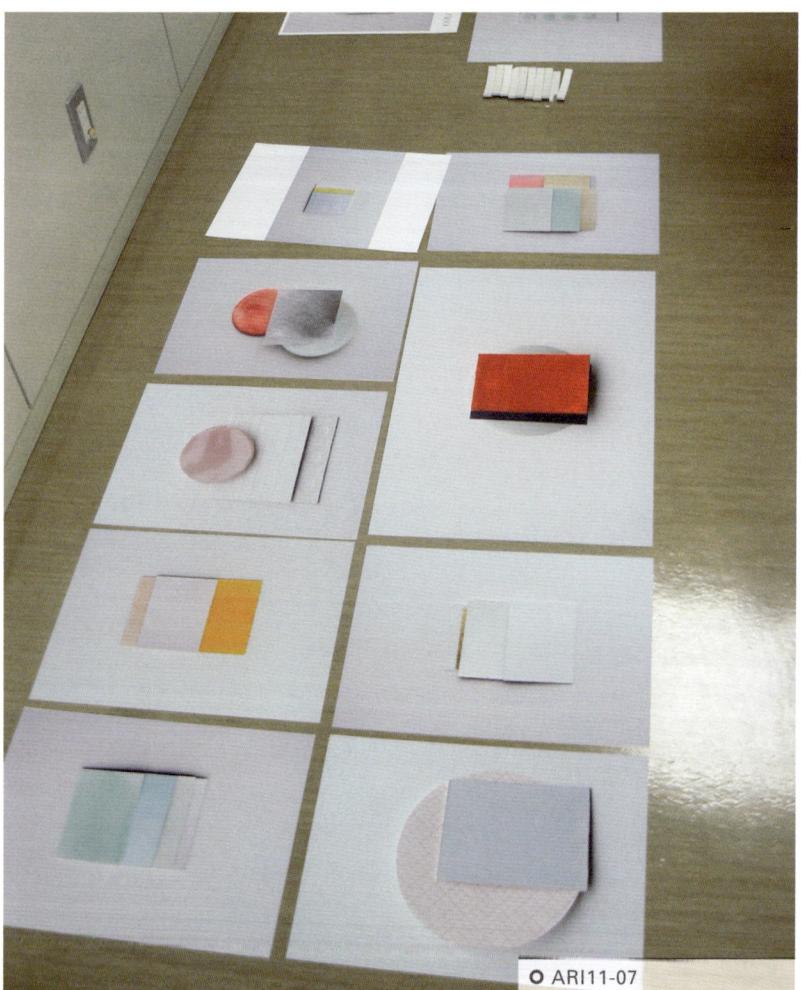

O ARI11-07

O ARI11-07

○ ARI11-07

○ ARI11-07

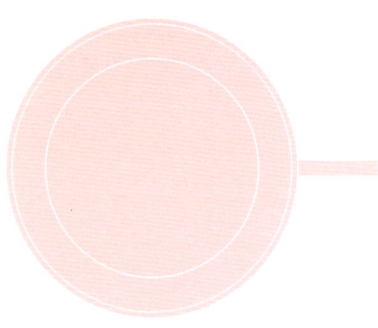

○ ARI11-09

○ ARI11-09

◑ ARI13-12

● ARI12-04

○ ARI11-07

○ ARI11-07

○ ARI11-07

● ARI12-02

O ARI11-07

O ARI08-06

O ARI11-09

O ARI11-09

168

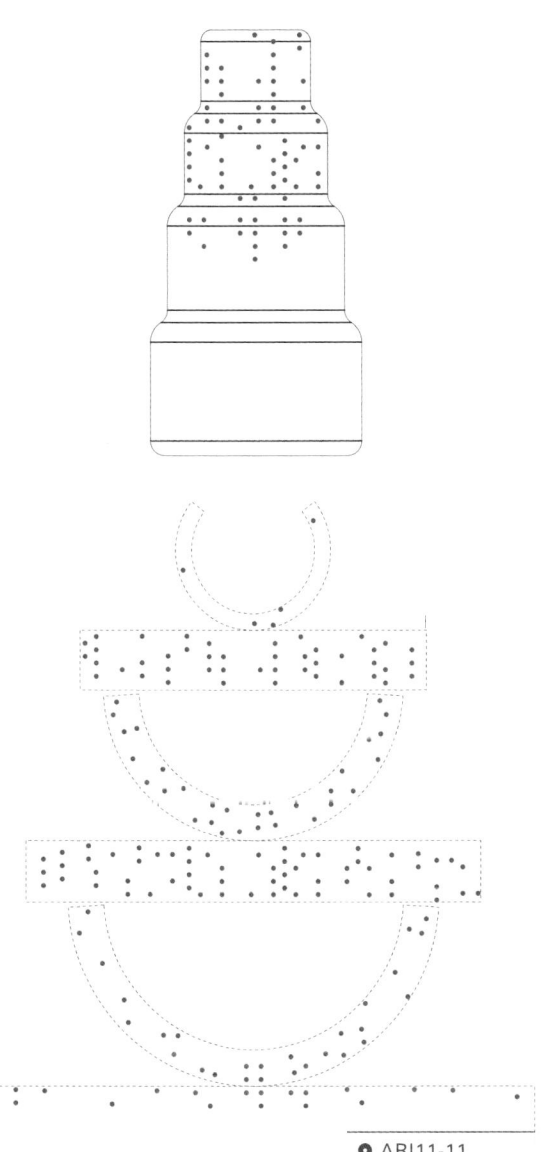

● ARI11-11

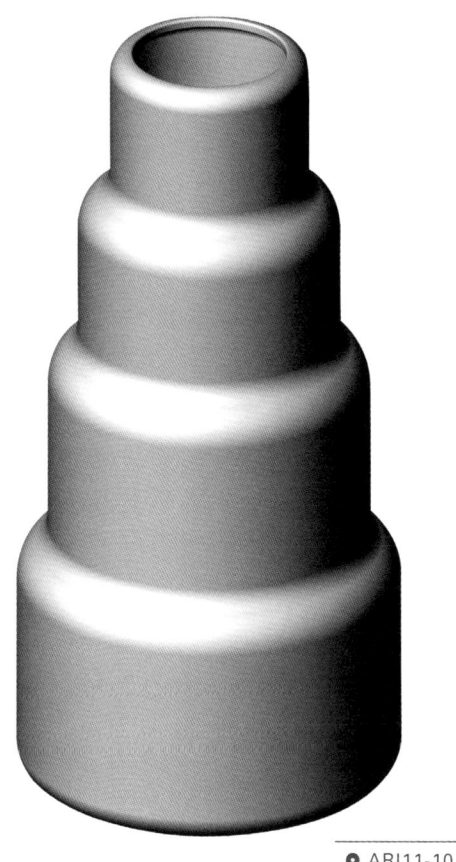

● ARI11-10

● ARI13-12

● ARI12-04

● ARI13-10

● ARI12-02

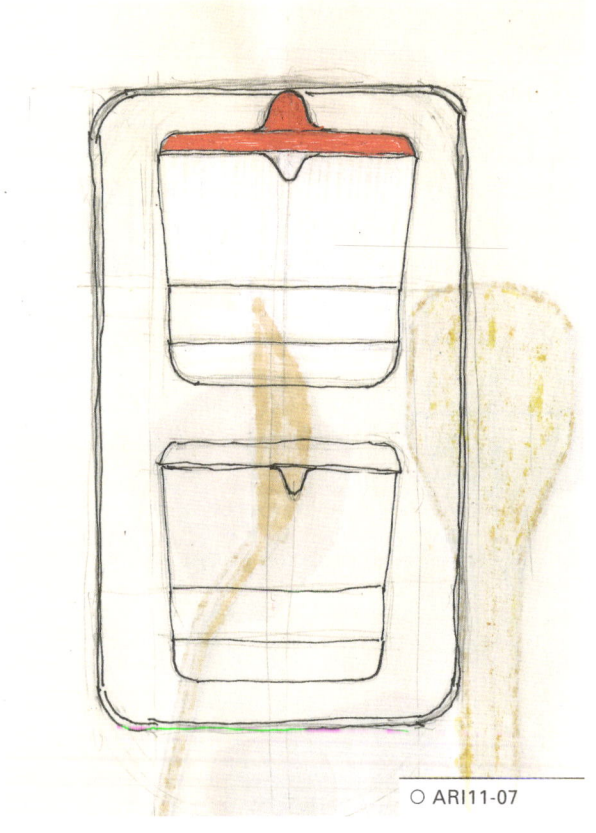
○ ARI11-07

● ARI12-04

170

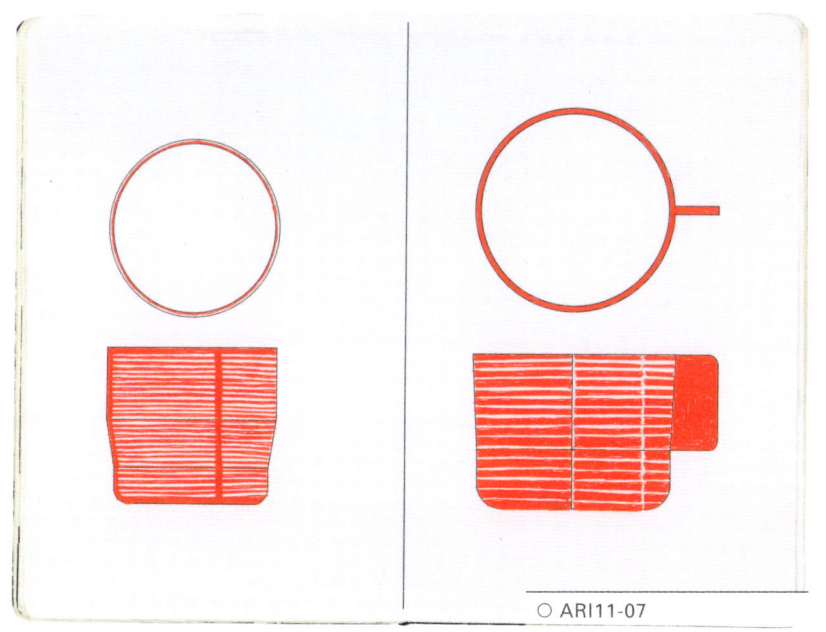

○ ARI11-07

◉ ARI11-10

● ARI12-02

○ ARI11-09

ARI12-02

ARI12-02

ARI12-02

ARI12-02

172

ARI12-02

ARI12-02

ARI12-02

ARI12-02

173

ARI12-02

ARI11-07

ARI11-07

ARI11-07

ARI12-02

175

ARI13-12

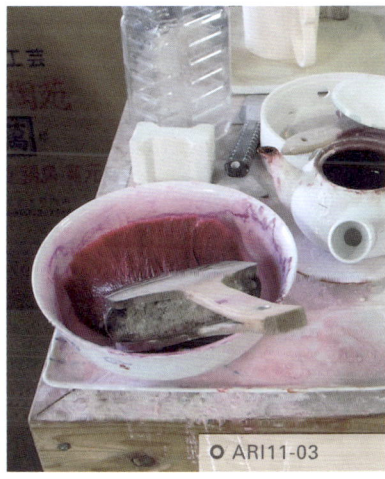

ARI11-03

ARI12-02

● ARI11-12

● ARI13-12

● ARI11-08

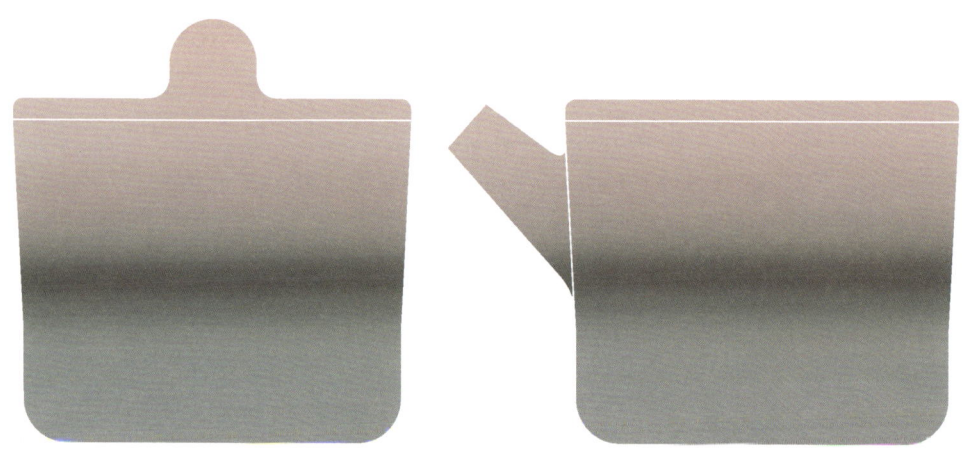

● ARI11-09

178

● ARI12-04

● ARI12-02

ARI13-12

ARI13-12

180

● ARI13-10

● ARI13-10

● ARI13-10

● ARI13-10

184

○ ARI11-06
Colours distilled from
decorations on historic
Arita masterpieces,
painted in watercolour
June 2011

○ ARI11-07
Composition of matt and
high-gloss colour finishes,
painted on cardboard and
with gold leaf detail
July 2011

○ ARI11-07
Composition of hand-painted
colours on cardboard from
colour research conducted
for Colour Porcelain
July 2011

○ ARI11-07
Colour compositions in matt
white, light-yellow and blue
with silver leaf
July 2011

○ ARI11-07
Colour compositions in
keeping with the water-
colours distilled from Arita
masterpieces
July 2011

○ ARI11-07
Soft matt colour composition
from a study conducted into
the suitability of colours for
Colour Porcelain
July 2011

○ ARI11-07
From white to yellow,
cardboard colour samples for
colour composition
July 2011

○ ARI11-07
Fluorescent-pink, matt-
beige and matt-grey colour
composition
July 2011

◉ ARI11-08
Porcelain models made
on the basis of cardboard
colour samples
August 2011

◉ ARI11-08
Example of aquarelle-blue
glaze and drawing-paper
transfer on porcelain
August 2011

◉ ARI11-08
Underglaze in light-purple &
salmon and high-gloss, soft-
pink glaze samples
August 2011

◉ ARI11-10
Discussing the Colour
Porcelain designs and foam
models in Kyoto, Japan
October 2011

◉ ARI11-08
Glaze samples in high-gloss
red, matt beige and light-
purple
August 2011

◉ ARI11-08
Porcelain models made on
the basis of colour research
on cardboard
August 2011

○ ARI11-06
Colours distilled from
decorations on historic Arita
masterpieces, painted in
watercolour
June 2011

○ ARI11-09
Handmade foam models of
Flower Vase Low, deep plate,
bowl and espresso cup
September 2011

● ARI12-04
Detail of Flower Vase Low,
matt light-purple with silver
stripes
April 2012

● ARI12-04
Detail of Flower Vase High,
matt-grey with aquarelle-blue
April 2012

● ARI12-04
Detail of Flower Vase Low,
plain with high-gloss soft-
pink gradient
April 2012

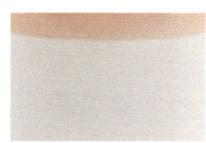

● ARI12-04
Detail of mug,
plain with soft-pink
April 2012

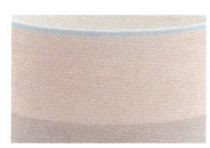

● ARI12-04
Detail of teacup, light-blue
line, matt light-pink and
light-purple
April 2012

● ARI12-04
Detail of Flower Vase Low
in aquarelle-blue
April 2012

● ARI12-04
Detail of coffee cup with
saucer in yellow-ochre,
pink and aquarelle-blue
April 2012

● ARI12-04
Detail of mug, plain with blue
April 2012

● ARI12-04
Detail of coffee cup with saucer,
plain with aquarelle-blue
April 2012

● ARI12-04
Detail of mug,
matt light-yellow
April 2012

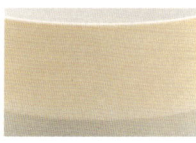

● ARI12-04
Detail of teacup,
matt-grey with salmon
April 2012

● ARI12-04
Detail of plate,
pink with matt-grey
April 2012

● ARI12-04
Detail of tea-light holder,
yellow-ochre with light-pink
April 2012

● ARI12-04
Detail of teapot with plain
lid and aquarelle-blue body
April 2012

● ARI12-04
Detail of teacup, plain
with aquarelle green
April 2012

● ARI12-04
Detail of tea-light holder
in aquarelle-blue
April 2012

● ARI12-04
Detail of espresso/sake cup,
matt green with aquarelle-
blue glaze
April 2012

● ARI12-04
Detail of milk/soy jug,
light-purple, light-yellow
and yellow-ochre
April 2012

● ARI12-04
Detail of teapot with
plain high-gloss body
and matt-grey lid
April 2012

● ARI12-04
Detail of bowl, plain with
orange with matt-grey lid
April 2012

● ARI12-04
Detail of Flower Vase,
plain, high gloss
April 2012

● ARI12-04
Detail of espresso/sake
cup, matt and high-gloss
light-pink
April 2012

● ARI12-04
Detail of milk/soy jug,
matt light-purple with
matt light-yellow
April 2012

● ARI12-04
Detail of bowl with
brown stripes
April 2012

● ARI12-04
Detail of mug plain high gloss
April 2012

● ARI12-04
Detail of coffee cup with
saucer, plain with matt-brown
and aquarelle-green gradient
April 2012

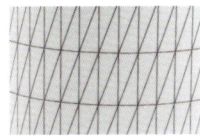

● ARI12-04
Detail of container with
grid and coloured lid
April 2012

● ARI12-04
Detail of bowl, plain with
aquarelle-blue high-gloss lid
April 2012

● ARI12-04
Detail of Flower Vase High,
plain with red dot pattern
April 2012

● ARI12-04
Detail of espresso cup, matt
and high-gloss light-yellow
April 2012

● ARI12-04
Detail of Flower Vase High,
matt and high-gloss light-pink
April 2012

● ARI12-04
Detail of mug,
brown with grey
April 2012

● ARI12-04
Detail of tea-light holder,
plain with salmon and
white stripes
April 2012

● ARI12-04
Detail of candlestick in
aquarelle-blue with matt-grey
April 2012

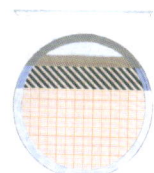

○ ARI11-08
Sketches of different colours
and patterns made with felt-tip
pen, marker, drawing pen
and tape
August 2011

◐ ARI11-10
Design of platter with grid
and high-gloss, aquarelle-
blue edge
October 2011

● ARI12-04
Tea-light holder with pink
stripes from the Colour
Porcelain collection
April 2012

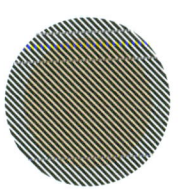

◐ ARI11-10
Design of large plate from
the 'Extraordinary' series with
grid, salmon-coloured circles
and aquarelle-blue edge
October 2011

◐ ARI11-10
Discussing the Colour
Porcelain designs and foam
models in Kyoto, Japan
October 2011

○ ARI11-09
Detail of design with grid
September 2011

◐ ARI11-10
Discussing the colours of
the glaze and the possibility
of using multiple layers
October 2011

● ARI12-04
Blue mug
April 2012

○ ARI11-09
Design of tea light candle
holder
September 2011

○ ARI11-09
Design of tea light holder
September 2011

◐ ARI12-06
Discussing the handle and
size of the teapot in Kyoto,
Japan
October 2011

○ ARI11-09
Sketches showing various
options for attaching the
teapot's handle
September 2011

○ ARI11-09
Handmade foam model
of teapot small
September 2011

○ ARI11-07
Pages from sketchbook.
Sketches with teapot design
and black & white copy of
traditional Japanese fabric
patterns from the last century
July 2011

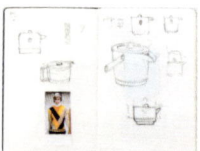

○ ARI11-07
Pages from sketchbook.
Sketches of different teapot
designs
July 2011

○ ARI11-07
Pages of sketchbook.
Sketches of teapot designs
July 2011

○ ARI11-09
Handmade foam models
of teapot, platter and tea-
light holder
September 2011

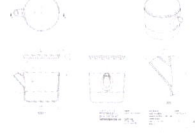

◉ ARI11-10
Technical drawing of milk
jug from Colour Porcelain
October 2011

○ ARI11-09
Design of sugar bowl and
milk jug, with glaze code
Indication
September 2011

◉ ARI11-07
Discussing the colours of the
colour composition in order
to find corresponding glaze
colours in the Arita laboratory
July 2011

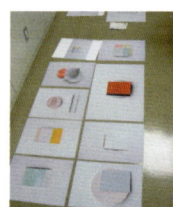

◉ ARI11-07
Colour compositions from
the colour research book
for Colour Porcelain
July 2011

◉ ARI11-07
Jotting down the relevant
glaze codes
July 2011

◉ ARI11-07
Plates with a collection
of different glaze colours
July 2011

◉ ARI11-07
Discussing the corresponding
cardboard colour sample
July 2011

○ ARI11-09
Design of coffee cup
September 2011

○ ARI11-09
Foam models of teacup,
mug and cup with saucer
September 2011

◉ ARI13-12
Production of coffee cups
at the Arita factory in Japan
December 2013

● ARI14-04
Coffee cup and saucer
in light-pink from the Colour
Porcelain collection
April 2014

○ ARI11-07
Composition from colour and
structure research for Colour
Porcelain
July 2011

○ ARI11-07
Cardboard samples in warm-
yellow, matt light-purple and
soft-pink
July 2011

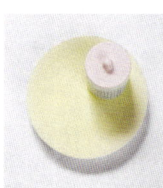

● ARI12-02
Yellow platter from the
'Minimal' series and container
with grid and soft-pink lid,
photography Inga Powilleit (IP)
February 2012

○ ARI11-07
Composition of hand-painted
colours on cardboard; colour
research conducted for Colour
Porcelain
July 2011

○ ARI11-07
Colour research on cardboard
to determine the porcelain
colours
July 2011

○ ARI11-09
Foam model of
Flower Vase Low
September 2011

○ ARI08-06
Cardboard models for size,
proportions and curves of
high vase
June 2008

○ ARI11-09
Design of Flower Vase Low
– matt soft-purple underglaze
with platinum lustre
September 2011

◉ ARI11-11
Drawing and ultimate result
of dot pattern on high vase
November 2011

◉ ARI11-10
3D rendering of high vase
from the Colour Porcelain
collection
October 2011

◉ ARI13-12
Unglazed, baked high vases
before masking and glazing
December 2013

● ARI12-04
Flower Vase High
April 2012

● ARI13-10
Products from the Colour
Porcelain collection in use,
photography Ariko Inaoka (AI)
October 2013

● ARI12-02
Bowl, mug and deep plate with red dot from the Colour Porcelain collection (IP)
February 2012

○ ARI11-07
Page from sketchbook. Sketch of sugar bowl and milk jug
July 2011

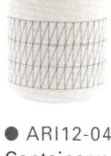

● ARI12-04
Container with red, high-gloss lid
April 2012

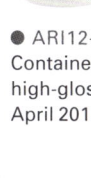

○ ARI11-07
Pages from sketchbook. Sketch with designs of small espresso cup and cup with handle
July 2011

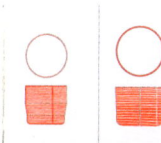

● ARI11-10
Design of bowl with lines
October 2011

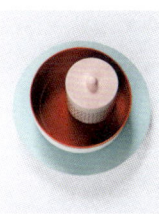

● ARI12-02
Matt-blue platter, bowl with red, high-gloss interior and container with matt-pink lid (IP)
February 2012

○ ARI11-09
Design of container
September 2011

● ARI12-02
Izumi Mountain in Arita, where in 1616 a Korean potter named Ri Sampei discovered porcelain (IP)
February 2012

● ARI12-02
The stones that are used as raw material for the unique Arita porcelain (IP)
February 2012

● ARI12-02
Flower Vase Large in the workshop of 1616/Arita Japan, where the stones are ground into powder (IP)
February 2012

● ARI12-02
The bags of porcelain clay are transported to the various ateliers (IP)
February 2012

● ARI12-02
Stones are ground into porcelain powder in the Arita factory (IP)
February 2012

● ARI12-02
Gathering the porcelain powder with a fork-lift truck (IP)
February 2012

● ARI12-02
The machine in which the porcelain powder is mixed with water for the production of clay loaves (IP)
February 2012

● ARI12-02
View inside the Arita factory (IP)
February 2012

● ARI12-02
The square porcelain clay loaves are formed in the machine (IP)
February 2012

○ ARI11-07
Detail of plaster injection moulds used in porcelain production
July 2011

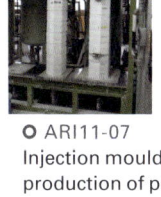

○ ARI11-07
Opening the injection moulds
July 2011

○ ARI11-07
Injection moulds for the production of porcelain
July 2011

● ARI12-02
The 1616 Arita logo is hand-stamped onto plates designed by Teruhiro Yanagihara (IP)
February 2012

● ARI12-02
Overview of the entire Colour Porcelain collection in the factory's workshop (IP)
February 2012

● ARI13-12
Unglazed, baked lids of the container before glazing
December 2013

○ ARI11-03
Tools for masking the products, allowing the different glaze colours to be applied separately
March 2011

● ARI12-02
Scholten & Baijings' Flower Vase Low is provided with a masking coating before a partial glaze is applied (IP)
February 2012

● ARI11-12
Very first prototypes of Flower Vase Low and mug
December 2011

● ARI13-12
Teacups/Japanese tea bowls with different glaze combinations
December 2013

● ARI11-08
Colour samples of matt and high-gloss porcelain glazes
August 2011

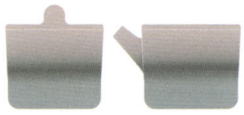

○ ARI11-09
Design of sugar bowl,
milk jug and platter
September 2011

● ARI12-04
Pink/grey flat plate from
Colour Porcelain from
the 'Colourful' collection
April 2014

● ARI12-02
Deep plate in pink and blue;
deep plate with platinum
lustre in combination with
a light-purple espresso/sake
cup (IP)
February 2012

◑ ARI13-12
Production of mugs with and
without masking, in the Arita
factory, Japan
December 2013

◑ ARI13-12
Even the bottom of the mugs
is provided with a masking
layer before the glaze is applied
December 2013

◑ ARI13-12
Production of bowls
December 2013

◑ ARI12-02
Glazing process (IP)
February 2012

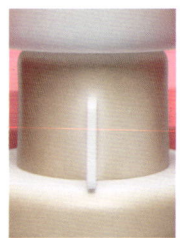

● ARI13-06
Details. The picture is part
of a series of images made
by photographers Scheltens
& Abbenes. It was
commissioned by the Art
Institute of Chicago, especially
for the 'Colour Installation'
exhibition by Scholten & Baijings
September 2013 – February 2014

● ARI13-10
Colour Porcelain
in use in Japan (AI)
October 2013

● ARI13-10
Container with grid and red
lid and all the mugs from the
Colour Porcelain collection
(AI)
October 2013

● ARI13-10
Container, teacup with light-
blue line, matt light-pink and
light-purple and three bowls
from the Colour Porcelain
collection (AI)
October 2013

● ARI13-10
Different items from the
Colour Porcelain collection
(AI)
October 2013

● ARI13-10
Colour Porcelain in use in a
Japanese kitchen (AI)
October 2013

● ARI12-08
Colour Porcelain,
specially photographed
by Scheltens & Abbenes
for T: *New York Times Style
Magazine*
August 2012

COLOUR ONE FOR MINI

COLOUR ONE FOR MINI (2012)
Industrial Product
Concept car and research into the materials, shapes and colours
   of the various car parts
Materials/Techniques: Various
Colours: Various
Client/Brand: BMW Group/MINI (Germany)

'And then you get to design a MINI!' This invitation from Adrian van Hooydonk (Senior Vice President of BMW Group Design) and Anders Warming (Head of MINI Design) to design a concept car for MINI came as a big surprise, says Scholten. 'It was an open invitation, we were allowed to work on all possible aspects and didn't have to take any technical requirements into account.'

Those who stick to the beaten track and don't have the courage to dream will never innovate. Scholten & Baijings also believe that those who don't dirty their hands during the design process won't be able to create. For them, every design process is a work in progress. Therefore, the strength of the Colour One for MINI project lies in its open, investigative character. Not a single part of the car was considered an immutable given. Everything was questioned. Scholten & Baijings' concept car is a store of innovative ideas.

Layer by layer, the designers dissected the MINI so as to penetrate to the core of the iconic design. Their new MINI was then rebuilt from the ground up. This process involved asking many questions, such as 'Why does car design tend to be so generic?', 'Why is a wheel always made up of a rim and a black rubber tyre?', 'Why are the fabrics used in cars always so neutral in terms of colour and ambience?' and 'Can we design parts that are functional both inside and outside the car?' The questions led to an unusual approach to car design, and an equally unusual result, in which various parts acquired almost autonomous qualities. For instance, storage compartments were replaced by Nomadic Pockets, which can be mounted in the car with magnets or taken out to serve as bags. The steering wheel can be clicked into place on either side of the car. The wheels were moulded in transparent coloured plastic. The bumper was transformed from a nondescript functional object into a brightly coloured, visual element.

The typical Scholten & Baijings colour palette has been applied here as well. The tailgate, for example, has been crumpled and finished in gold leaf, while the whole of the exterior was painted a light grey-blue. Gold and pale-pink geometric patterns, reminiscent of various Scholten & Baijings fabric designs, were used to embellish the safety belts. Baijings: 'Often cars have an aggressive look. We wanted our MINI to be kinder and gentler, more homely. We applied our own DNA. In the end, it is the client who consciously chooses. So we needed to strike a delicate balance between the image the car already had and our own interpretation.'

What is particularly remarkable about this new MINI is its outer skin, which was perforated with 12,500 holes, allowing smells from outside the car to penetrate inside. The holes also create a visual play of light and shadow, and function as an organic ventilation system. Scholten: 'We knew these were strange ideas to a car manufacturer, but in the meantime the MINI experts are seriously studying the possibilities we have introduced.'

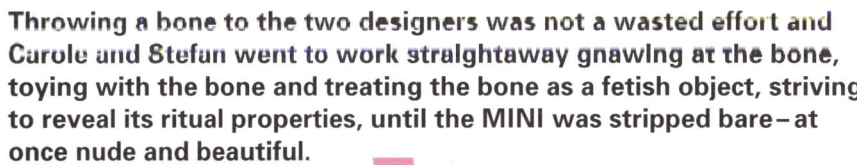

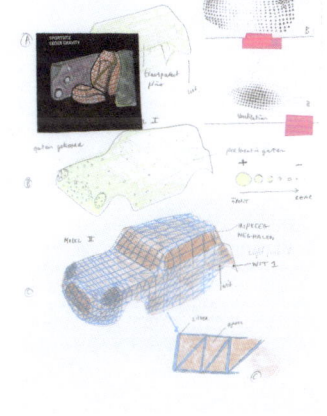

Throwing a bone to the two designers was not a wasted effort and Carole and Stefan went to work straightaway gnawing at the bone, toying with the bone and treating the bone as a fetish object, striving to reveal its ritual properties, until the MINI was stripped bare – at once nude and beautiful.
— Lidewij Edelkoort, Trend Forecaster

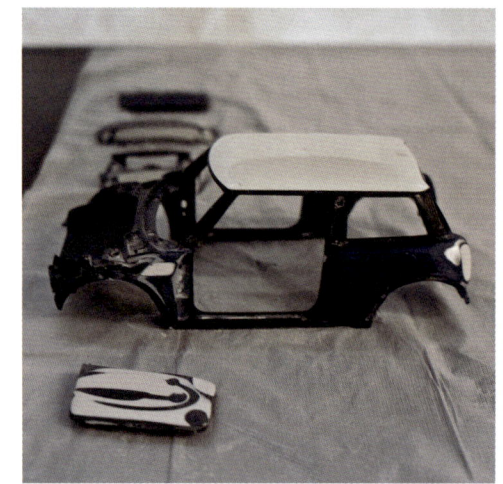

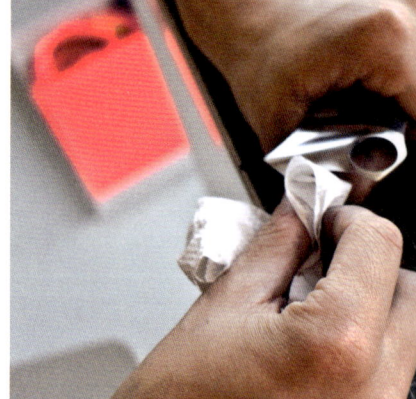

We always build our models in the studio, and we also produce things there. But this was really taking it to the extreme.
— Stefan Scholten

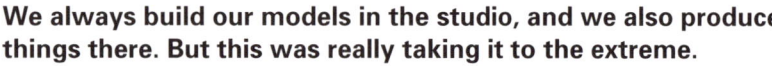

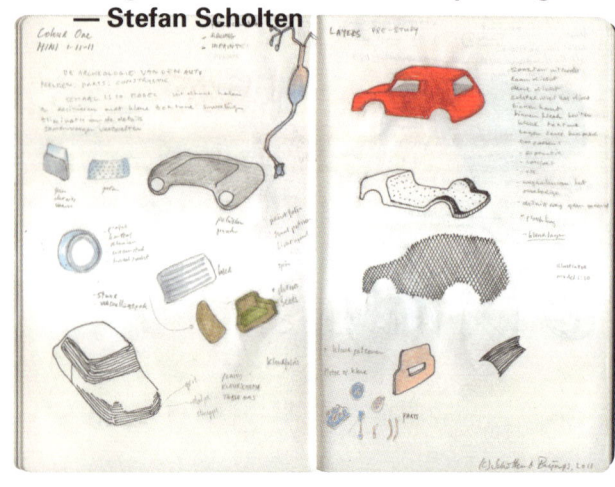

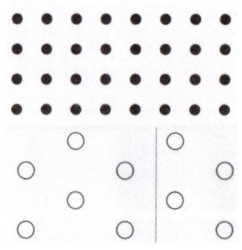

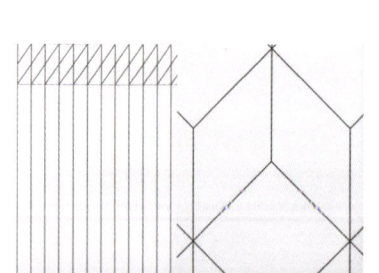

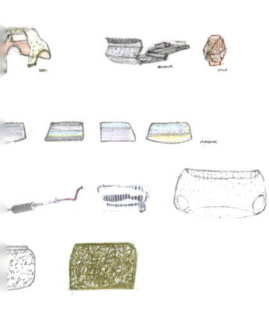

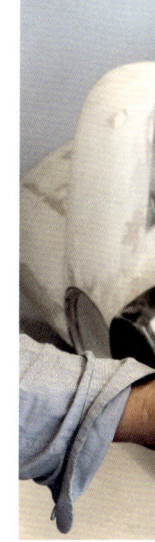

Why can't wheel and rim be moulded from one piece of material?
What's wrong with perforated bodywork and a gradient paint job?
— 'Colour One' for MINI in *Frame*, Issue 87

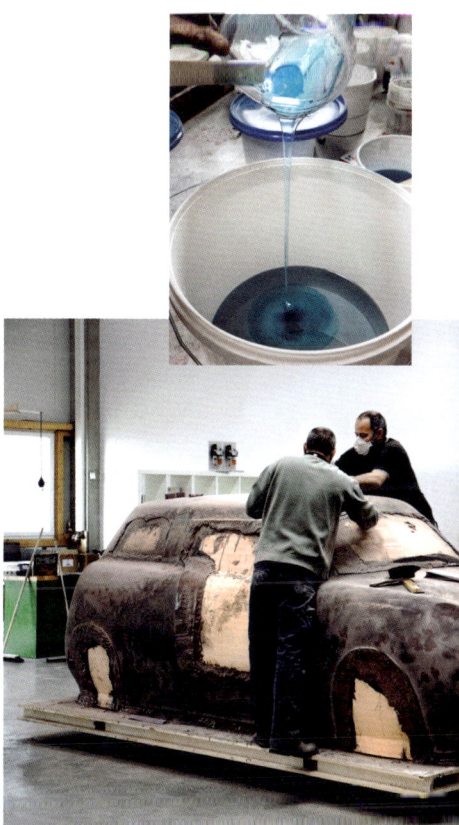

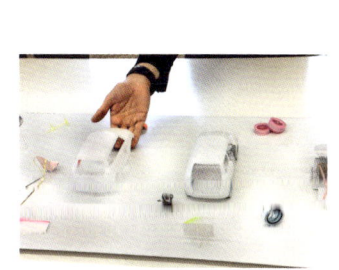

They created a one-on-one sketchbook for a car, where the process was the design laid bare. For the sake of research, they chose abstraction.
— Lidewij Edelkoort, Trend Forecaster

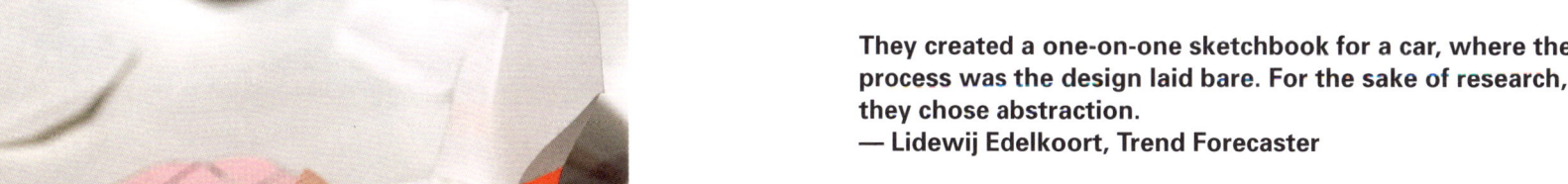

The 'Colour One' for MINI was given 12,500 perforations, changing the colour of the bodywork depending on your perspective and the incidence of light.
— Stefan Scholten

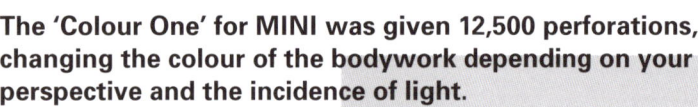

The stitching on the seat's textile upholstery was made by hand. It's a bit irregular, but we really like that. It's important to have something personal as a counterweight to all the mass-produced perfection.
— Carole Baijings

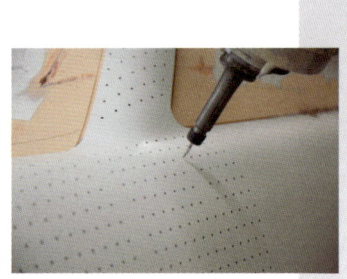

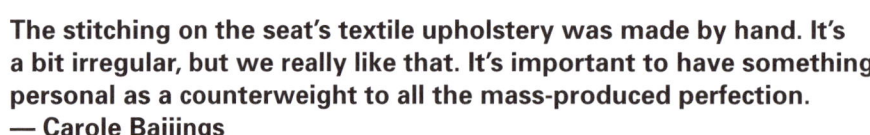

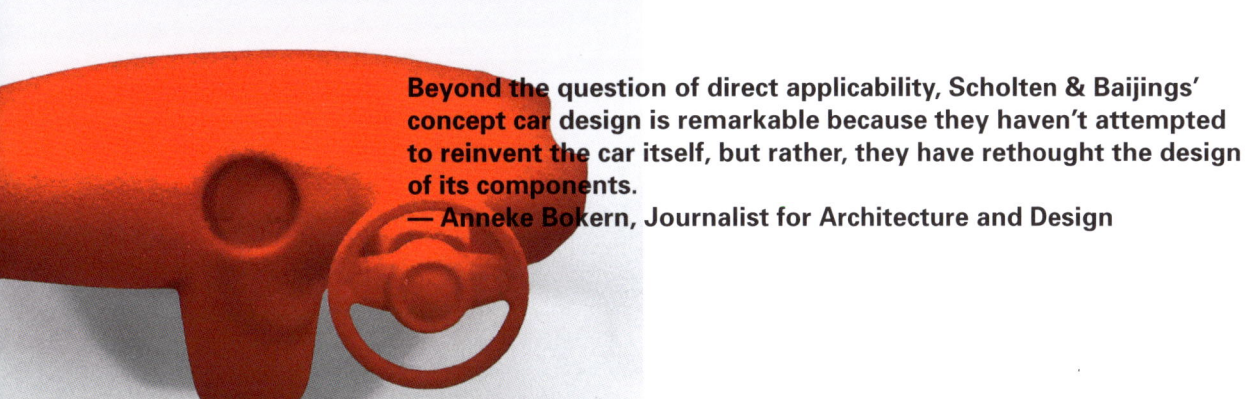

Beyond the question of direct applicability, Scholten & Baijings' concept car design is remarkable because they haven't attempted to reinvent the car itself, but rather, they have rethought the design of its components.
— Anneke Bokern, *Journalist for Architecture and Design*

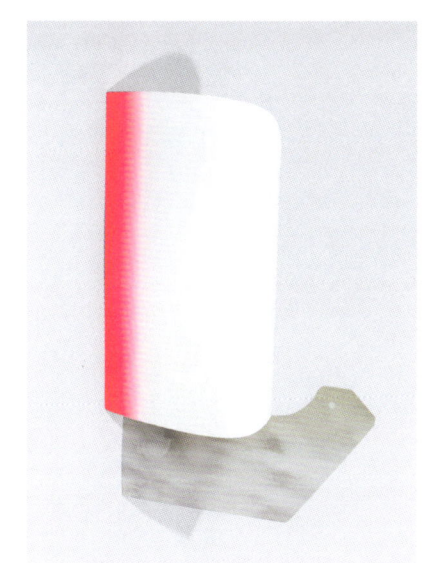

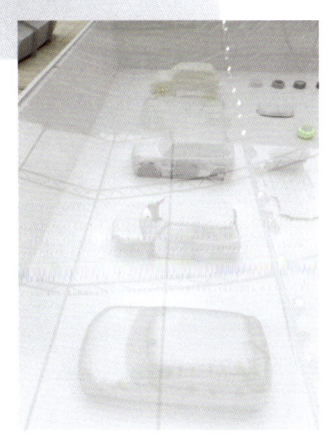

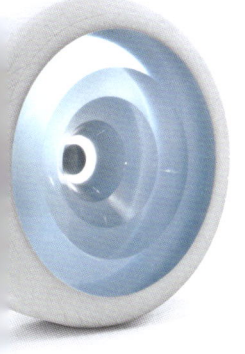

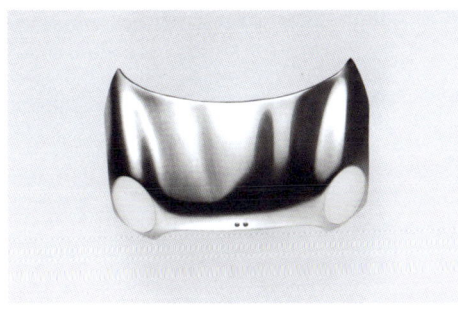

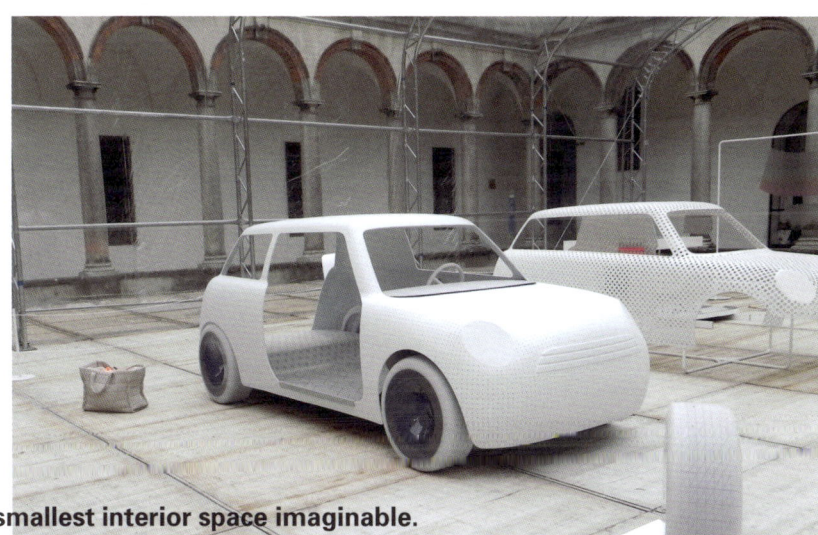

A car has the smallest interior space imaginable.
— Carole Baijings

201

MIN11-10

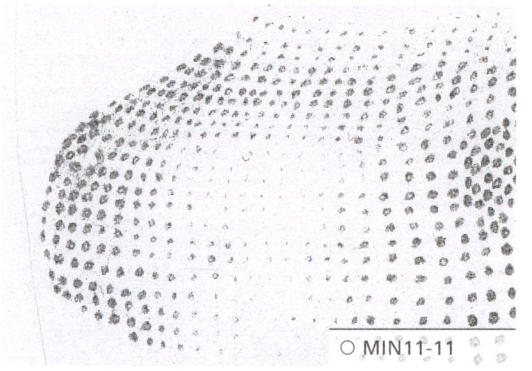

○ MIN11-11

○ MIN11-10

○ MIN11-12

○ MIN11-12

○ MIN11-12

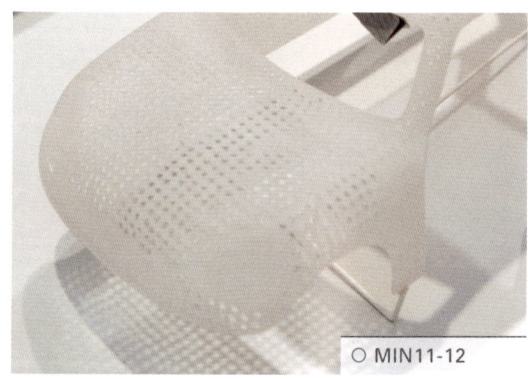

○ MIN11-12

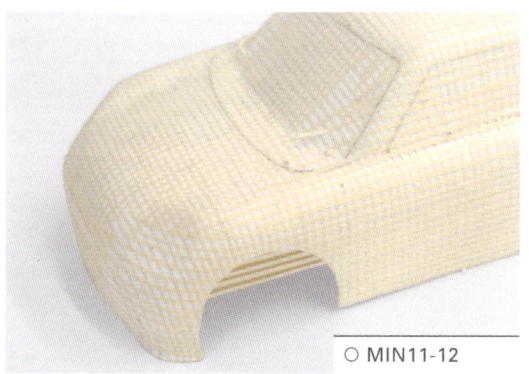

○ MIN11-12

● MIN12-04

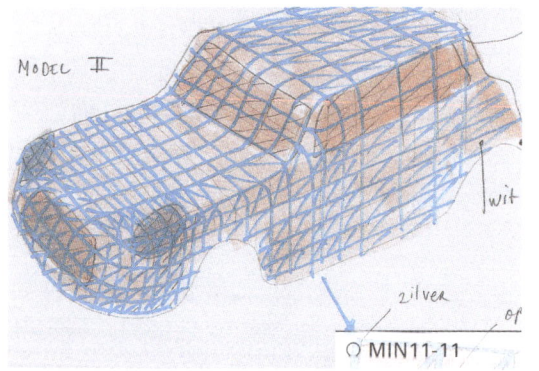

MODEL II

zilver

○ MIN11-11

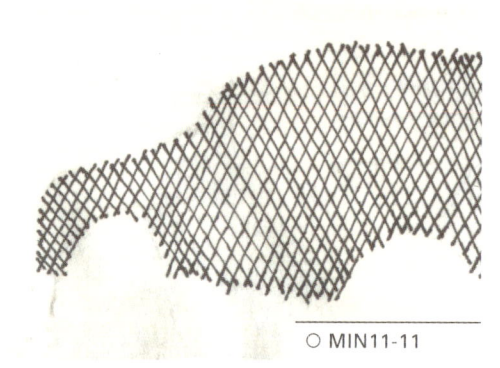

○ MIN11-11

204

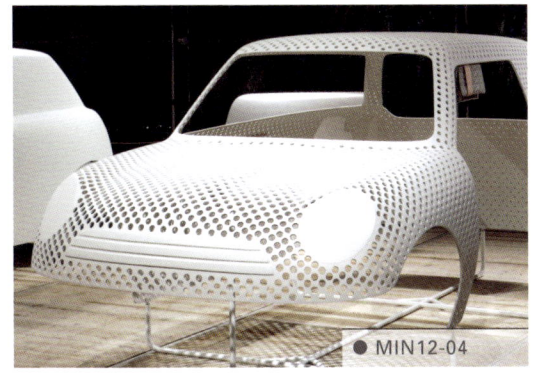

● MIN12-04

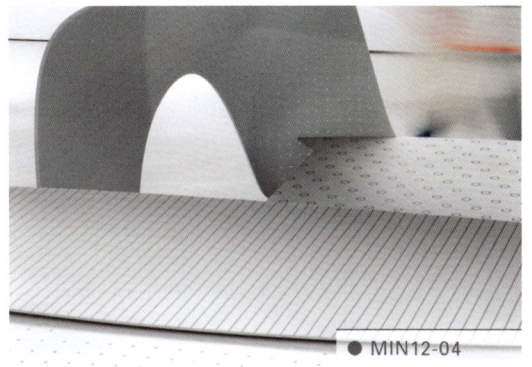

● MIN12-04

COLOUR ONE FOR MINI BY SC

● MIN13-02

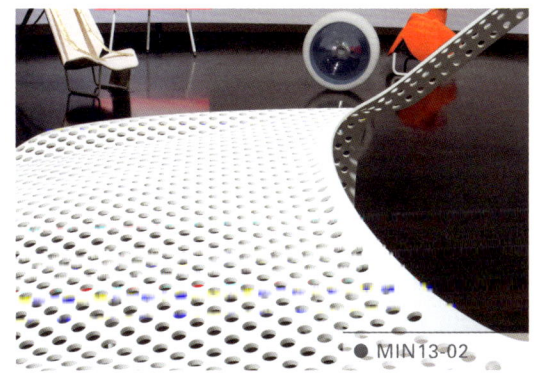

● MIN13-02

● MIN12-04

FOR MINI BY SCHOLTEN & BAIJING

● MIN13-02

● MIN12-04

FOR MINI BY SCHOLTEN & BAI NGS

● MIN13-02

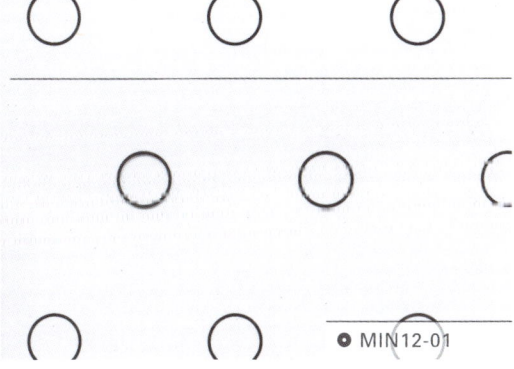

● MIN12-01

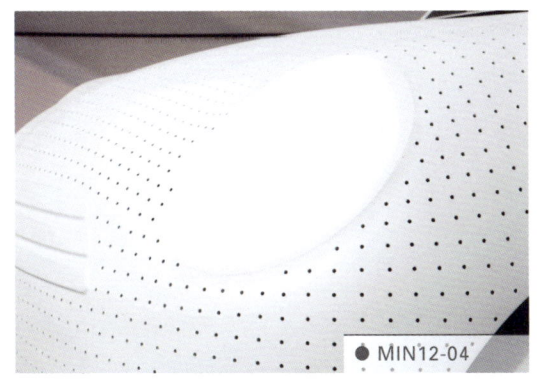

● MIN12-04

● MIN12-04

MIN12-03

MIN12-03

MIN12-03

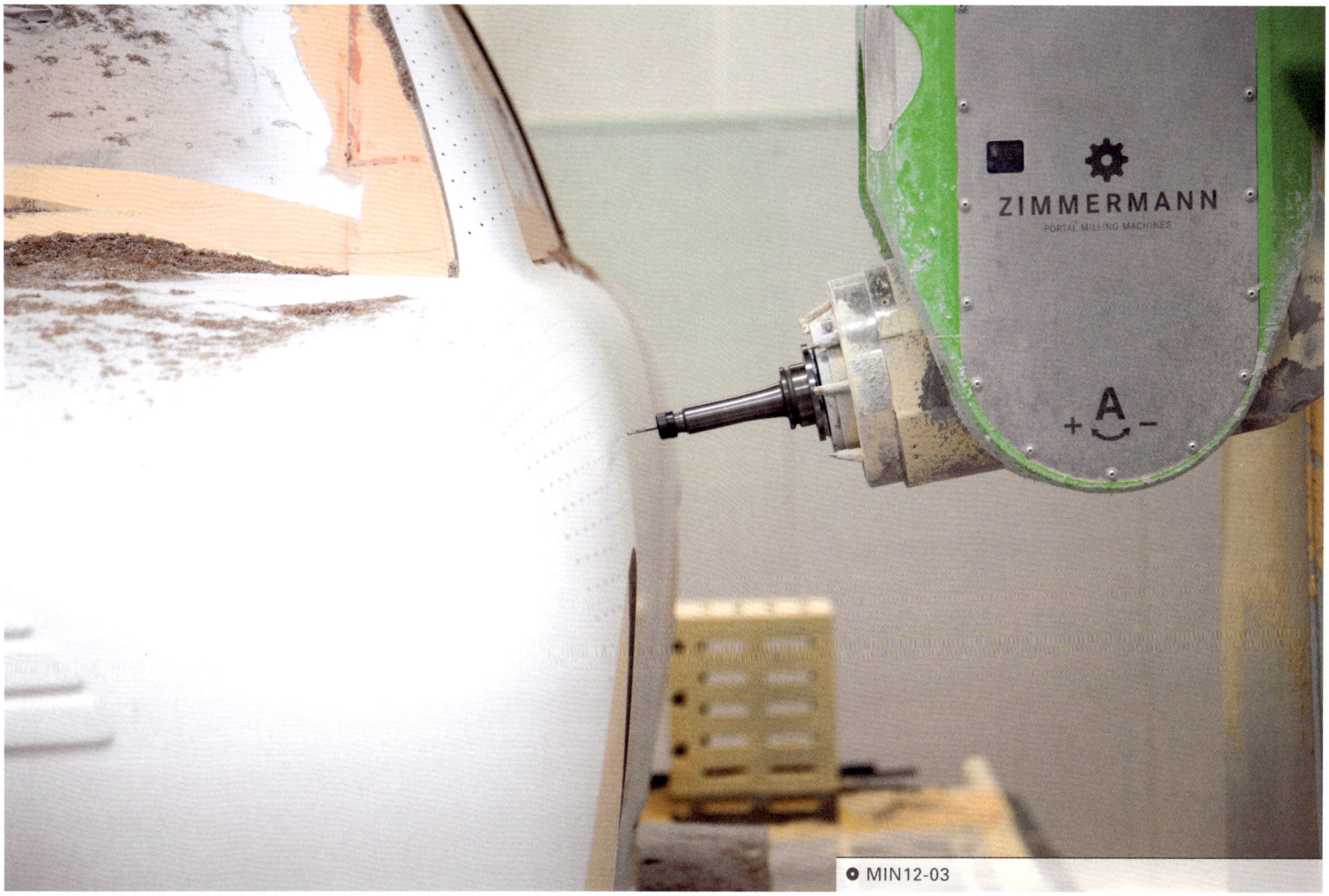

ZIMMERMANN
PORTAL MILLING MACHINES

+ A −

● MIN12-03

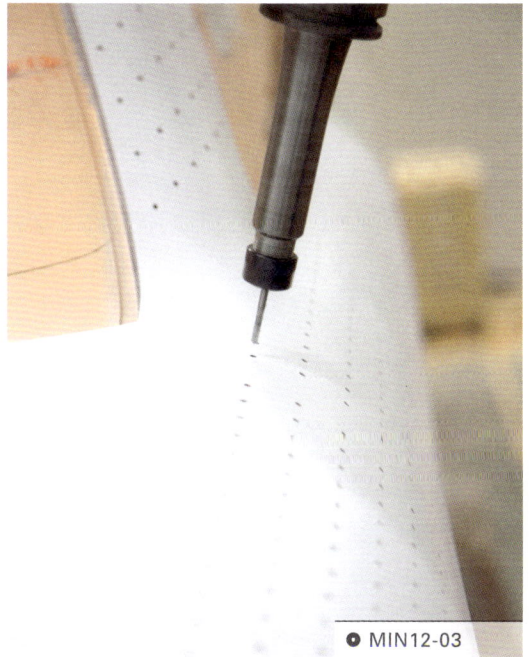

● MIN12-03

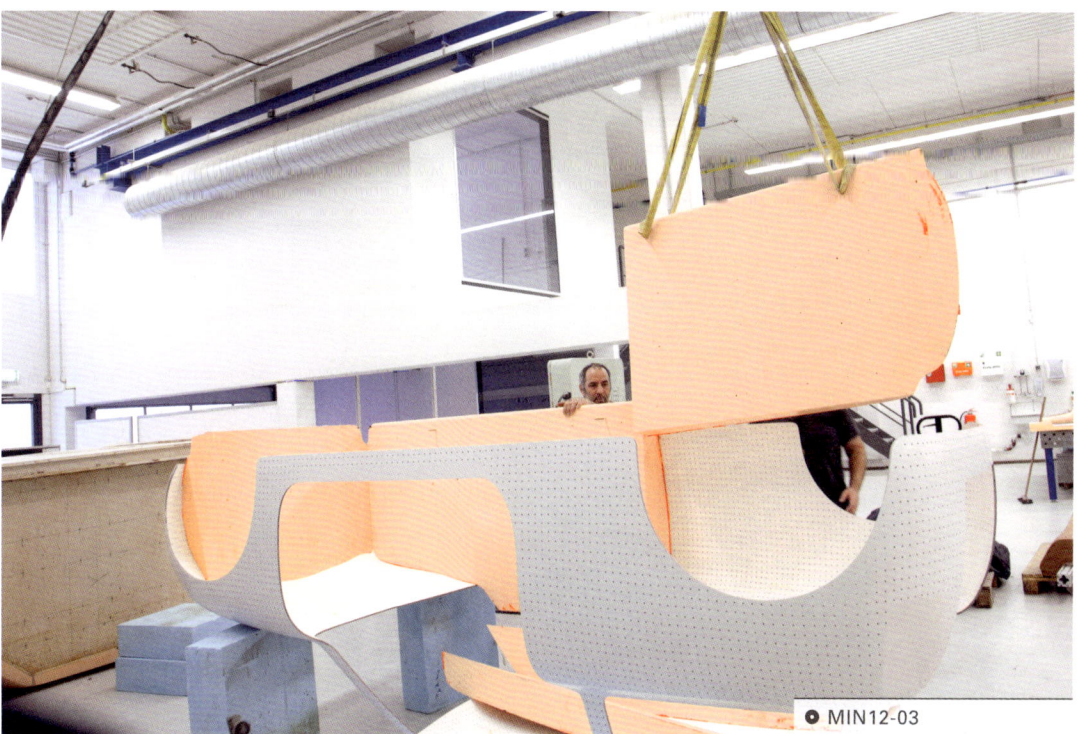

● MIN12-03

207

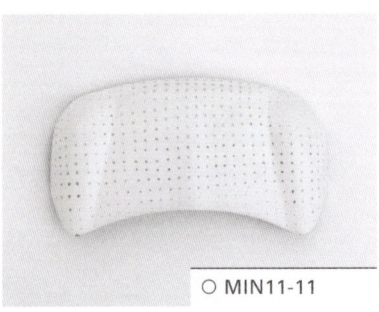

○ MIN11-11

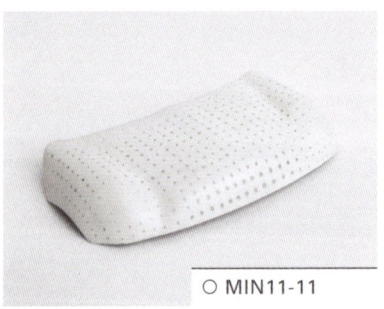

○ MIN11-11

○ MIN11-11

○ MIN11-11

○ MIN11-11

○ MIN11-10

○ MIN11-10

○ MIN11-12

○ MIN11-10

○ MIN11-10

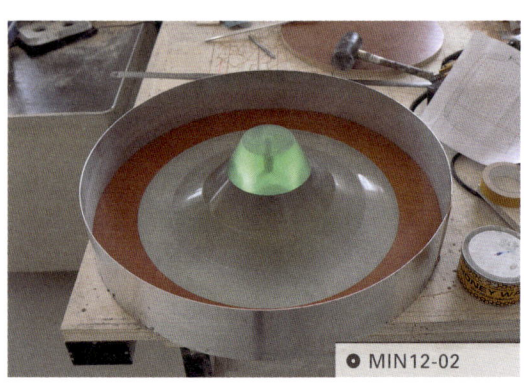

● MIN12-02

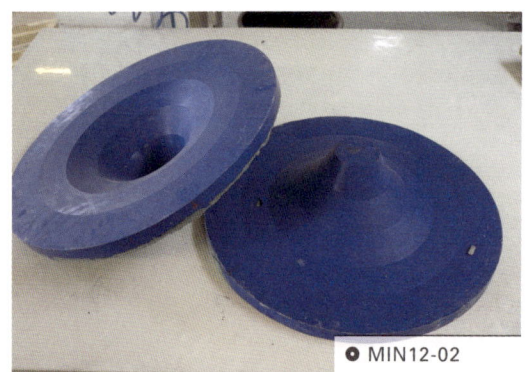

● MIN12-02

● MIN12-02

● MIN12-02

● MIN12-02

● MIN12-04

● MIN12-04

● MIN13-02

● MIN13-02

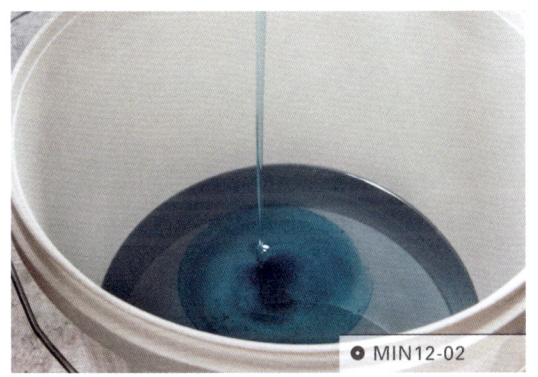

● MIN12-02

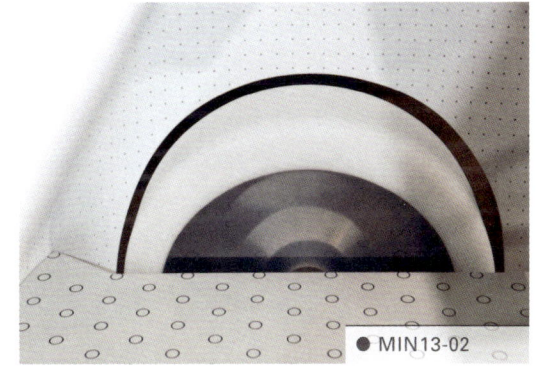

● MIN13-02

● MIN12-02

● MIN12-04

● MIN12-04

● MIN12-02

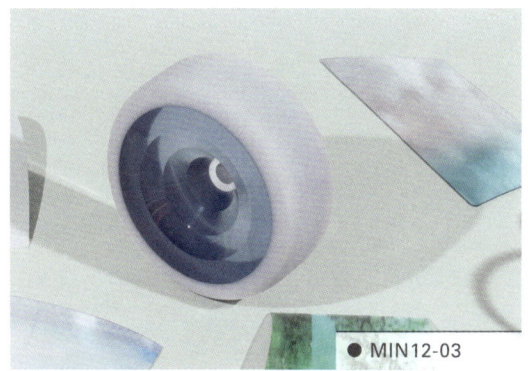

● MIN12-03

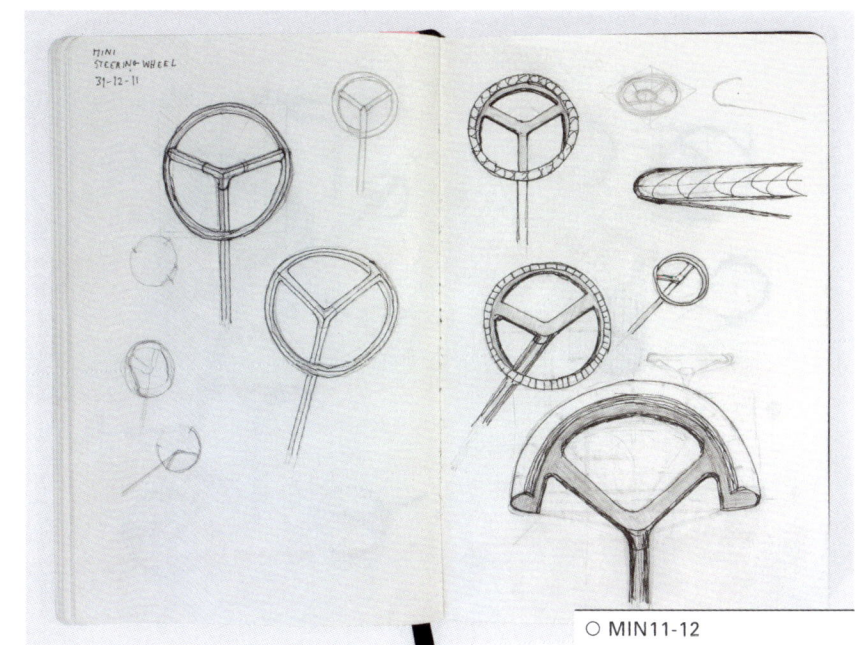

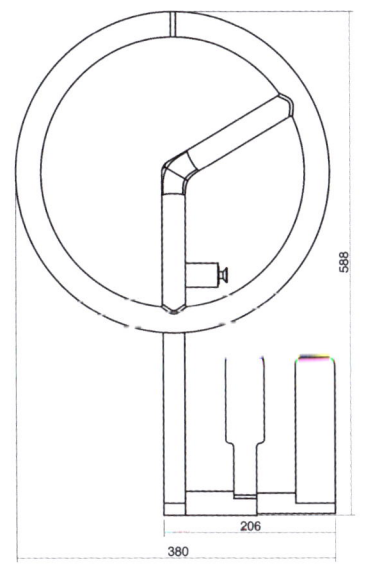

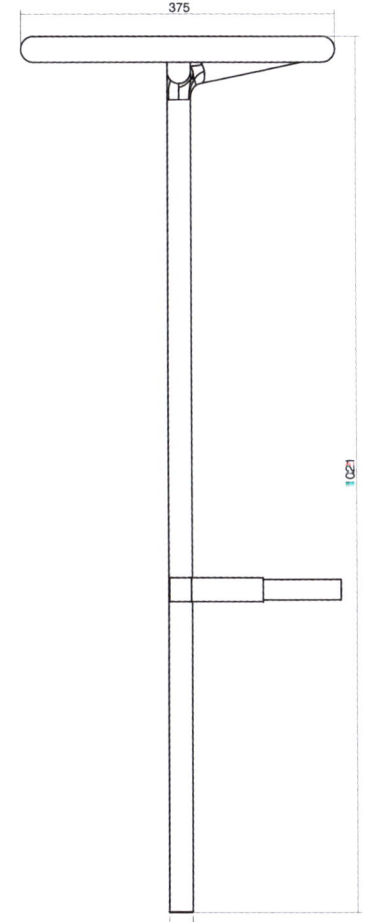

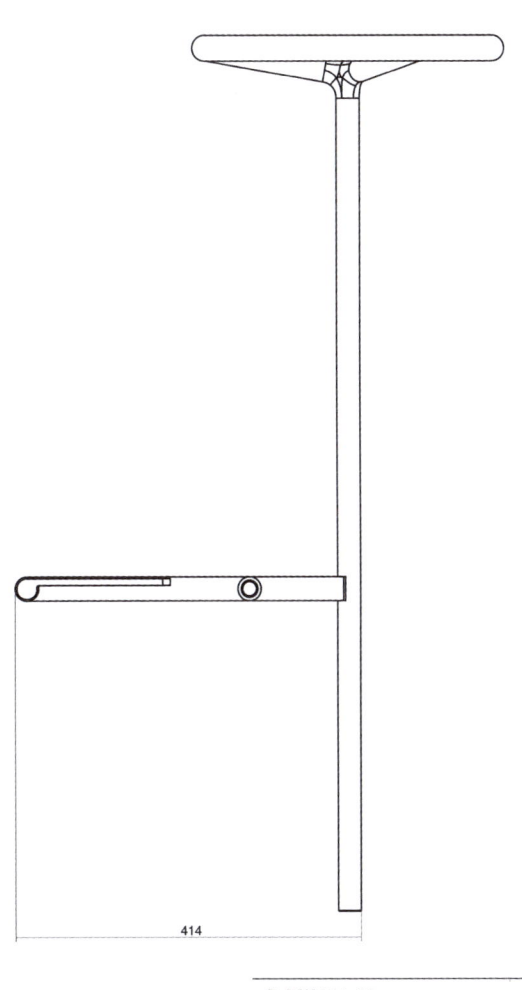

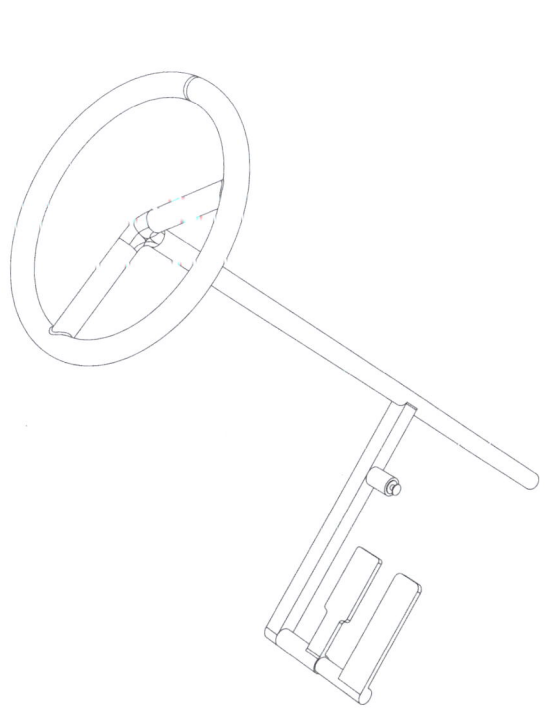

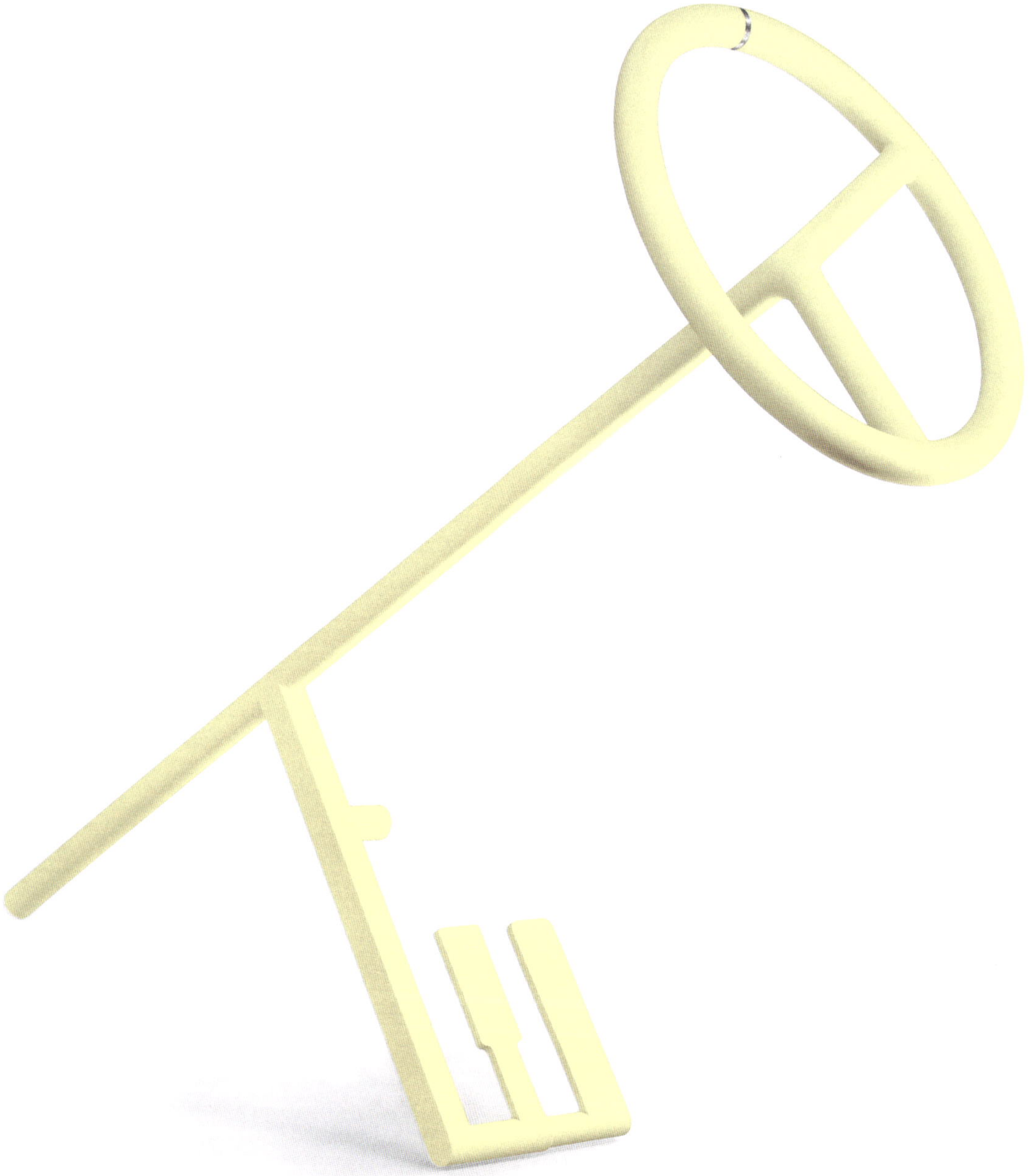

● MIN12-04

○ MIN11-12

MIN12-04

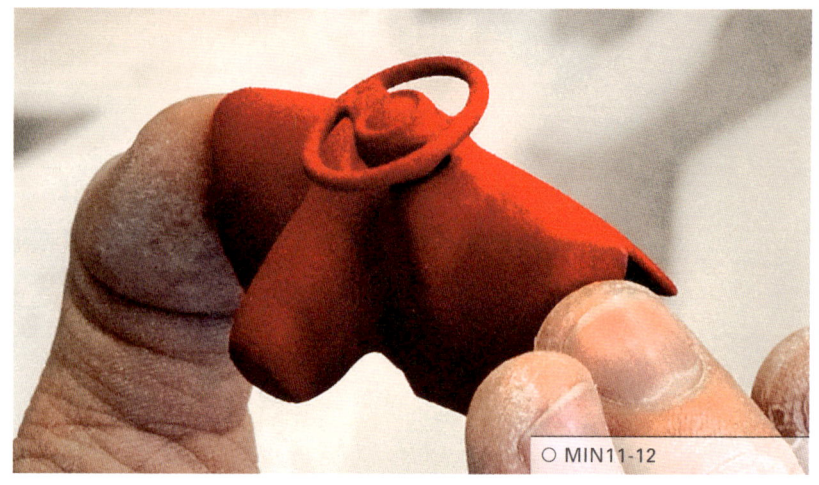

○ MIN11-12

○ MIN11-12

● MIN12-02

216

○ MIN11-12

○ MIN11-11

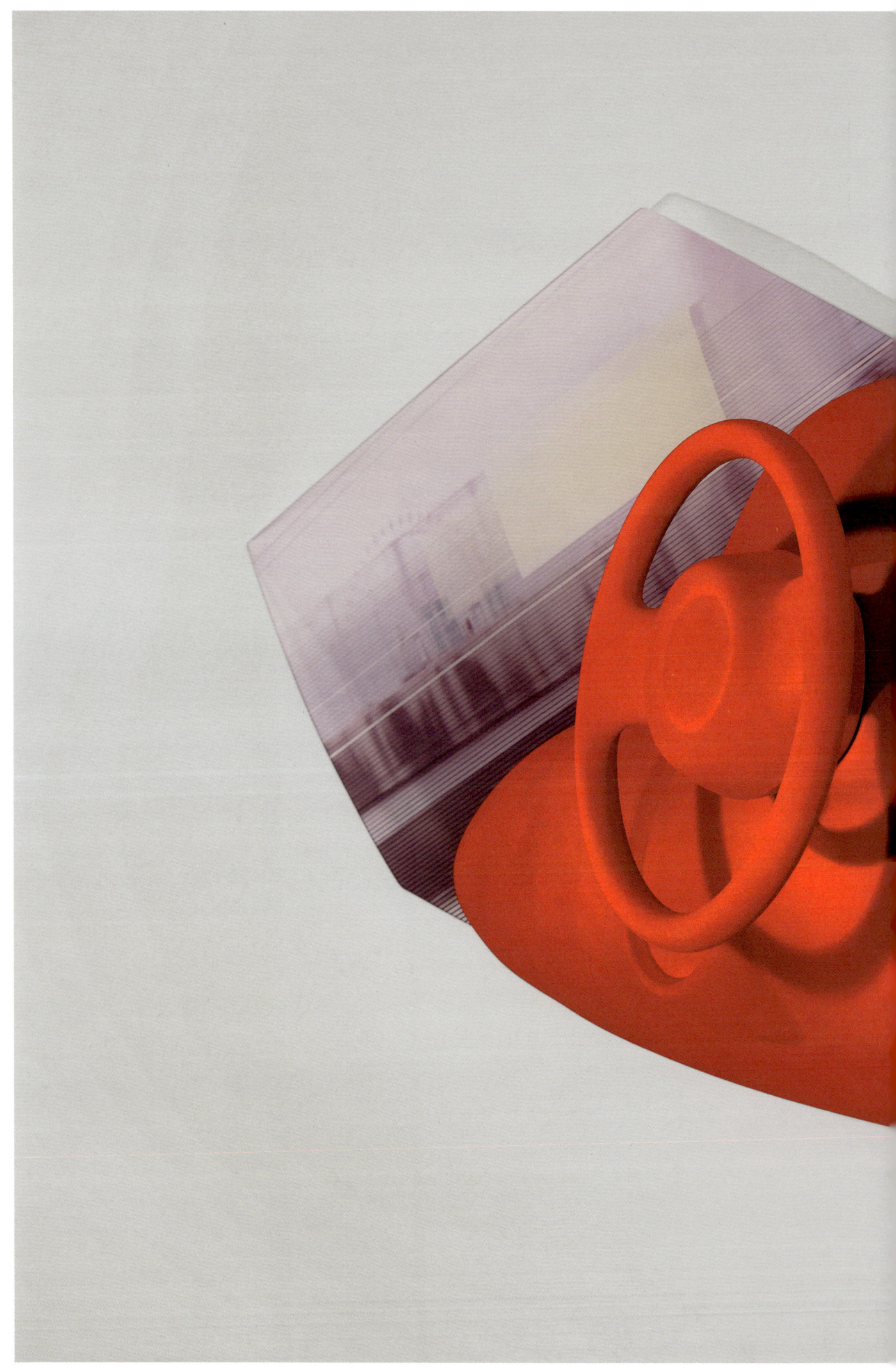

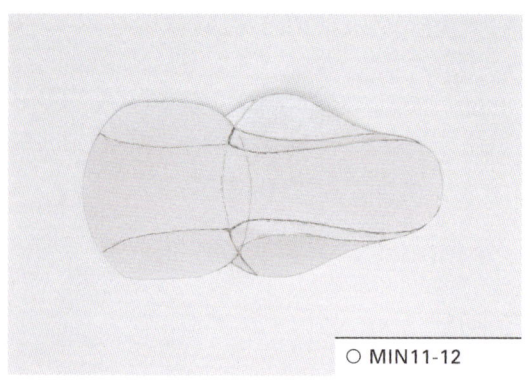

○ MIN11-12

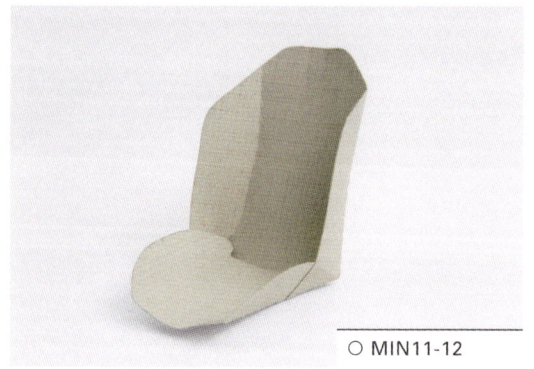

○ MIN11-12

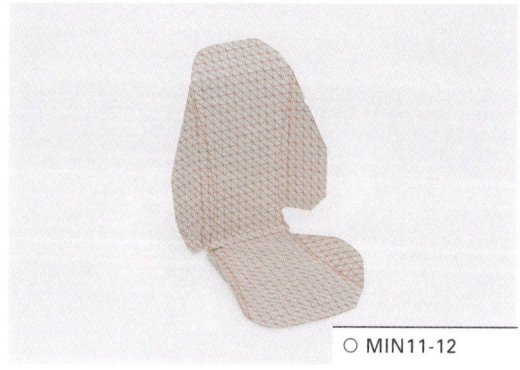

○ MIN11-12

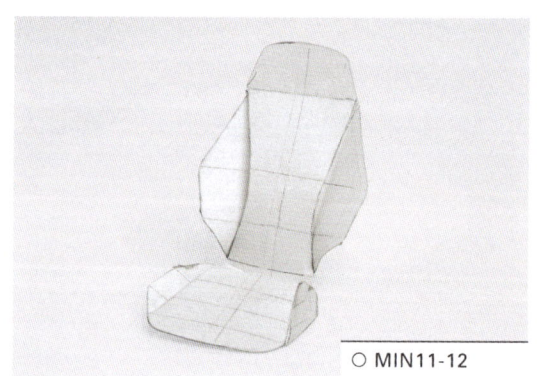

○ MIN11-12

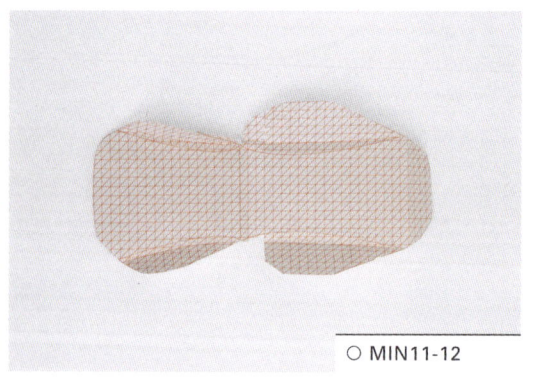

○ MIN11-12

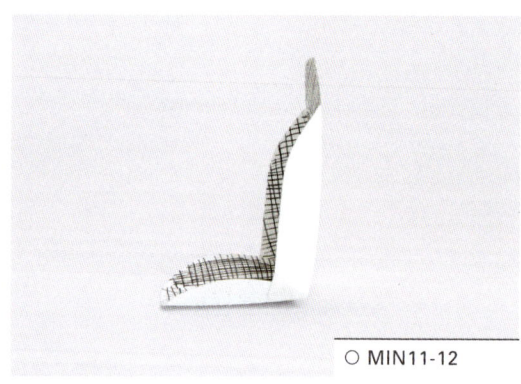

○ MIN11-12

○ MIN11-12

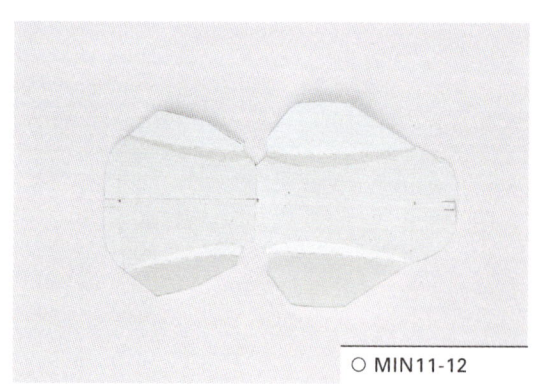

○ MIN11-12

○ MIN11-12

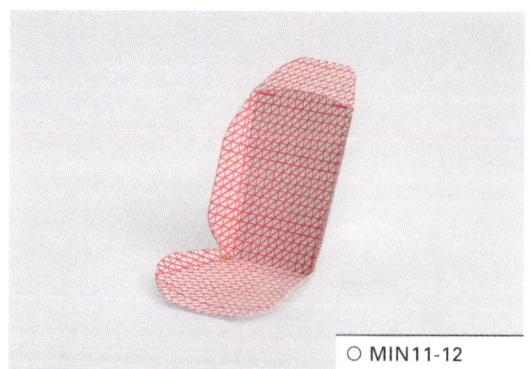

○ MIN11-12

MIN11-12

FRAGILE AND THIS
COLOUR ONE FOR M...
SCHOLTEN & BAIJING...
PART: STEERING WHEEL

MIN12-04

○ MIN11-12

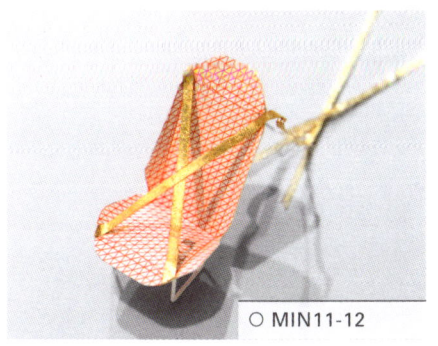

○ MIN11-12

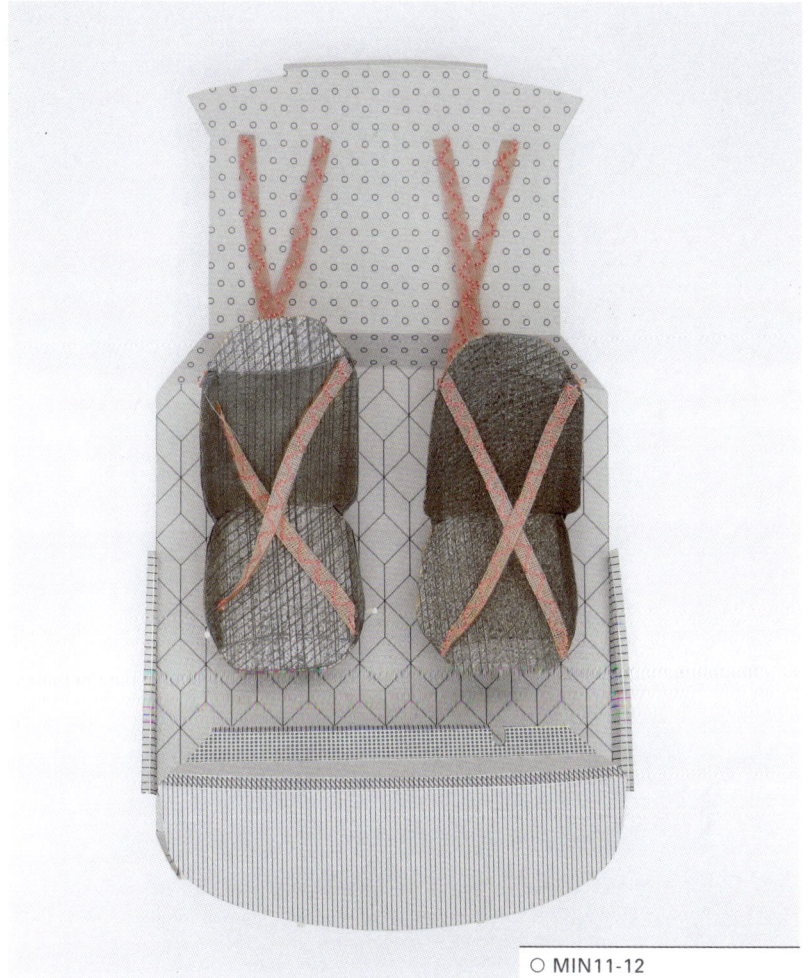

○ MIN11-12

◉ MIN12-01

○ MIN11-12

● MIN12-02

● MIN12-02

○ MIN11-12

● MIN13-02

224

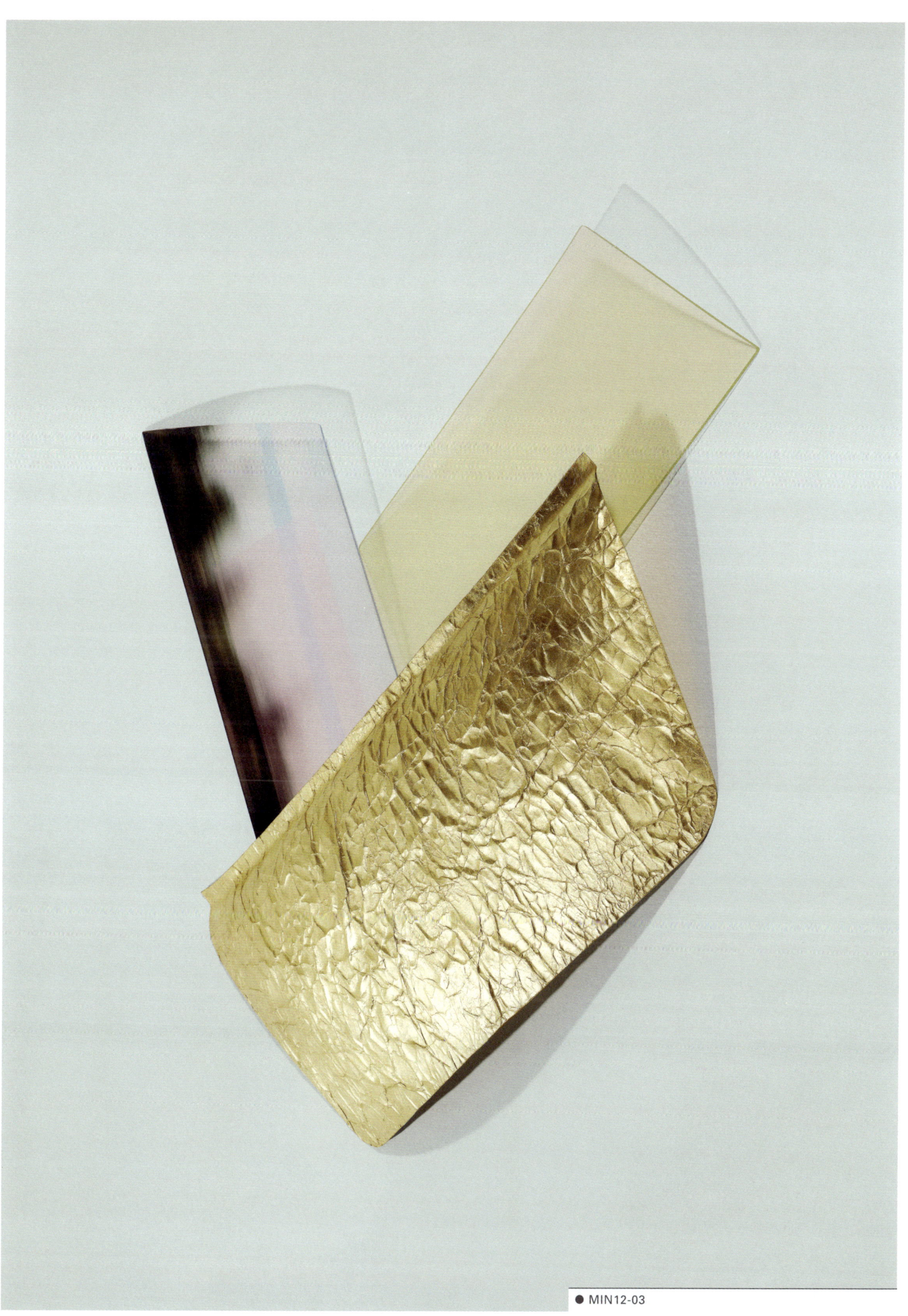

● MIN12-03

○ MIN12-02

● MIN11-11

● MIN12-04

○ MIN11-12

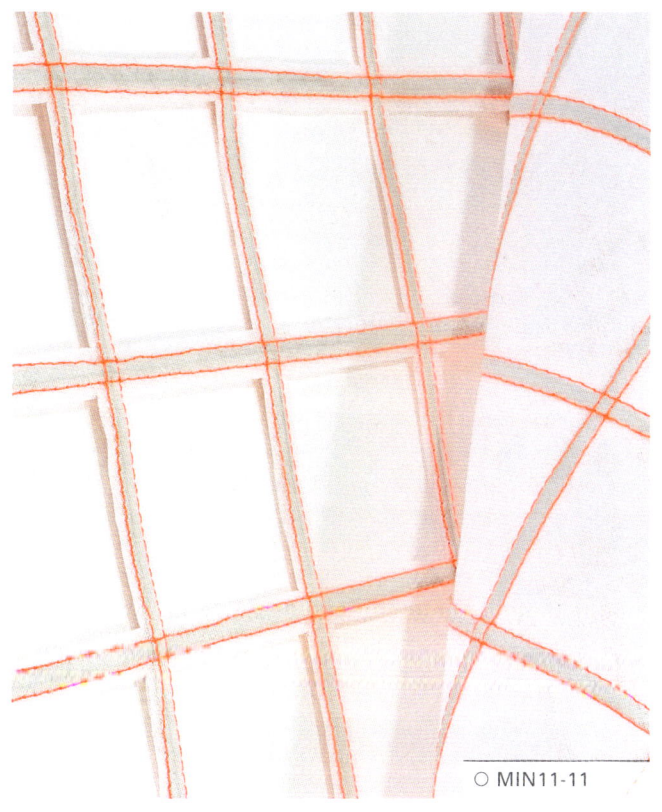

○ MIN11-11

○ MIN12-01

O MIN12-01

● MIN12-04

● MIN12-03

○ MIN11-12

● MIN13-02

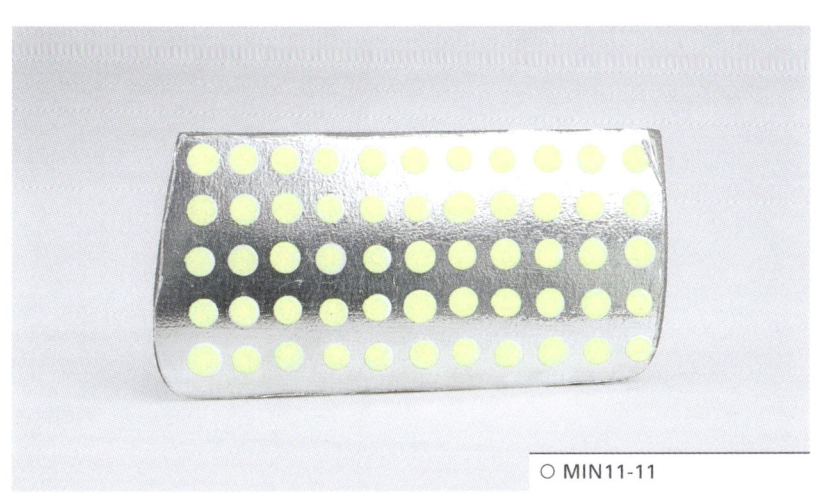

○ MIN11-11

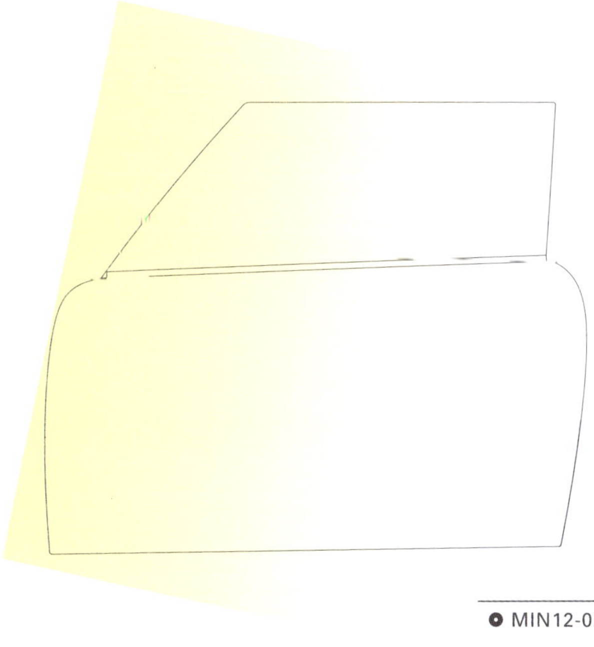

● MIN12-02

231

○ MIN11-12

○ MIN11-10

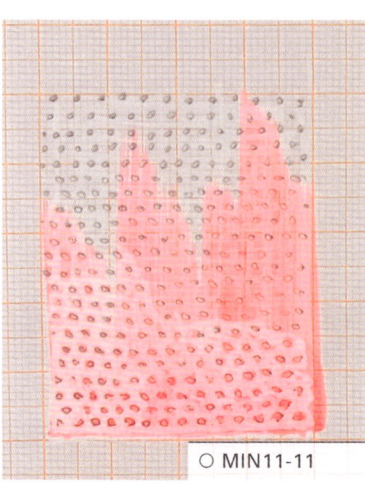

○ MIN11-11

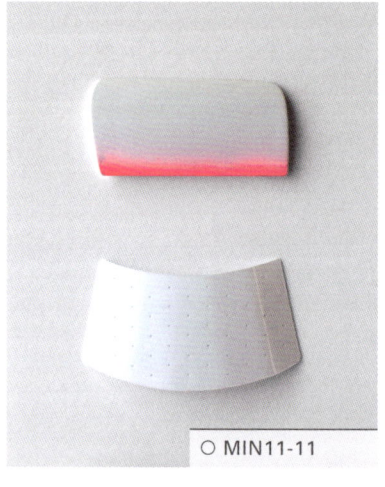

○ MIN11-11

○ MIN11-11

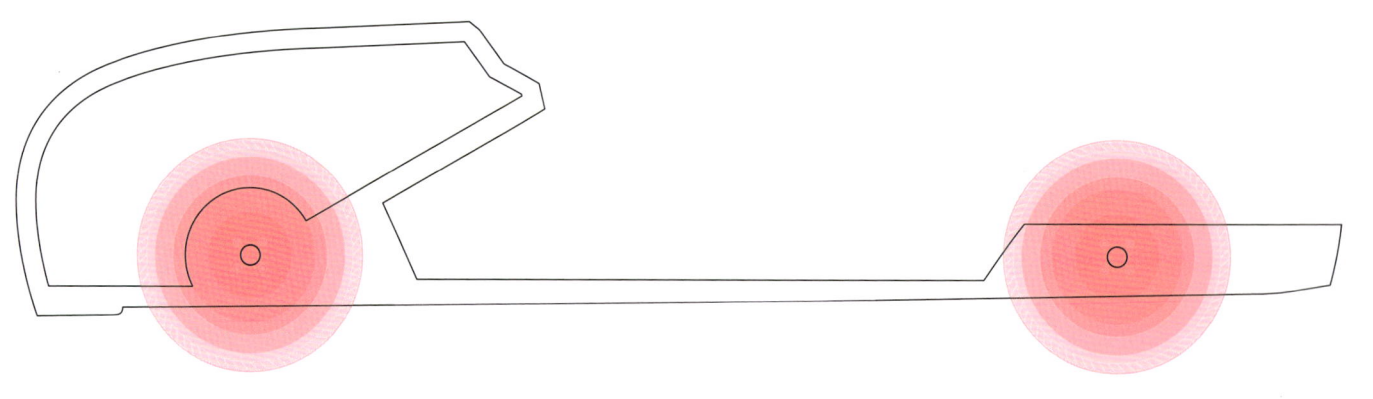

○ MIN11-12

● MIN12-03

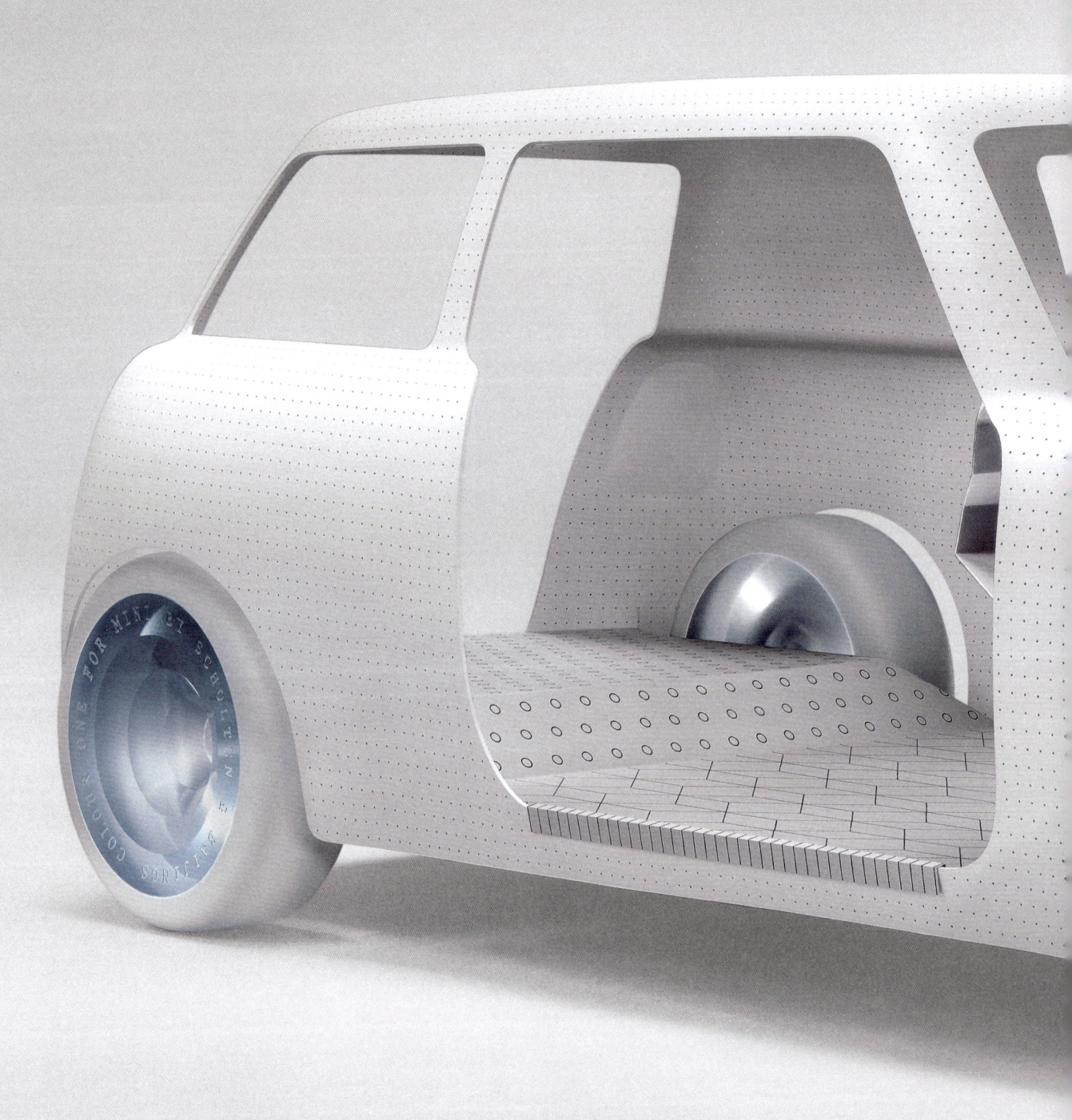

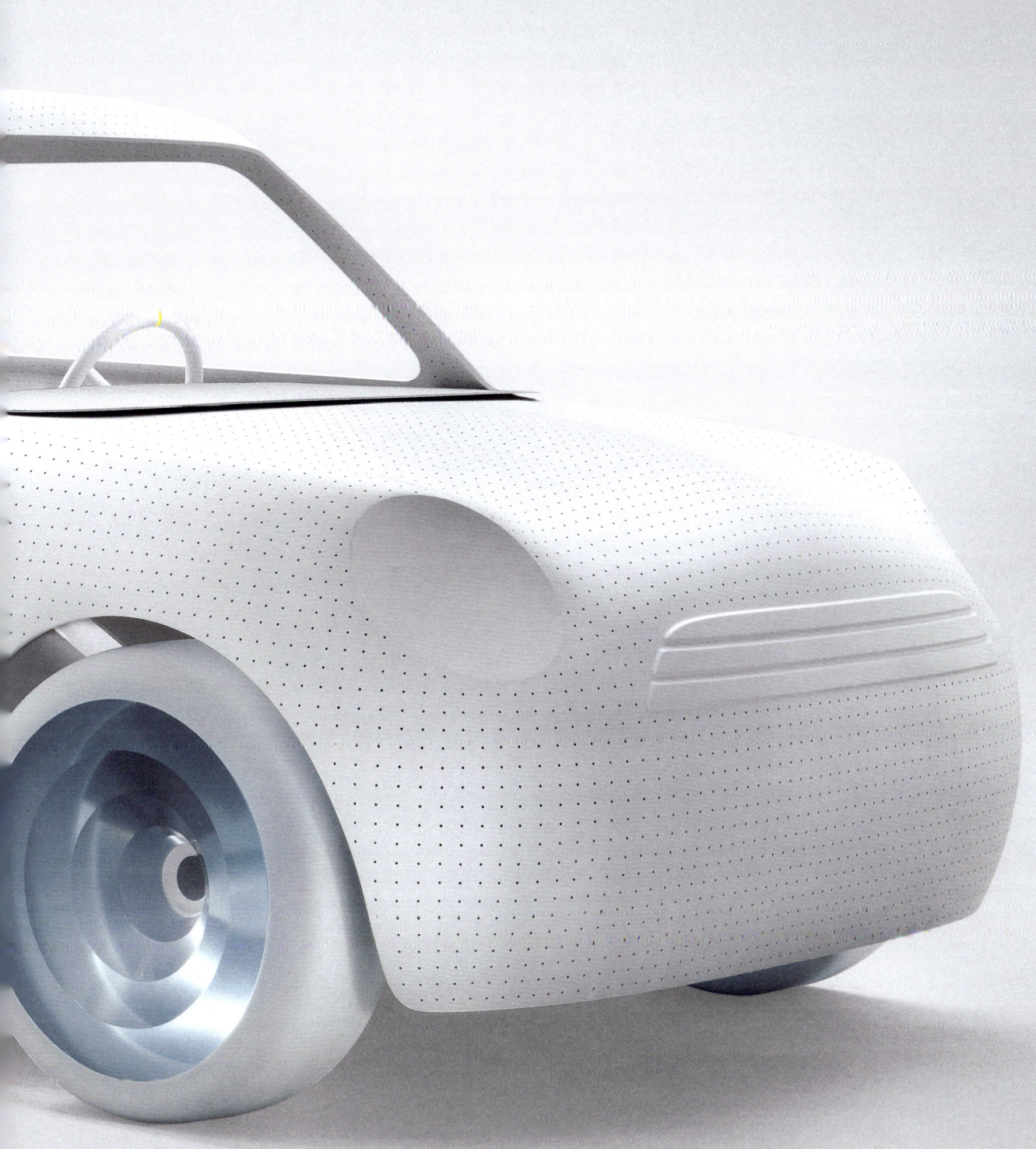

● MIN12-04

○ MIN11-10
All the components of
the dismantled MINI ONE,
1:18 scale model
October 2011

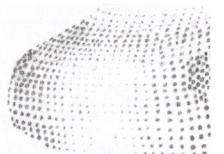

○ MIN11-11
Sketch of the holes in
the car's Shell
November 2011

○ MIN11-10
MINI ONE, 1:18 scale model,
peeled like an onion
October 2011

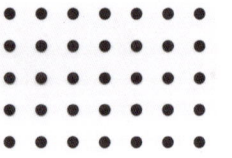

○ MIN11-12
Dot pattern in 'Colour One'
for MINI's Interior Sheet
December 2011

○ MIN11-12
Shell, 1:18 scale model
of papier-mâché, viewed
from top
December 2011

○ MIN11-12
Shell, 1:18 scale model of
papier-mâché, fluorescent
yellow inside
December 2011

○ MIN11-12
Shell, 1:18 scale model,
made by hand in the studio
December 2011

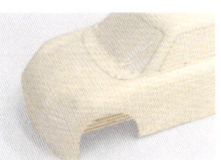

○ MIN11-12
Tape-covered, vacuum-formed
1:18 scale model for positioning
the holes to be drilled
December 2011

● MIN12-04
Shell with gradient hole
pattern, ranging from large
to small, presented in Milan
during the Salone del Mobile
April 2012

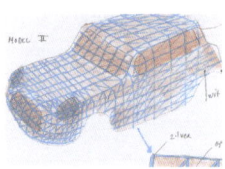

○ MIN11-11
Sketch of Shell with grid
pattern
November 2011

○ MIN11-11
Detail from sketchbook.
Sketch of Grid Shell
November 2011

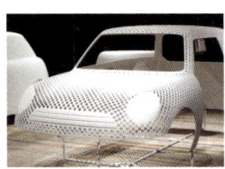

● MIN12-04
Shell with a gradient hole
pattern and Nomadic Pockets,
presented in Milan during
the Salone del Mobile 2012
April 2012

● MIN12-04
Details of the holes in the
exterior and Interior Sheet
patterns of the Concept Car
for MINI. Photography Inga
Powilleit (IP)
April 2012

● MIN13-02
Shell with a gradient hole
pattern and Nomadic Pockets,
exhibited at the BMW Museum
in Munich
February 2013

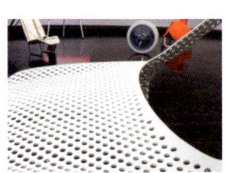

● MIN13-02
Detail of the Shell with holes
at BMW Museum
February 2013

● MIN12-04
Shell and Concept Car, with
door and colour gradient in
the background. 'Colour One'
for MINI in Milan
April 2012

● MIN13-02
Different angle of Shell with
holes at BMW Museum
February 2013

● MIN12-04
Stefan and Carole examine
Shell during assembly (IP)
April 2012

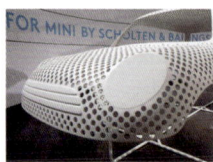

● MIN13-02
Detail of grille and headlight
in Shell at BMW Museum
February 2013

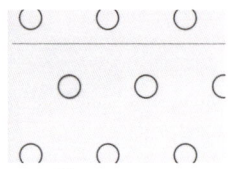

◉ MIN12-01
Dot pattern of Interior Sheet
January 2012

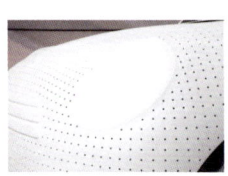

● MIN12-04
Dot pattern with headlights
of the Concept Car
April 2012

● MIN12-04
Shell with a gradient hole
pattern and Nomadic Pockets.
Photography MINI (M)
April 2012

◉ MIN12-03
Foam model of the Concept
Car at the prototype workshop
in Munich (M)
March 2012

◉ MIN12-03
Assembly of the front of the
Concept Car, cut out of foam
(M)
March 2012

◉ MIN12-03
Hand-sanded clay model
of the Concept Car at
the prototype workshop
in Munich (M)
March 2012

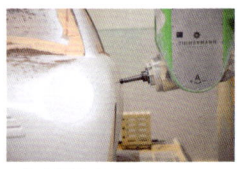

◉ MIN12-03
Drilling 12,500 holes at
the prototype workshop
in Munich (M)
March 2012

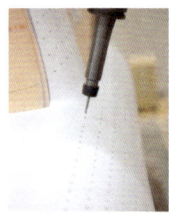

◉ MIN12-03
Drilling thousands of holes
in the Concept Car's Shell
with a robot arm (M)
March 2012

◉ MIN12-03
Removing the interior form from
the Concept Car's Shell (M)
March 2012

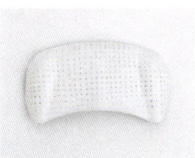

○ MIN11-11
Hole pattern applied in pencil
on shaved 1:18 scale model of
motor hood
November 2011

○ MIN11-11
Front of motor hood with
hand applied dot pattern
November 2011

○ MIN11-11
Sketch of motor hood
and doors for Art Parts
November 2011

○ MIN11-11
Hand-sanded motor hood
of 1:18 scale model without
headlights
November 2011

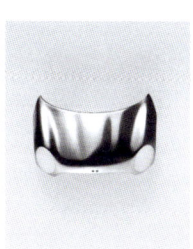

○ MIN11-12
Polished motor hood with
acrylic headlights of MINI One
Art Parts at a scale of 1:18 (M)
December 2011

○ MIN11-11
Sketches of the 'Colour One'
for MINI wheel
November 2011

○ MIN11-10
Painted rubber tyre and cast
scale models of the wheel
October 2011

○ MIN11-10
Cast colour samples for
the wheel
October 2011

○ MIN11-12
Cast wheel, 1:18 scale model,
on the Conceptual Concept
Car (IP)
December 2011

○ MIN11-10
Cast colour samples for
the wheel in gradient hues
October 2011

○ MIN11-10
1:18 scale model of coloured
wheel for 'Colour One' for
MINI/ cast wheel, 1:18 scale
model, for the Conceptual
Concept Car
October 2011

◉ MIN12-02
Mould for casting the wheels
February 2012

◉ MIN12-02
Parts of the mould used
for casting the 'Colour One'
for MINI wheels
February 2012

◉ MIN12-02
First casting of the synthetic
wheel with colour samples
and 1:18 scale model of the
Concept Car (IP)
February 2012

◉ MIN12-02
Vincent de Rijk cuts a
synthetic disc for the wheel
with millimetre precision (IP)
February 2012

◉ MIN12-02
Parts of the synthetic wheel
in Vincent de Rijk's workshop
February 2012

◉ MIN12-04
Wheel cast in one piece from
a combination of different
synthetic materials (M)
April 2012

◉ MIN12-04
Concept Car exhibited in
a paddock setting during
the Salone del Mobile in Milan
(M)
April 2012

◉ MIN13-02
Wheel cast in one piece
presented at the BMW
Museum
February 2013

◉ MIN13-02
Concept Car presented
at the BMW Museum
February 2013

◉ MIN12-02
Determining the formula
for the wheel's colour (IP)
February 2012

◉ MIN13-02
Wheels viewed from the
inside of the Concept Car
February 2013

◉ MIN12-02
Stefan and Carole with the
first casting of the synthetic
wheel in Vincent de Rijk's
workshop (IP)
February 2012

◉ MIN12-04
'Colour One' Concept Car
for MINI (M)
April 2012

◉ MIN12-04
Wheel cast in one piece from
a combination of different
synthetic materials, at the
presentation of 'Colour One'
for MINI in Milan (M)
April 2012

◉ MIN12-02
The prototype and samples
of the wheel for MINI
with 1:18 scale model of
the Concept Car (IP)
February 2012

● MIN12-03
Detail of Wheel,
photographed by
Scheltens & Abbenes (S&A)
March 2012

● MIN12-03
Wheel with Landscape
Window (S&A)
March 2012

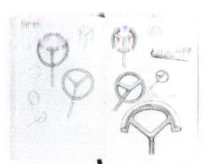

○ MIN11-12
Pages from sketchbook.
Sketches of the steering
wheel for 'Colour One'
for MINI
December 2011

◉ MIN11-12
Technical drawings
of the steering wheel
December 2011

◉ MIN11-12
3D drawing of the steering
wheel for 'Colour One' for
MINI
December 2011

● MIN11-12
Steering wheel with pedals (M)
December 2011

○ MIN11-12
Colour samples for
the steering wheel
December 2011

● MIN12-04
Detail of the Concept Car.
Aluminium Interior Sheet
with grid pattern and steering
wheel with pedals (IP)
April 2012

○ MIN11-12
Art Part, dashboard,
1:18 scale model (IP)
December 2011

○ MIN11-12
View through studio
to workshop (IP)
December 2011

○ MIN12-02
Pigments of the bumper
in fluorescent orange
at Scholten & Baijings'
workshop (IP)
February 2012

○ MIN11-12
Shaving the steering wheel
by hand (IP)
December 2011

○ MIN11-11
Art Part, dashboard,
1:18 scale model
November 2011

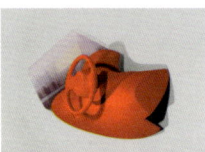

● MIN12-03
Dashboard with colour
pigments and Landscape
Window (S&A)
March 2012

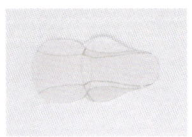

○ MIN11-12
Paper model of car seat
December 2011

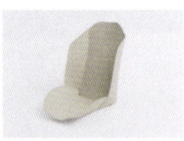

○ MIN11-12
Cardboard model of car seat
December 2011

○ MIN11-12
Paper model of car seat
with grid pattern
December 2011

○ MIN11-12
1:18 scale model in paper
with folding lines
December 2011

○ MIN11-12
Paper model of car seat
with grid pattern
December 2011

○ MIN11-12
Hand-drawn structure
inside the 1:18 scale model
of car seat
December 2011

○ MIN11-12
1:18 scale model of car seat
with fluorescent-pink accents
December 2011

○ MIN11-12
White paper layout of car seat
December 2011

○ MIN11-12
Cardboard back of car seat
December 2011

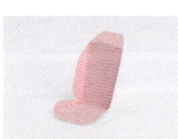

○ MIN11-12
Paper model of car seat with
hand-drawn, fluorescent-pink
grid pattern
December 2011

● MIN11-12
Cardboard prototype of car
seat with soft-grey leather
embroidered in-house by hand
with silver threads, and soft-
pink, geometric-patterned
safety belts at Scholten &
Baijings' studio (IP)
December 2011

● MIN12-04
Backs and seat cushions
of the various car seats (IP)
April 2012

○ MIN11-12
Sketch sheet with
drawings of car seat
December 2011

○ MIN11-12
1:18 scale model car seat
for 'Colour One' for MINI
December 2011

○ MIN11-12
1:18 scale model of Interior
Sheet with grid pattern. Paper
car seats covered in silver leaf
and with handmade soft-pink,
geometric-patterned safety
belts
December 2011

● MIN12-01
Technical drawing of car seat
for 'Colour One' for MINI
January 2012

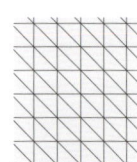

○ MIN11-12
Test grid pattern on aluminium
for Interior Sheet
December 2011

● MIN12-02
Crumpled cardboard
for Art Part, rear door
February 2012

○ MIN12-02
Applying gold leaf to rear door
February 2012

○ MIN11-12
Safety belt samples (IP)
December 2011

● MIN13-02
Self-made canvas grid fabric
with fluorescent-orange yarns
and safety belt of crumpled
cardboard with gold leaf
February 2013

● MIN12-03
Rear door with Landscape
Windows (S&A)
March 2012

○ MIN12-02
Prototype of Big Bag
– Nomadic Pockets at
Scholten & Baijings'
workshop
February 2012

○ MIN11-11
Cutting out the grid sheet
stitched in silver thread for
Nomadic Pockets
November 2011

● MIN12-04
Big Bag – Nomadic Pockets,
at the presentation of 'Colour
One' for MINI in Milan (M)
April 2012

○ MIN11-12
1:18 scale model of Big Bag
– Nomadic Pockets
December 2011

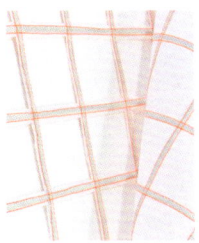

○ MIN11-11
Grid made in-house
for Nomadic Pockets
November 2011

○ MIN12-01
Cardboard model
of clutch/sun visor
January 2012

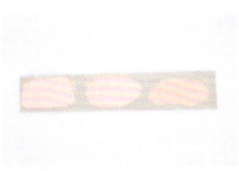

◉ MIN12-01
Colour tests for clutch
– Nomadic Pockets
January 2012

● MIN12-04
(Scale) models of Nomadic
Pockets and sketches for
'Colour One' for MINI,
presented in Milan during
the Salone del Mobile (M)
April 2012

● MIN12-03
Nomadic Pockets (S&A)
March 2012

● MIN12-03
Door with window and
colour gradient, and
Landcape Window (S&A)
March 2012

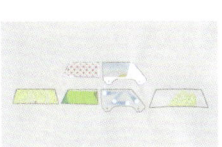

○ MIN11-12
Sketches for Landscape
Windows
December 2011

● MIN13-02
Landscape Window; in the
background a car door with
yellow colour gradient, at the
presentation of 'Colour One'
for MINI at the BMW Museum
February 2013

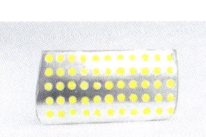

○ MIN11-11
1:18 scale model of door
with fluorescent-yellow dots
November 2011

◉ MIN12-02
Technical drawing of door
with window and colour
gradient
February 2012

○ MIN11-12
Fabric samples (IP)
December 2011

○ MIN11-10
Cast wheel, 1:18 scale model,
for the Conceptual Concept Car
October 2011

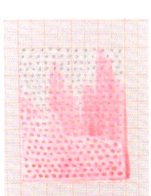

○ MIN11-11
Dot pattern with fluorescent-
pink colour gradient
November 2011

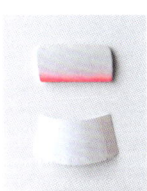

○ MIN11-11
1:18 scale model of door
with colour gradient and
paper window
November 2011

○ MIN11-11
Structure created with
fluorescent-pink tape
November 2011

○ MIN11-12
Cross section of car body
with pink wheels
December 2011

● MIN12-03
Door with colour gradient and
Landscape Window (S&A)
March 2012

● MIN12-03
Art Parts for 'Colour One'
for MINI (S&A)
March 2012

● MIN12-04
'Colour One' Concept Car for
MINI (M)
April 2012

● MIN12-04
'Colour One' for MINI by
Scholten & Baijings presented
in a paddock setting during the
Salone del Mobile in Milan (M)
April 2012

TEA WITH GEORG

TEA WITH GEORG (2013)

Industrial Product
Unlimited edition. The set consists of several items, including a teapot, cups,
   saucers and a warming plate
Materials/Techniques: Strained stainless steel, porcelain, glazes and
   transfers, plastic/etching
Colours: The grey colour of stainless steel, the greyish-white colour of
   porcelain with blue gradations, platinum lustre, and black transfers
Client/Producer: Georg Jensen (Denmark)

Tea with Georg is a family of unique, disparate parts. As befits any family, each item has its own character. The name of the tableware refers to Georg Jensen, the founder of the eponymous Danish company, which traditionally specializes in high-quality silver and metalworking.

Scholten & Baijings were commissioned to design a 'contemporary tea set', which launched them into an investigation of the famous Japanese tea ceremony. They decided to combine the subdued aesthetic of Japanese tea sets, as well as the sophisticated rituals they inspire, with European tea customs. And because the designers themselves are not only avid tea drinkers, but coffee drinkers as well, they chose to expand the tea set with cappuccino and espresso cups.

The collection features a variety of old craft techniques, all of which were revived to reflect the qualities of the Georg Jensen label: handcrafted metalwork, precision in design and a fine surface finish. The forms are simple, archetypal: a specific material was carefully selected for each item, in order to do justice to its intended function. For instance, the designers chose stainless steel for the teapot and the double espresso cup, porcelain and tinted glazes for the saucers, and plastic for the lids of the jars.

The set features remarkable details, such as soft colour gradients and a black grid which turn each porcelain object into a unique piece. Some decorations reappear in different guises. Take, for example, the etched steel line that runs towards the centre of the espresso saucer, a detail that is repeated in platinum lustre on the porcelain teacup.

New techniques such as computer-aided design are quite useful, but we're not focused on these tools. We care about skills. Working by hand provides very direct feedback.
— Stefan Scholten

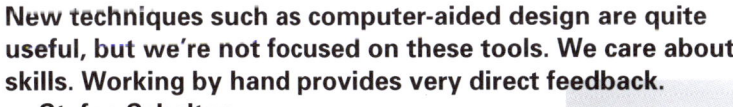

We choose to look for solutions in cooperation with industry. That's where the greatest challenges lie, as well as the greatest opportunities.
— Stefan Scholten

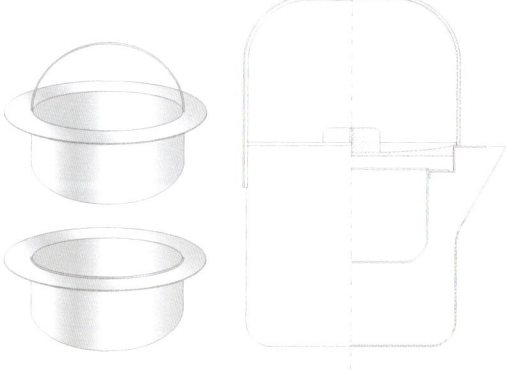

With an acute expertise in manipulating colour, they take an interest in material innovation and are also adroit at paring their work down to essential forms.
— Zoë Ryan, Curator of Architecture and Design at the Art Institute of Chicago

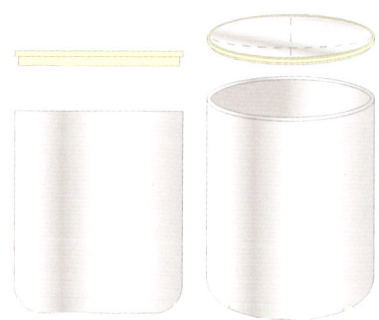

The collection is nuanced in its mix of cultural references. A teapot features elements of an archetypal tetsubin (cast-iron teapot) in its spout, lid and bridging handle, but then distilled in its round, minimal form.
— Conor Burke, Journalist

Tactility, vital in Japanese tea ceremonies, manifests itself in the matte and gloss finishes of the teacups. Their solid handles mean the cup must be pinched between the fingers or cradled within the hand.
— Conor Burke, Journalist

● GEO12-09

● GEO12-09

○ GEO11-01

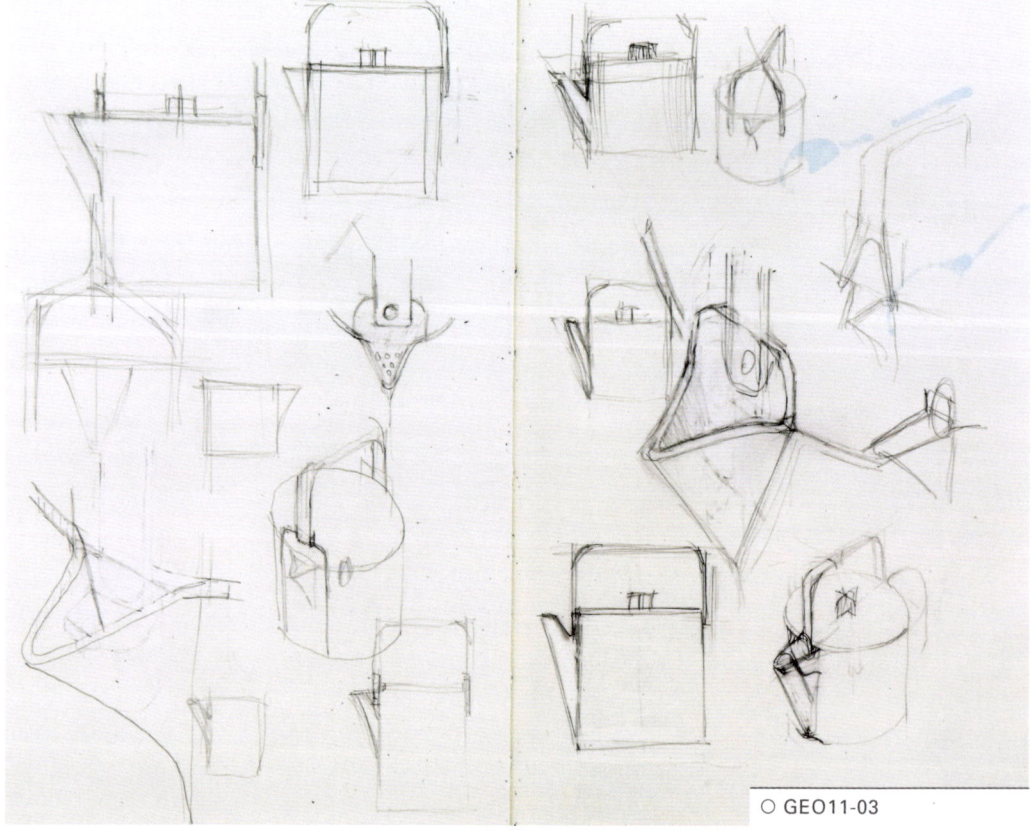

○ GEO11-03

○ GEO11-02

254

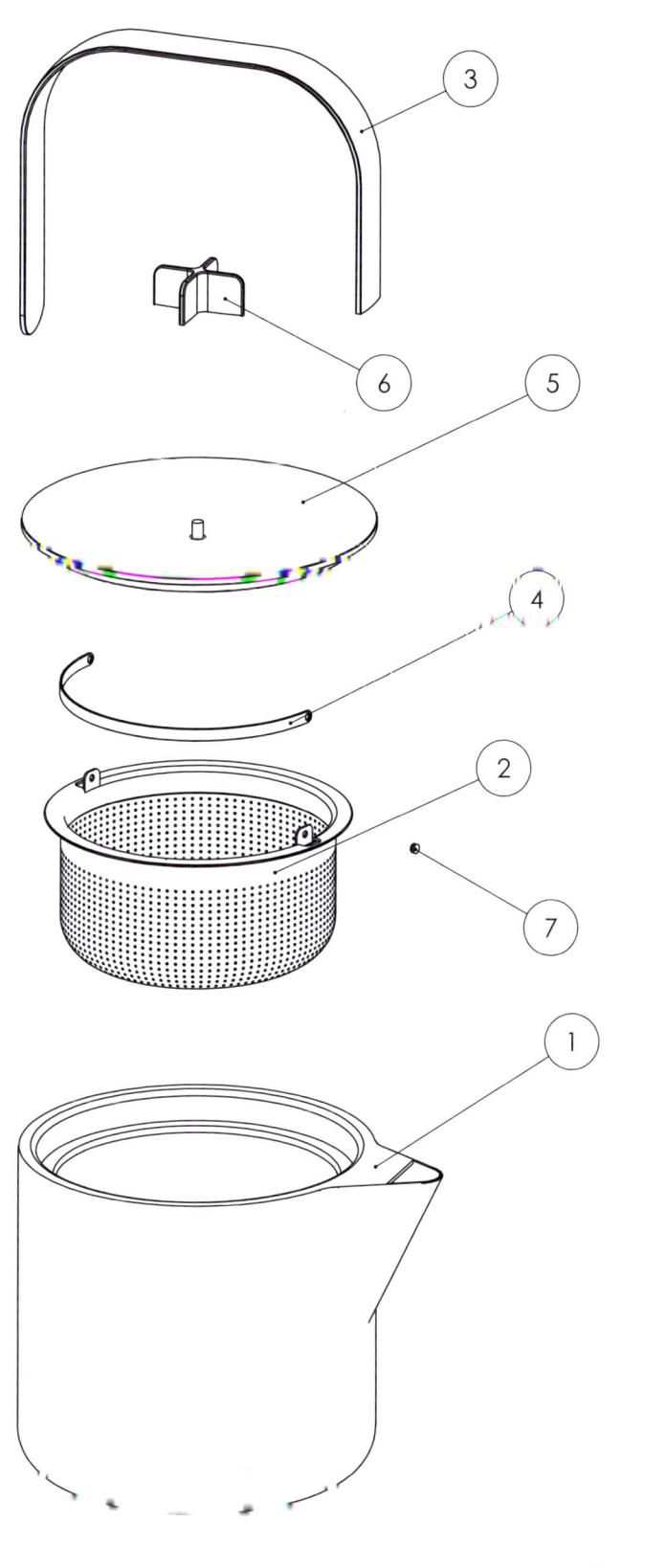

● GEO11-10

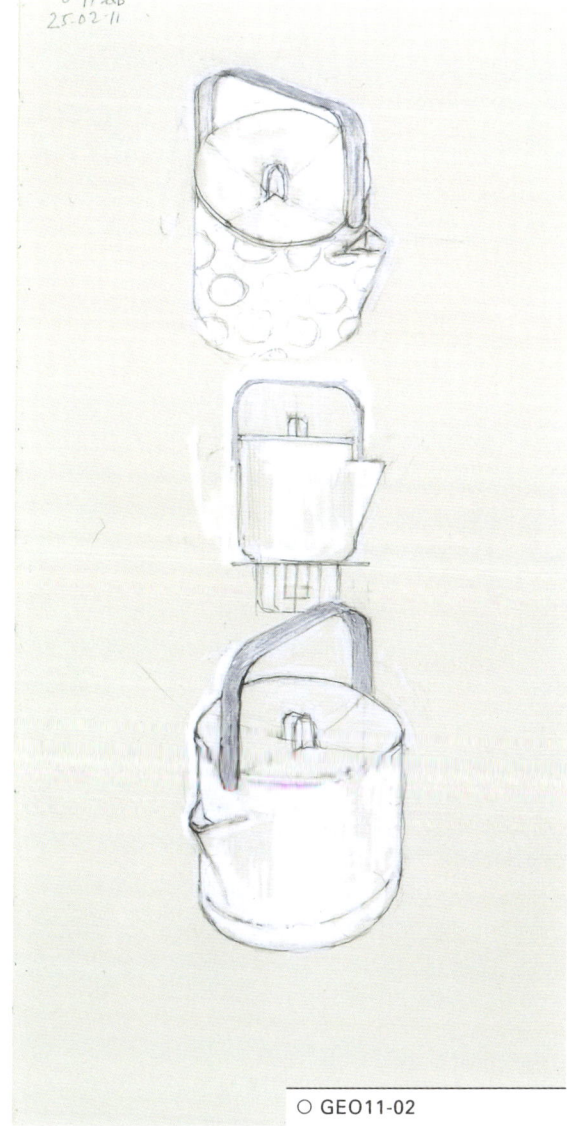

○ GEO11-02

● GEO13-04

○ GEO11-01

○ GEO11-03

○ GEO11-02

● GEO12-06

● GEO12-09

● GEO13-04

256

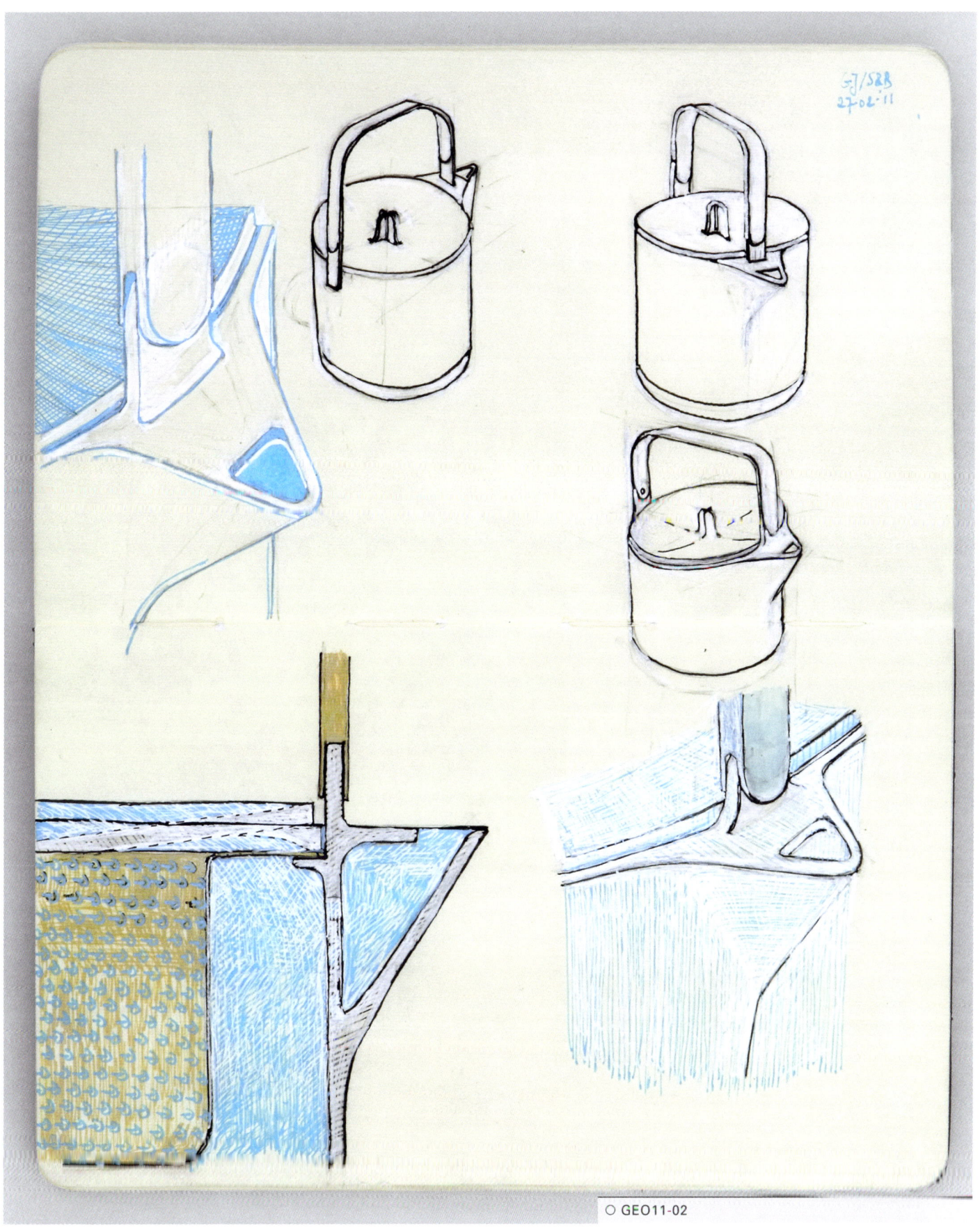

○ GEO11-02

○ GEO11-05

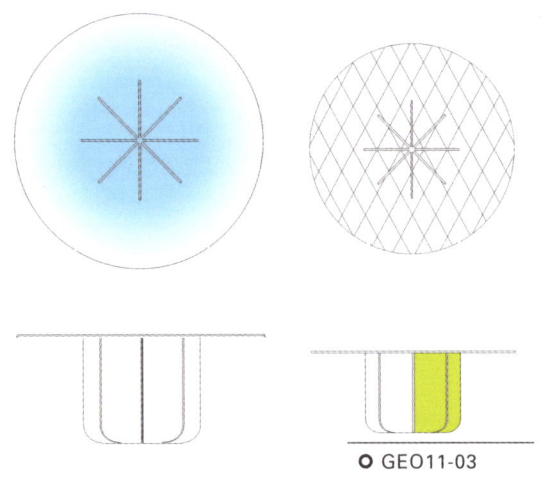

○ GEO11-03

○ GEO11-02

258

● GEO11-09

● GEO13-04

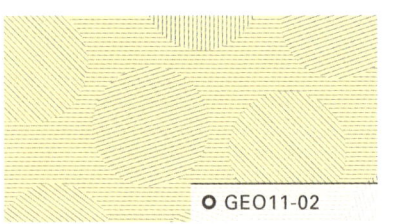

○ GEO11-02

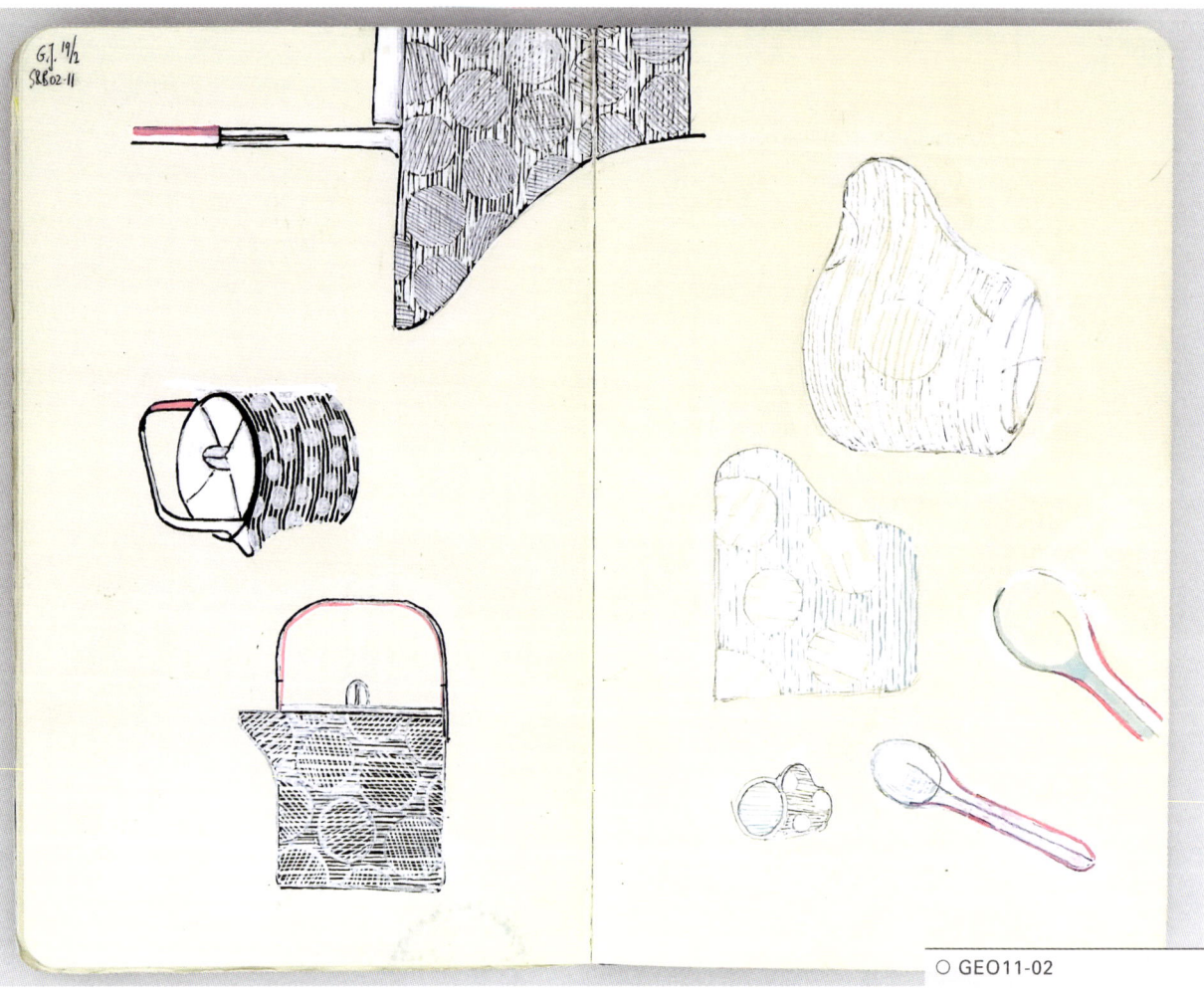

○ GEO11-02

○ GEO11-02

○ GEO11-02

O GEO11-02

● GEO13-04

● GEO12-09

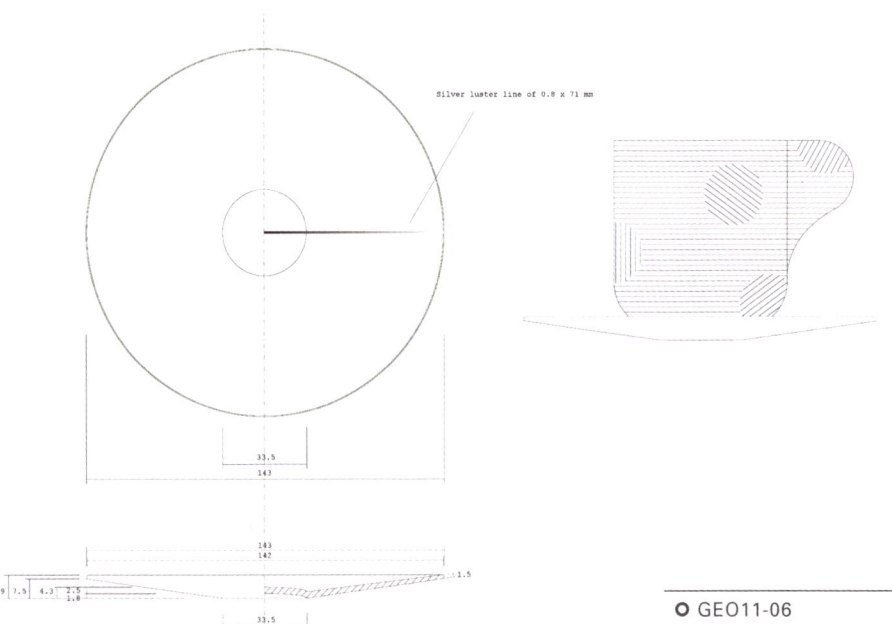

Silver luster line of 0.8 x 71 mm

○ GEO11-06

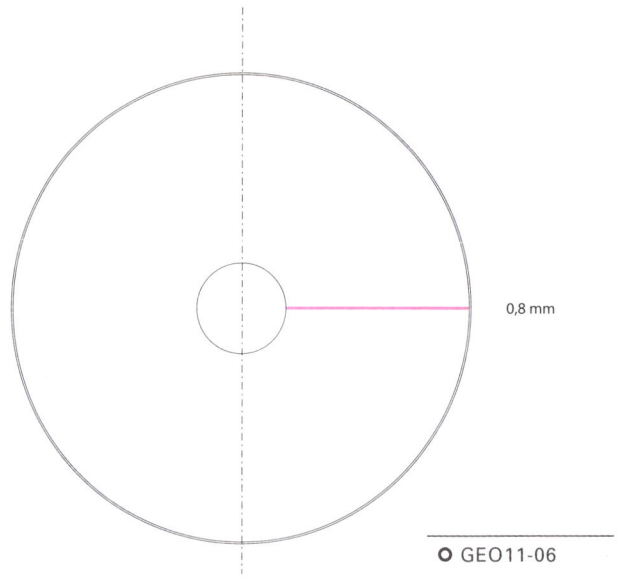

0,8 mm

○ GEO11-06

● GEO13-04

○ GEO11-02

● GEO12-09

○ GEO11-02

● GEO12-09

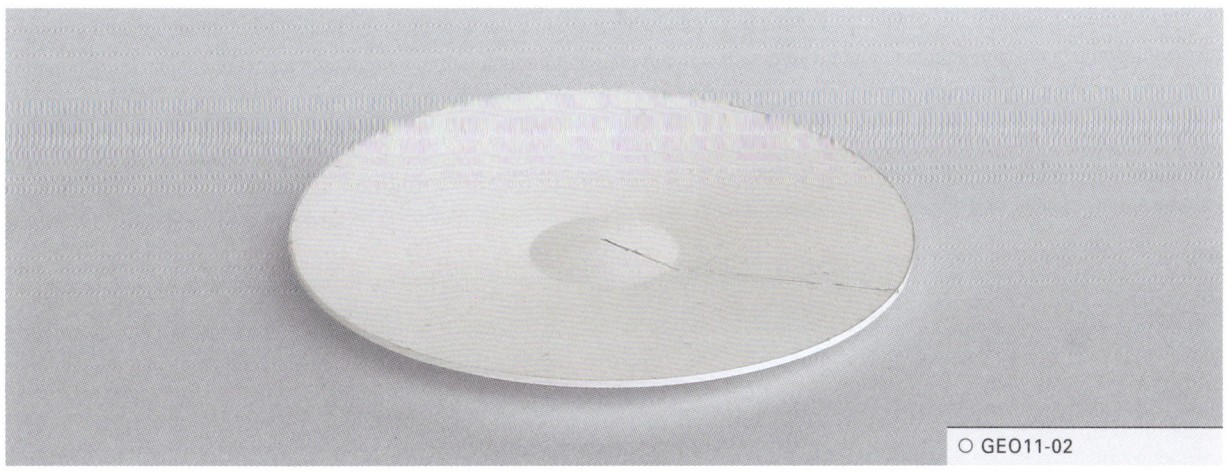

○ GEO11-02

○ GEO11-02

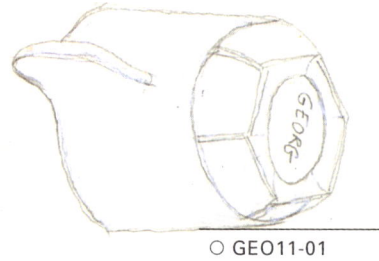

○ GEO11-01

○ GEO11-01

● GEO13-03

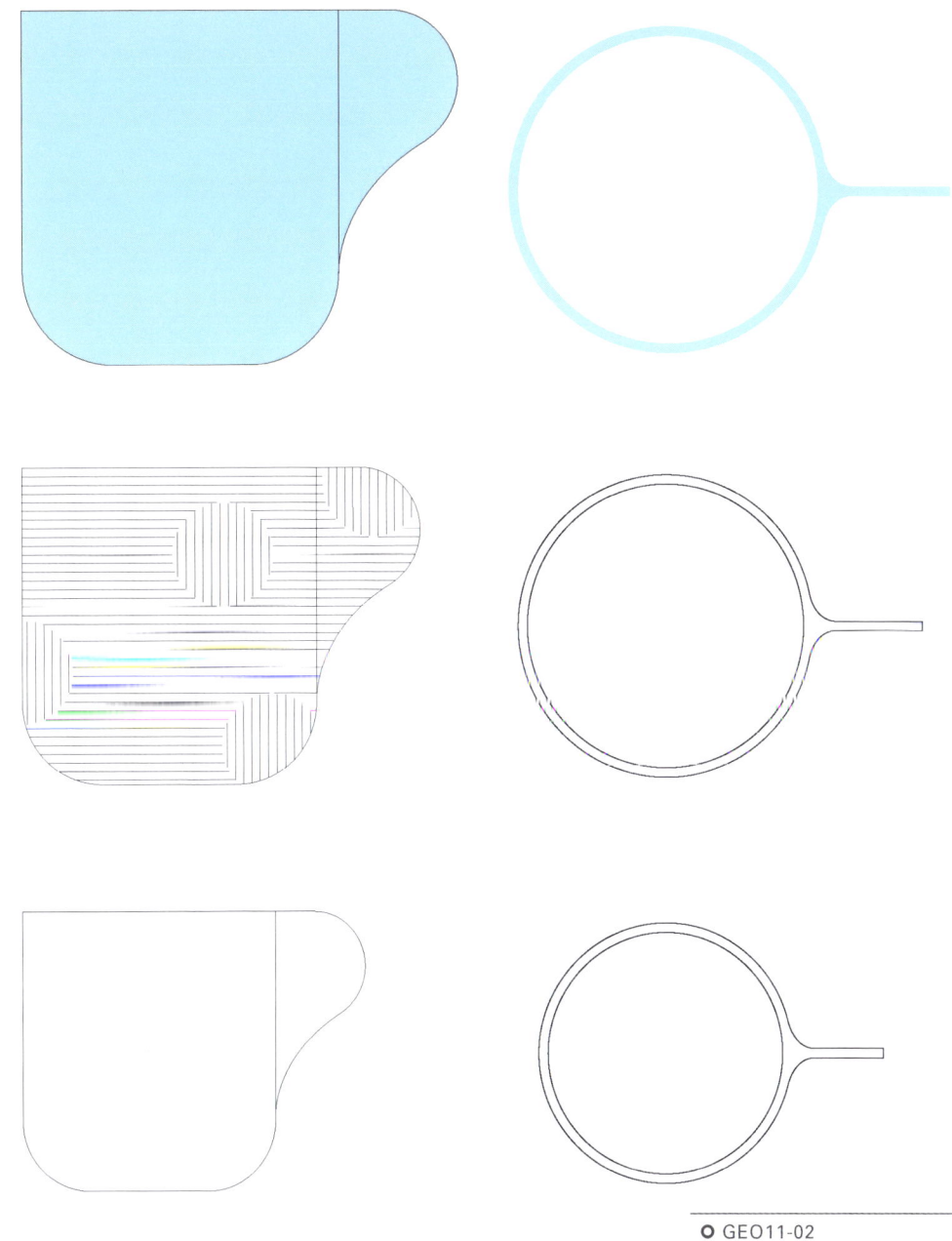

○ GEO11-02

○ GEO11-02

● GEO13-04

○ GEO11-02

● GEO13-04

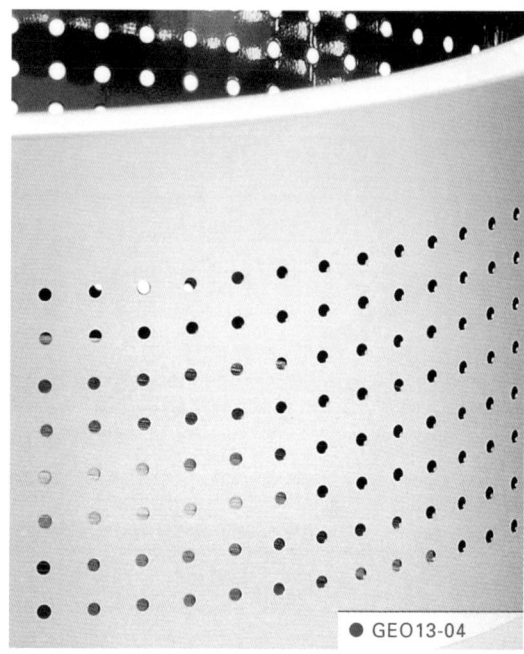

● GEO13-04

● GEO13-04

● GEO13-04

● GEO13-04

● GEO13-04

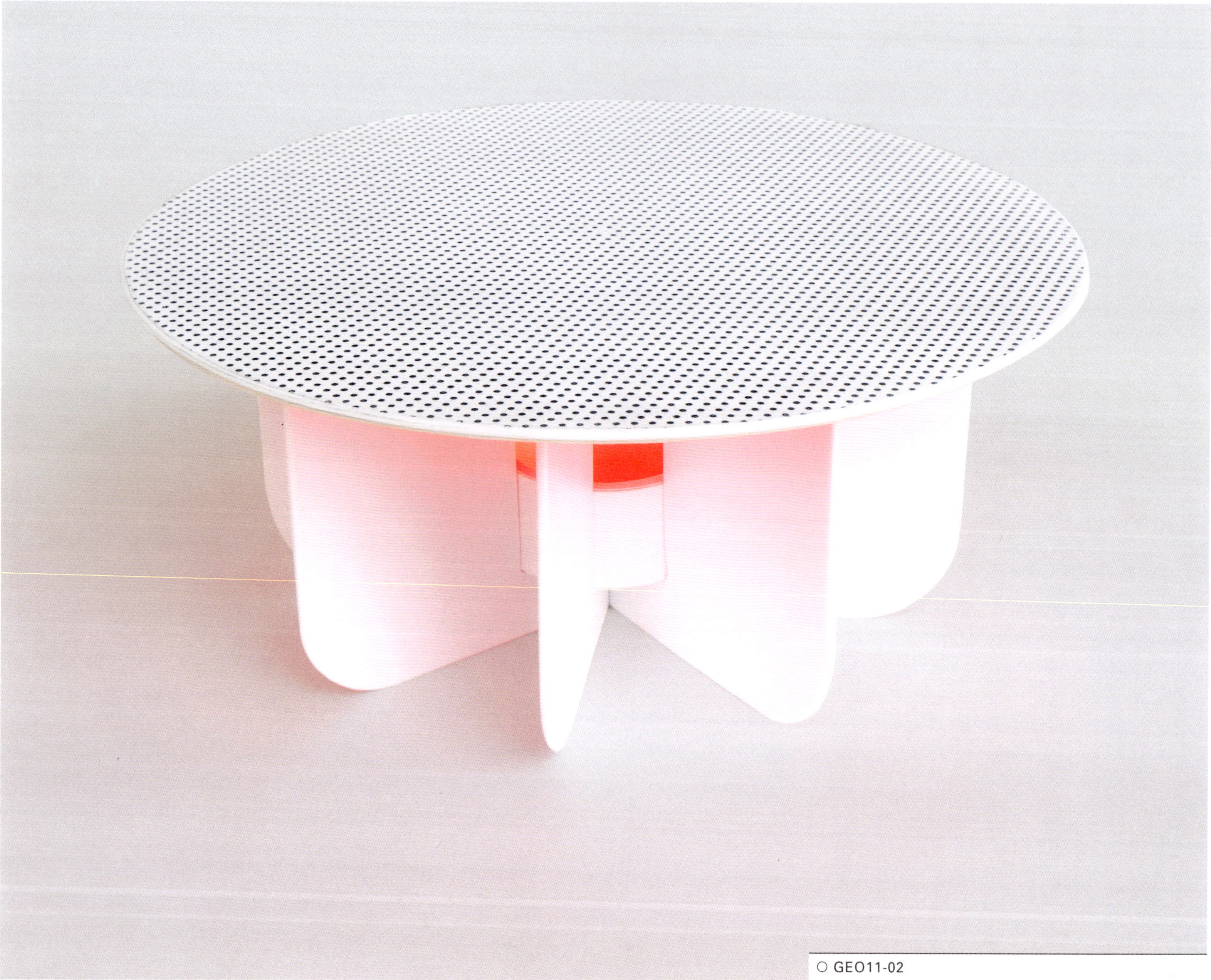

○ GEO11-02

○ GEO11-02

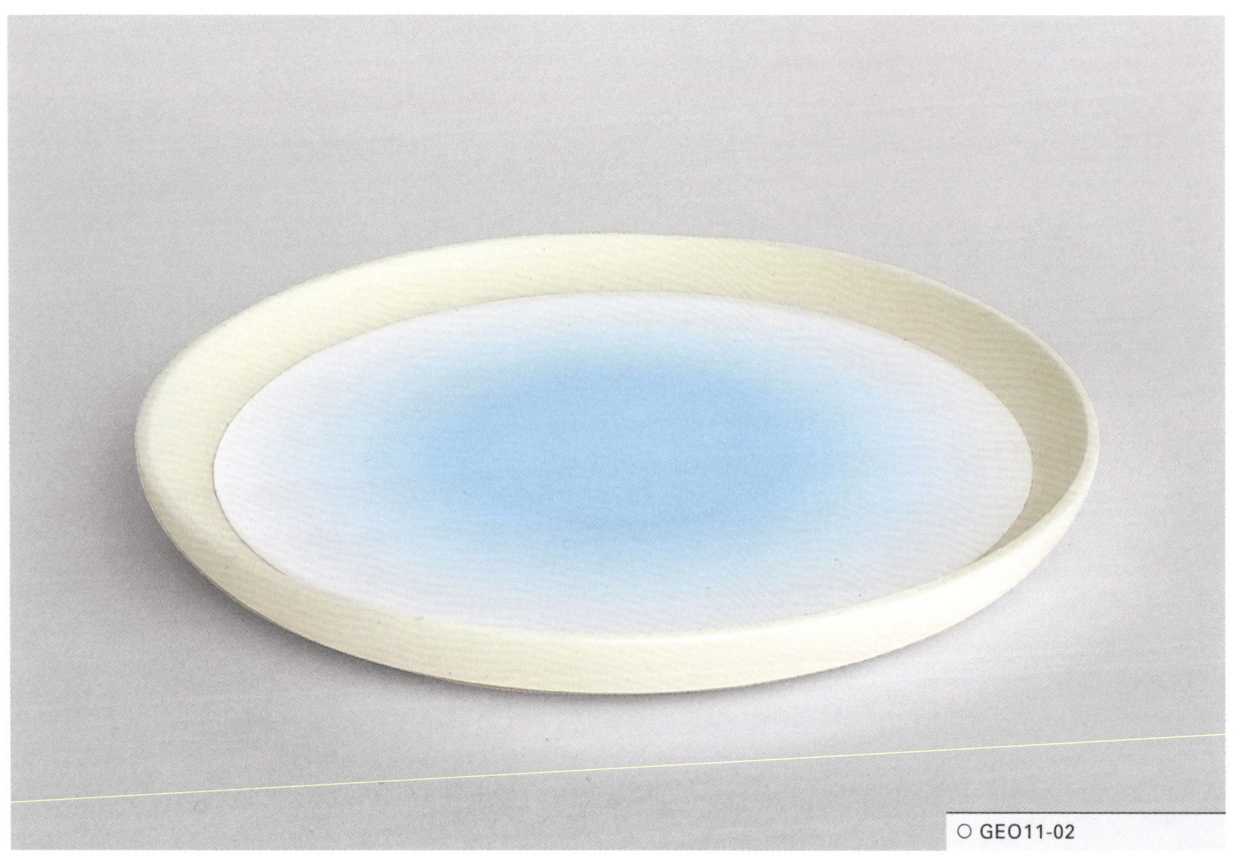

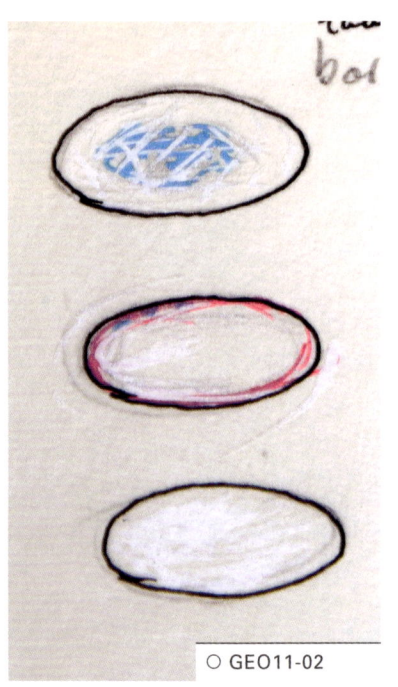

○ GEO11-02

○ GEO11-02

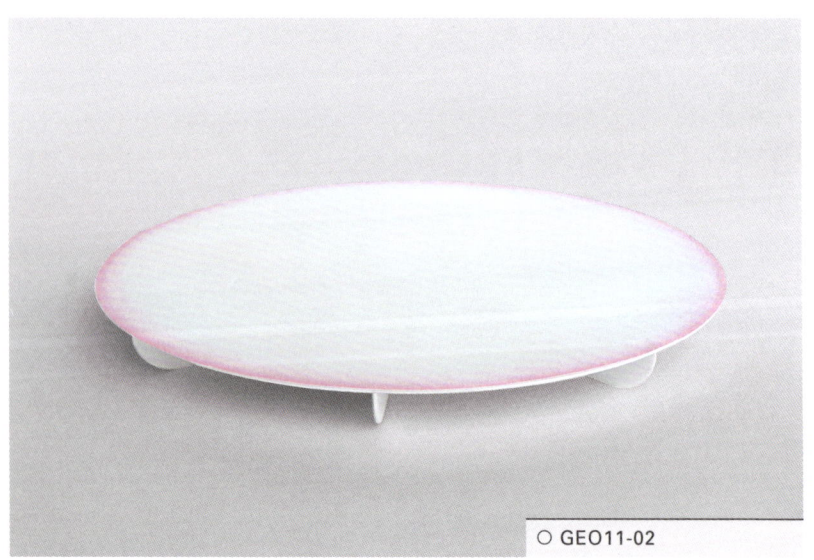

○ GEO11-02

○ GEO11-02

  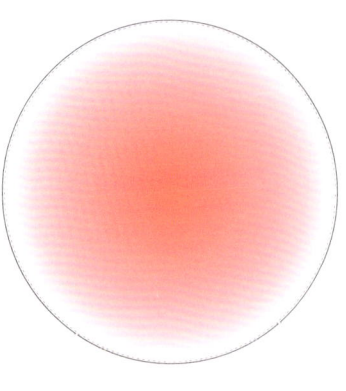

○ GEO11-06

271

● GEO12-09

Zonder
dekset

○ GEO11-02

○ GEO11-01

● GEO12-06

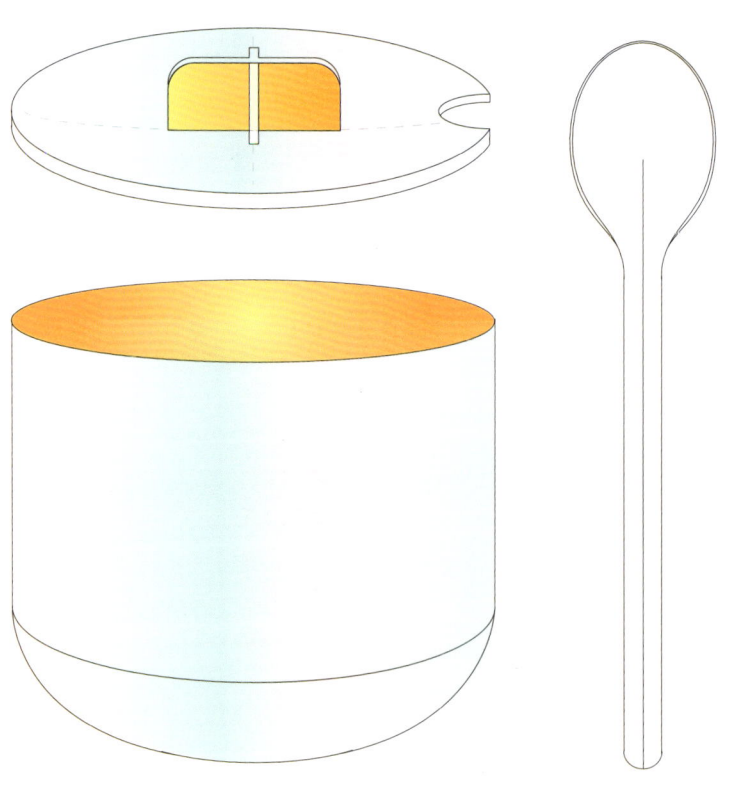

○ GEO11-02

272

GEO17-01

○ GEO11-02

○ GEO11-02

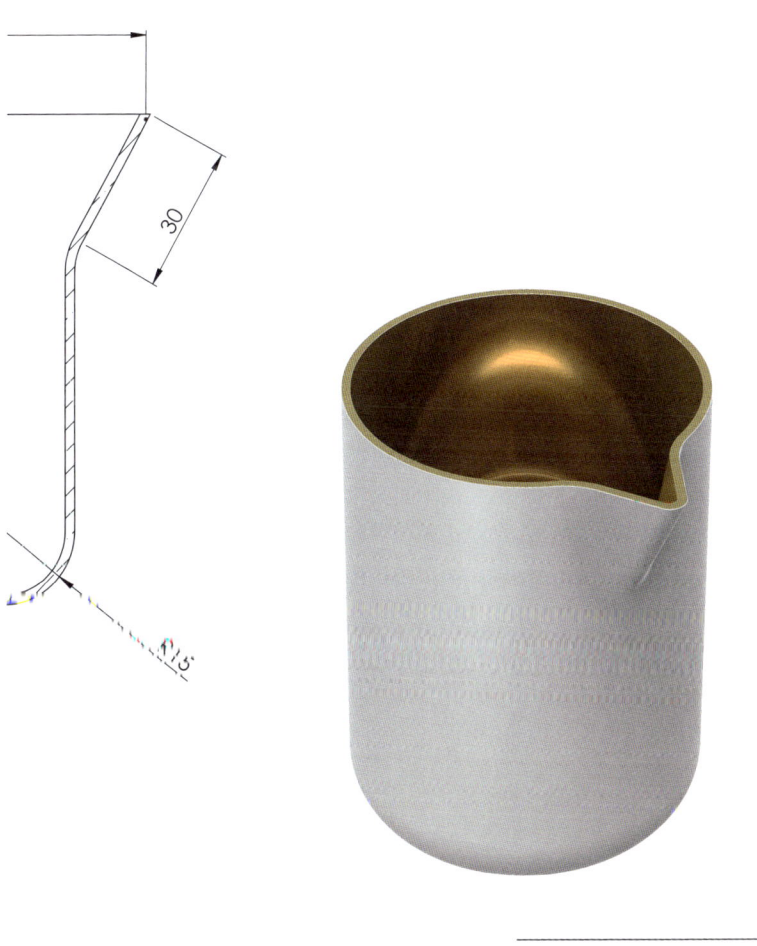

● GEO11-10

273

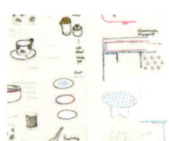

○ GEO11-02
Pages from sketchbook.
Designs from the Tea
with Georg collection
February 2011

◉ GEO12-09
Discussing the first industrial
prototypes at the Scholten &
Baijings studio
September 2012

◉ GEO12-09
Determining the use of colours
and materials for the Tea with
Georg collection, based on
drawings, material samples
and handmade foam models
September 2012

○ GEO11-01
First foam model of teapot
with paper print displaying
line pattern and dot structure
January 2011

○ GEO11-02
Foam model of teapot
lined with paper and
with removable handle
February 2011

○ GEO11-03
Pages from sketchbook.
Teapot with detail
drawings of spout
March 2011

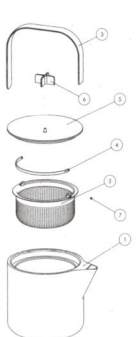

◉ GEO11-10
'Exploded view' of all of
the teapot components,
including sieve
October 2011

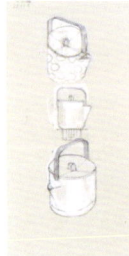

○ GEO11-02
Page from sketchbook.
Teapot with dot pattern
and various options for
the placement of the spout
February 2011

● GEO13-04
Spout detail of teapot from
the Tea with Georg collection
April 2013

○ GEO11-01
Spout detail of teapot
foam model with paper
print displaying line
pattern and dot structure
January 2011

○ GEO11-03
Spout detail of the ultimate
teapot foam model with
foam spout and paper print
displaying line and dot
structure
March 2011

○ GEO11-02
Spout detail of milk jug
foam model with gold leaf
February 2011

◉ GEO12-06
Spout detail of porcelain
milk jug with gold lustre
June 2012

◉ GEO12-09
3D rendering spout detail of
prototype of mirror-polished
stainless steel jug
September 2012

● GEO13-04
Spout detail of mirror-polished
stainless steel jug and lid with
blue acrylic top
April 2013

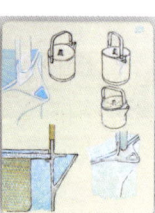

○ GEO11-02
Pages from sketchbook.
Teapot with details of spout,
handle and construction
February 2011

○ GEO11-05
Pages from sketchbook.
Various details for the
construction of the cake stand
May 2011

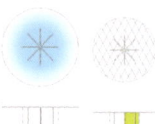

◉ GEO11-03
Artwork for cake stand
and teapot warmer
March 2011

○ GEO11-02
Polystyrene model
of cake stand with
blue colour gradient
February 2011

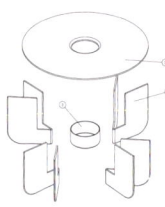

◉ GEO11-09
Technical drawing of the teapot
warmer's construction
September 2011

● GEO13-04
Teapot with teapot warmer
from the Tea with Georg
collection
April 2013

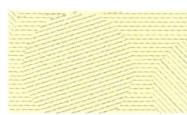

○ GEO11-02
Detail of line pattern and
dot structure for teapot
February 2011

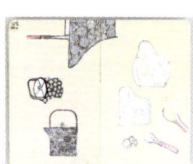

○ GEO11-02
Pages from sketchbook.
Teapot and espresso cups
with line pattern and dot
structure
February 2011

○ GEO11-02
Foam model of teapot with
paper print displaying line
pattern and dot structure,
and polystyrene teapot warmer
with dots and fluorescent-pink
reflecting base
February 2011

○ GEO11-02
Design drawing of line pattern
and dot structure composition
February 2011

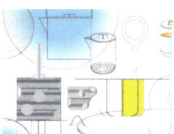

○ GEO11-02
Overview colours, structures
and forms designed for the Tea
with Georg collection
February 2011

● GEO13-04
Cake stand from the Tea with
Georg collection. White-matt
porcelain with a high-gloss
polished stainless steel foot
April 2013

◉ GEO12-09
Examining the prototypes of
the Tea with Georg collection.
Determining the colours
and materials for the acrylic
elements
September 2012

○ GEO11-06
Technical drawing of espresso
cup with pattern and saucer
with line detail
June 2011

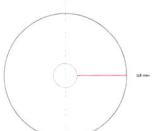

○ GEO11-06
Technical drawing of
fluorescent-pink line
on espresso saucer
June 2011

● GEO13-04
Teacup and saucer.
White porcelain with
platinum lustre line
April 2013

○ GEO11 02
Foam model of teacup
made in-house and by hand
February 2011

◉ GEO12-09
First porcelain prototype
of teacup and saucer with
flat ear handle
September 2012

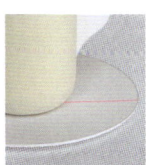

○ GEO11-02
Foam model of espresso
cup and paper saucer with
fluorescent-pink line
February 2011

◉ GEO12 09
First porcelain prototype of
espresso cup with platinum
lustre line
September 2012

○ GEO11-02
Paper saucer for espresso
cup with fluorescent-pink line
February 2011

○ GEO11-02
Foam model of espresso
cup lined with paper
February 2011

○ GEO11-01
From sketchbook.
First sketch of espresso
cup for Georg Jensen
January 2011

○ GEO11-01
Page from sketchbook.
First sketches of the
designs for the Tea with
Georg collection
January 2011

● GEO13-03
Cake plate and espresso cup,
photographed by Scheltens &
Abbenes 2013
March 2013

○ GEO11-02
Technical drawings of
espresso cup, coffee cup
and teacup
February 2011

○ GEO11-02
Ear handle detail of first
hand-turned foam model
February 2011

● GEO13-04
Ear handle detail of espresso
cup in mirror-polished stainless
steel
April 2013

○ GEO11-02
Detail of final prototype
of espresso cup in
Gesso-coated foam
February 2011

● GEO13-04
Platinum line on porcelain
saucer, reflected in white
porcelain teacup
April 2013

● GEO13-04
Detail of teapot's sieve
April 2013

● GEO13-04
Detail of reflection of
espresso saucer's line
in cup
April 2013

● GEO13-04
Reflection of teapot's side
seen on teapot warmer
April 2013

● GEO13-04
Reflection in cake stand's foot
April 2013

● GEO13-04
Reflection of teapot's
side with blue acrylic top
and handle of tea sieve
April 2013

● GEO13-06
Details. The picture is part of
a series of images made by
photographers Scheltens &
Abbenes. It was commissioned
by The Art Institute of Chicago,
especially for the 'Colour
Installation' exhibition by
Scholten & Baijings
September 2013 – February
2014

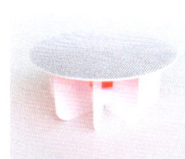

○ GEO11-02
First polystyrene model
of teapot warmer with dot and
reflecting fluorescent-pink base
February 2011

○ GEO11-02
First polystyrene model of
cake stand with fluorescent-
yellow ribs
February 2011

○ GEO11-02
Wooden trivet with reflecting
fluorescent-pink base
February 2011

○ GEO11-02
Second foam model of
teapot; inside of handle
in fluorescent-pink
February 2011

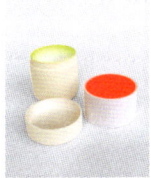

○ GEO11-02
Tea/coffee container consisting
of two pieces and a lid
February 2011

○ GEO11-02
Hand-turned foam model of
pastry plate with blue colour
gradient
February 2011

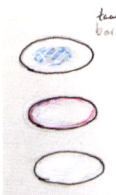

○ GEO11-02
Detail from sketchbook.
First sketch of pastry plates
in different colours and
gradients
February 2011

○ GEO11-02
Cake tray with pink colour
gradient, running
from outside to inside
February 2011

○ GEO11-02
Foam model of espresso cup
with blue colour gradient
February 2011

○ GEO11-06
Technical drawings of
pastry plates in different
colour gradients
June 2011

● GEO13-04
Cake tray with blue colour
gradient from the Tea with
Georg collection
April 2013

◐ GEO12-09
Discussing the various
material options for foam
models and colour samples
September 2012

○ GEO11-02
Detail from sketchbook.
Milk jug and sugar bowl
February 2011

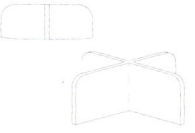

○ GEO11-01
Technical drawing of acrylic
top from the Tea with Georg
collection
January 2011

◐ GEO12-06
Three porcelain milk jugs
with different glaze options:
matt-gold, yellow-ochre and
gold-lustre
June 2012

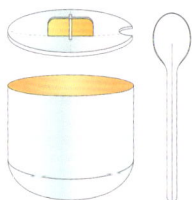

○ GEO11-02
Technical drawing of sugar
bowl from Tea with Georg
with golden interior, acrylic
top and folded spoon
February 2011

● GEO13-04
Jug with lid and acrylic top
from the Tea with Georg
collection
April 2013

○ GEO11-02
Foam model of sugar bowl
with lid and polystyrene top,
pasted with paper
February 2011

○ GEO11-02
Foam model of jug with lid
and polystyrene top, pasted
with paper
February 2011

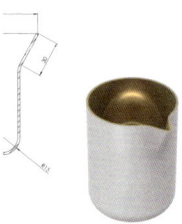

◐ GEO11-10
3D rendering of jug
October 2011

● GEO13-08
Teatime with Tea with Georg
collection in combination with
'Colour Glass' collection
for HAY and 'Fruit Party' for
Thomas Eyck. Photography
Inga Powilleit for Schöner
Wohnen November 2013
August 2013

● GEO13-03
Tea with Georg collection,
photographed by
Scheltens & Abbenes
March 2013

BLOCKS & GRID

BLOCKS & GRID (2014)

Industrial Product. Two different textile designs, each with an elongated
   pattern, executed in various colour schemes. Blocks measures 8.38 metres
   (27 feet 6 inches); Grid measures 8.38 metres (27 feet 6 inches)
Materials/Techniques: 92% wool, 8% nylon/woven textile
Colours: Blocks in five colours 001 (yellow), 002 (green), 003 (red), 004 (grey),
   005 (black-blue). Grid in six colours 001 (beige), 002 (yellow-green),
   003 (grey-green), 004 (orange-red), 005 (light blue), 006 (dark grey)
Client/Producer: Maharam (USA)

A hugely individualistic use of colour and an exceptionally high quality of crafts-manship and detailing are typical in the work of Scholten & Baijings. These qual-ities are the result of the intensive design process that takes place in both their studio and on the premises of the companies they work with. Through trial and error – the so-called *dirty hands* method – the designers explore the possibilities of materials and techniques. The sense of aesthetics and elegance generated by this approach is evident in all of their products and also typifies the Blocks & Grid collection they developed at the request of the textile company Maharam.

Almost every successful design starts with a clear assignment and a consci-entious client. Maharam is known as a world pioneer in the field of textile inno-vation: the company produces textiles designed by greats such as Charles and Ray Eames, Alexander Girard and Verner Panton, and currently works with contem-porary designers such as Hella Jongerius, Konstantin Grcic, and Paul Smith. The production itself is outsourced to the best manufacturers, including a variety of artisanal weavers with specialist expertise, as well as high-tech companies capable of translating the latest material innovations into modern fabrics.

Scholten: 'Maharam is a company with vision and cultural integrity – an ideal client that makes clear choices and formulates their commissions with preci-sion. They would, for instance, not give Paul Smith the same brief they would give us. Maharam protects the designers, analyses their specialties and asks specific questions that match their individual talents. They asked us to design an upholstery fabric using colours and geometric shapes, a so-called Colour Blocking. We were given *carte blanche* in terms of the realization of this com-mission. That is very important. To get the best out of yourself, you have to have a good brief and the client's trust. You have to be able to talk to each other.'

Baijings: 'We chose subtle colours. When we design a quilt or a pillow we can add spicy hues or even fluorescent colours. But furniture has a long life and upholstery should therefore have a timeless quality. For this collection we opted for colours that are close together.'

Scholten: 'Colour Blocking is a fashion concept from the 1970s, both in fashion design and in upholstery fabrics. The blocks are usually assembled to produce stark contrasts, the main concern being the composition of colours. We wanted to cast a new light on this theme by applying greater layering to the blocks of colour; as if they were not simply placed right next to each another, but partly overlapped.'

Baijings: 'Sometimes the colours seem to float above or overlap each other. In other places they almost imperceptibly blend into one another, as if painted onto a canvas by a painter.'

Scholten: 'In addition to this layering we wanted to create varying degrees of transparency. In our own studio, we discovered how the grid could beautifully reflect both this layering and the sense of transparency, whilst remaining graphically interesting. The density of the grid determines how one experiences colour and gives the colour a more airy appearance than a monochromatic colour plane.'

Baijings: 'We start every design with sketches and material experiments that we carry out in our own workshop. In the initial phase, we also look for suitable yarns and create a first colour palette. Then we involve other experts in the process. For *Blocks & Grid,* for example, we experimented on the machines of the TextielLab at the TextielMuseum in Tilburg, the Netherlands. We kept adjusting our design on the basis of these experiments, until the result matched our initial ideas.'

Scholten: 'The patterns and colour layers are complex. When Michael Maharam first saw our designs, he said right away, "You will need a machine that can bring the colour layering to life," and introduced us to a specialist weaving mill. Then we started the design process all over again. In close cooperation with the experts at the weaving mill, we set out to find the most beautiful colours, the best weaving solutions. Unlike the TextielLab where we made our first tests, this weaving mill has machines of which both the warp and the weft can be varied. This expanded our colour range and allowed us to create a richer layering. We then used these first samples as a basis from which to further elaborate the designs. This way of going back and forth between making tests and then reworking the design in our workshop is a long and intensive process, enabling us to really get to know and use the technical competence of a producer.'

Baijings: 'In a Mondrian painting, the composition fits perfectly within the parameters of the canvas. Making a composition for an upholstery fabric calls for an entirely different approach. We opted for an unusually long *repeat,* so that we can create individual differences within one product family.'

Scholten: 'That obviously took a lot of consideration, because a nine-metre piece of fabric that shows the whole *repeat* has to be just as interesting as a single metre of fabric. The effect of the compositions was examined through an endless number of tests on various scale models. All the *Blocks & Grid* fabrics can be combined with each other and the patterns always fit together seamlessly.'

Like a musical score, we create our own grammar of colours. This doesn't stop us from breaking our own rules or perpetually violating the codes, so that materials and colours help each other and evolve to create an overall harmony.
— Carole Baijings

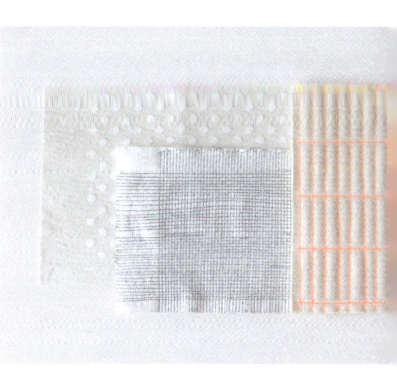

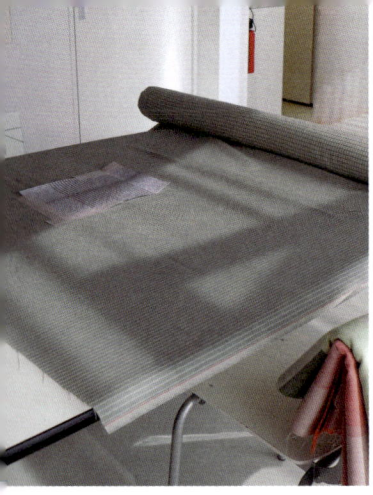

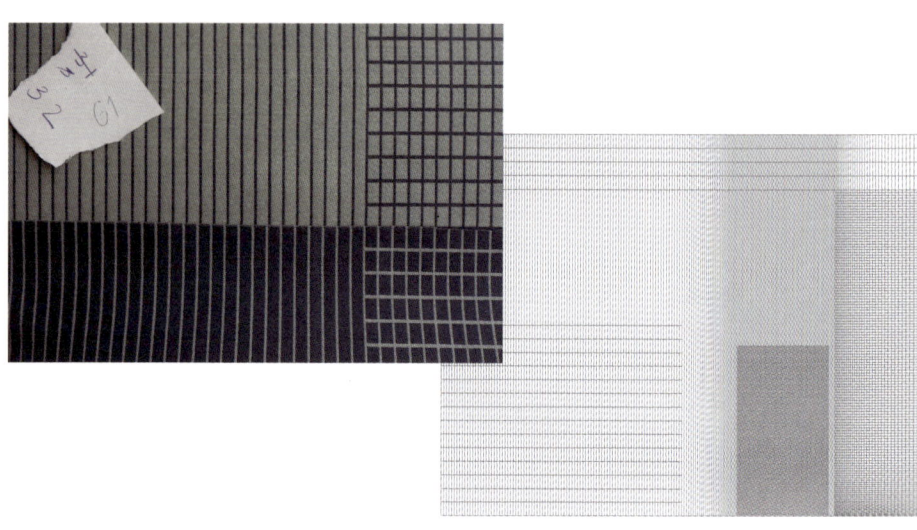

Their colourings don't have the clarity and rhythm of classic shades, but an airy, misty summer sunset look. They are impalpable haloes generated by a special grammar, hovering in the weight of matter.
— Cristina Morozzi, Journalist and Critic

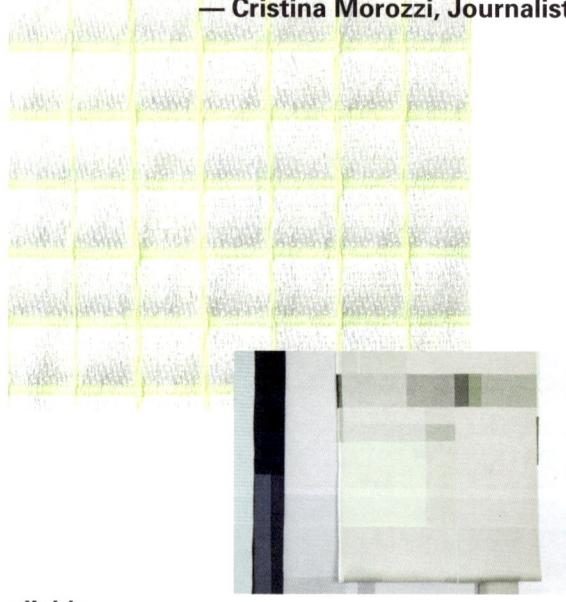

In their hands, colour becomes more pliable, more workable – more colourful.
— Crystal Bennes, Contributing Editor, *ICON* Magazine

We think in terms of colour—it's not an afterthought.
— Carole Baijings

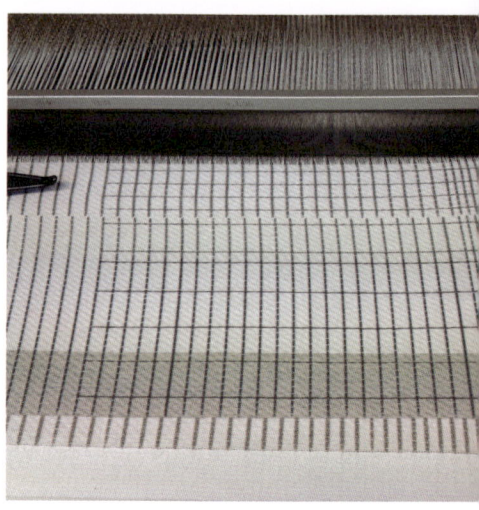

Working with the best companies helps to take us to the next level as designers.
— Stefan Scholten

Working with colour can be difficult because companies and craftspeople tend to use standard colours and are often not prepared to investigate new options. Basically, you need to work with people who also love colour.
— Stefan Scholten

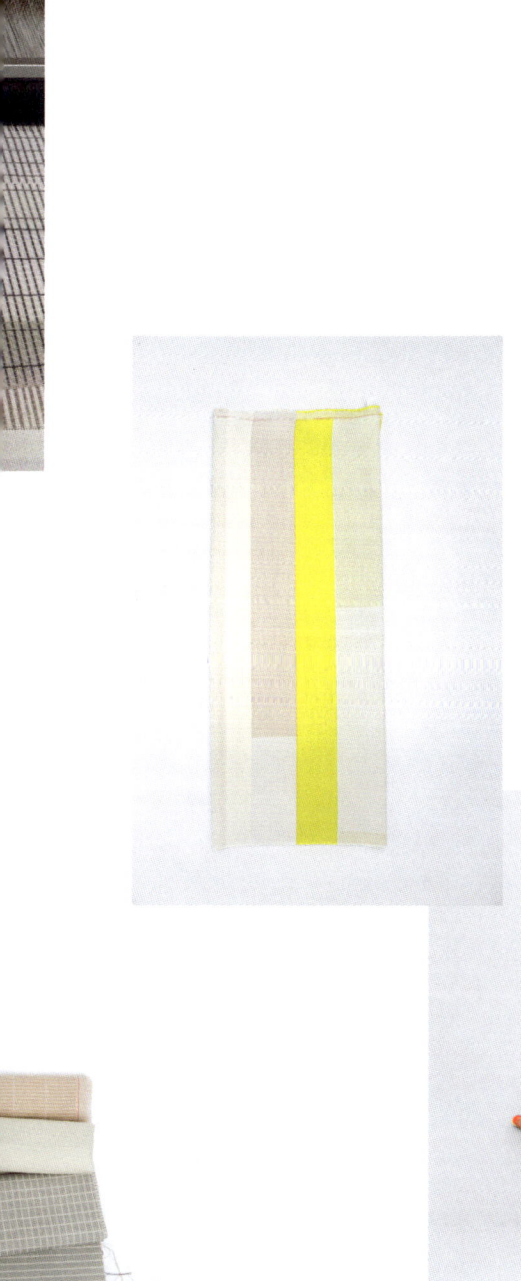

We make compositions instead of making people choose a colour.
People choose a mood, a tone, a feeling – not a colour. That's one
of the differences that distinguishes the way we work with colours.
— Carole Baijings

○ MAH12-03

○ MAH12-04

○ MAH12-04

290

○ MAH12-07

○ MAH12-07

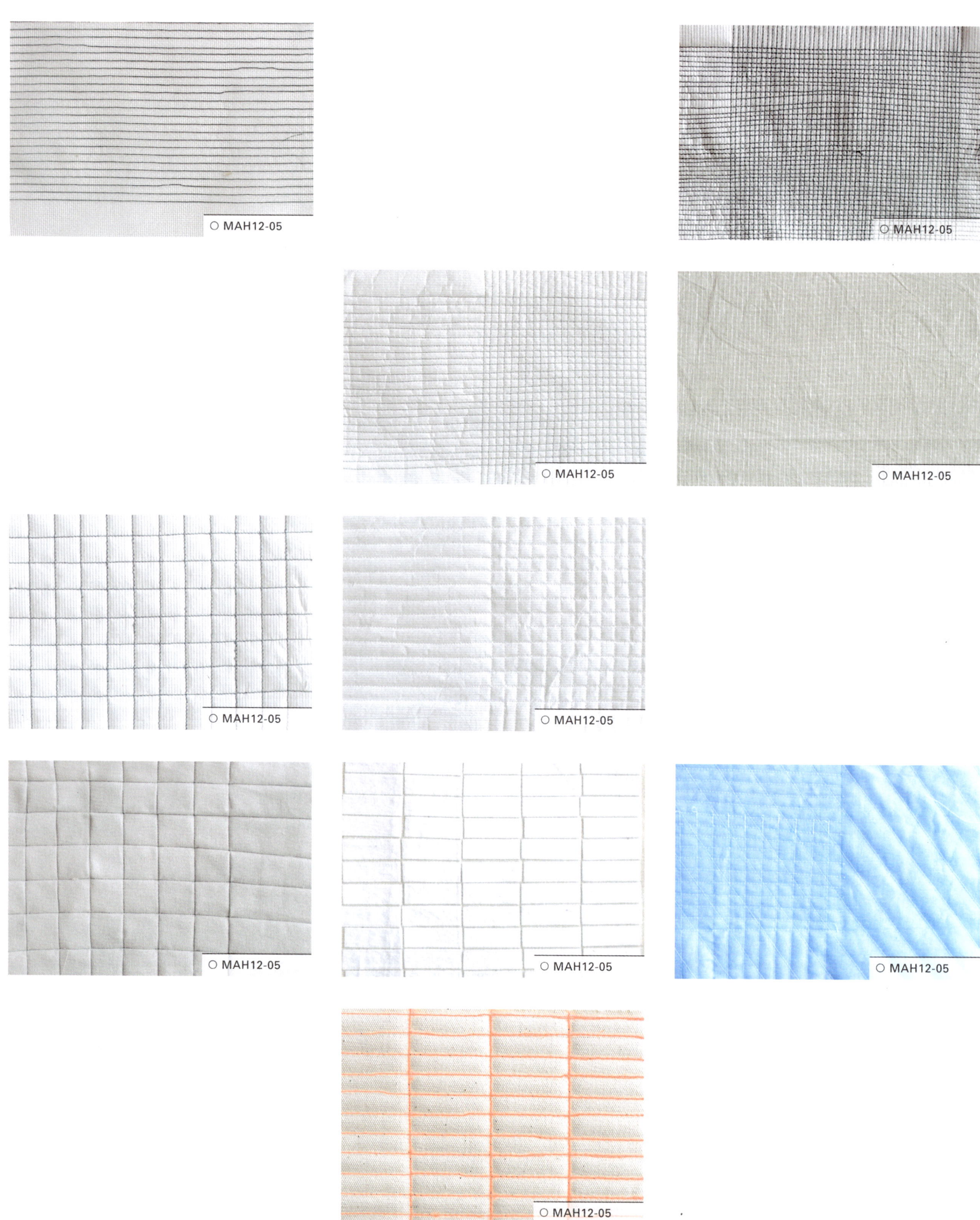

○ MAH12-05

○ MAH12-05

○ MAH12-05

○ MAH12-05

○ MAH12-05

○ MAH12-05

○ MAH12-05

○ MAH12-05

○ MAH12-05

○ MAH12-05

○ MAH12-05

○ MAH12-05

○ MAH12-05

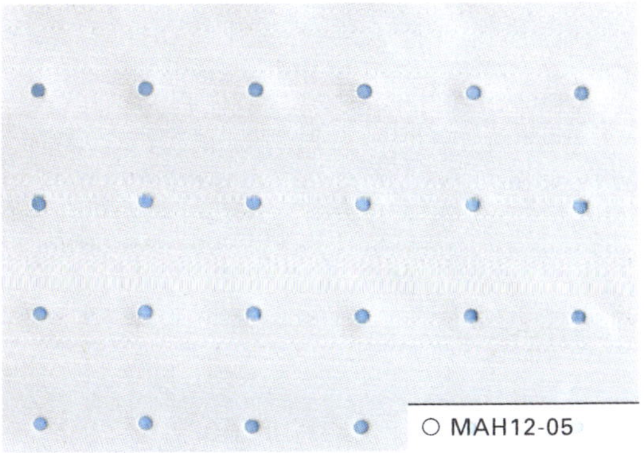

○ MAH12-05

○ MAH12-05

○ MAH12-05

○ MAH12-05

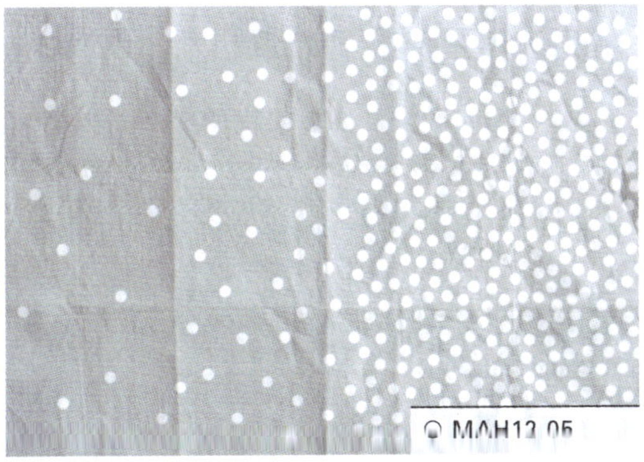

○ MAH12-05

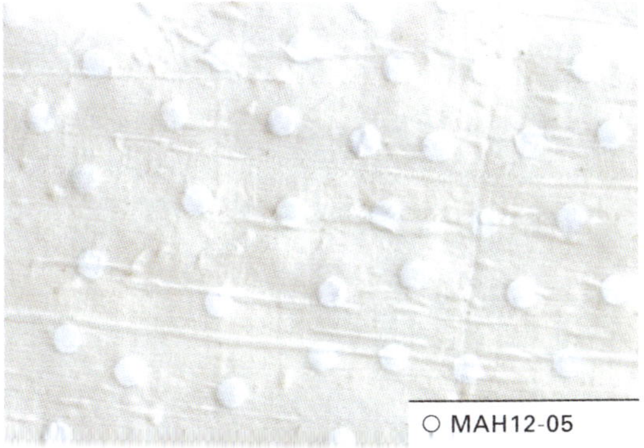

○ MAH12-05

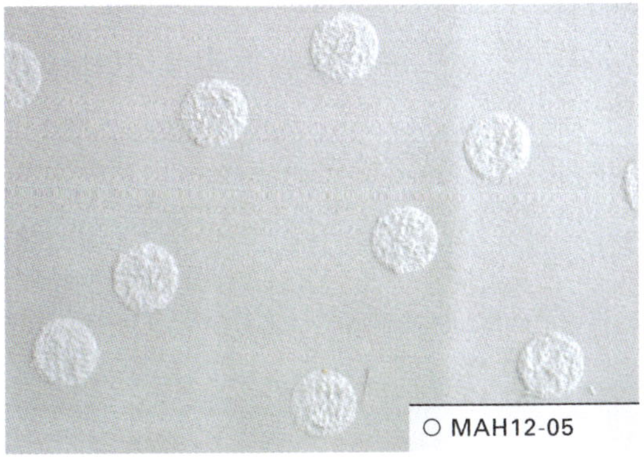

○ MAH12-05

○ MAH12-06

○ MAH12-06

○ MAH12-06

○ MAH12-06

○ MAH12-06

○ MAH12-06

○ MAH12-06

○ MAH14-01

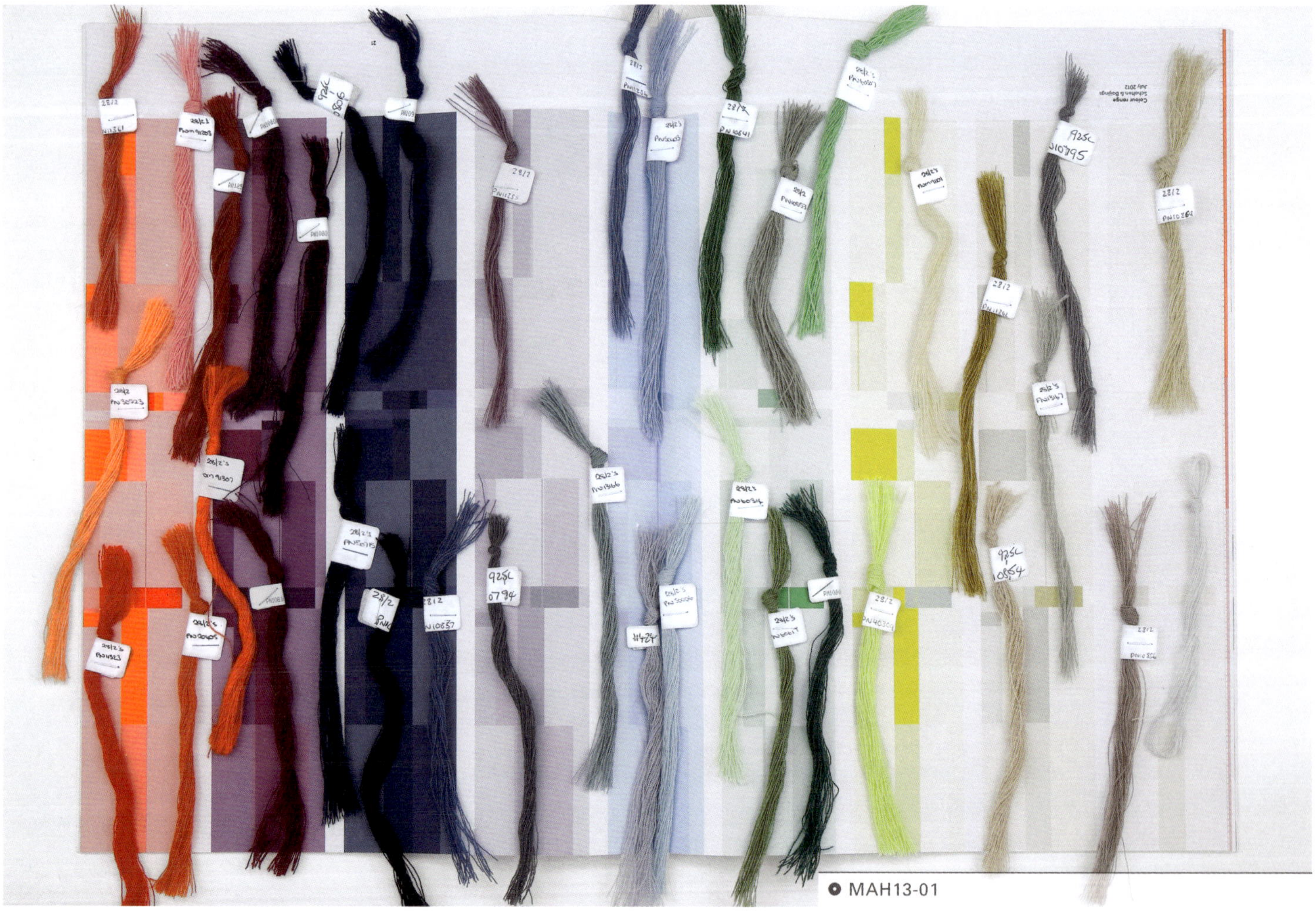

○ MAH13-01

● MAH13-08

● MAH13-08

● MAH13-08

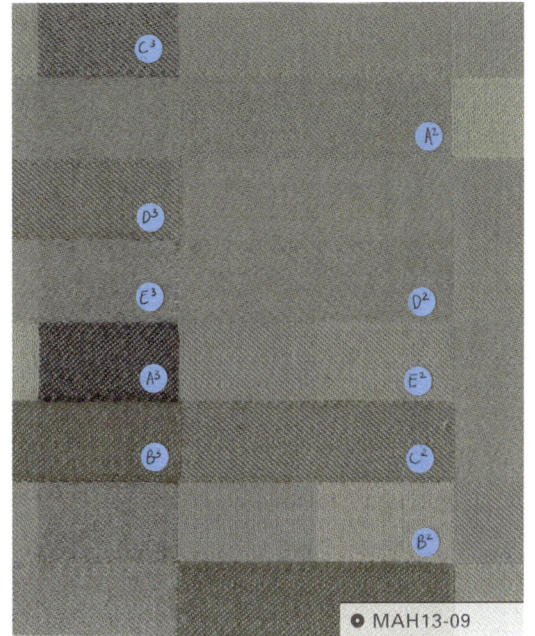

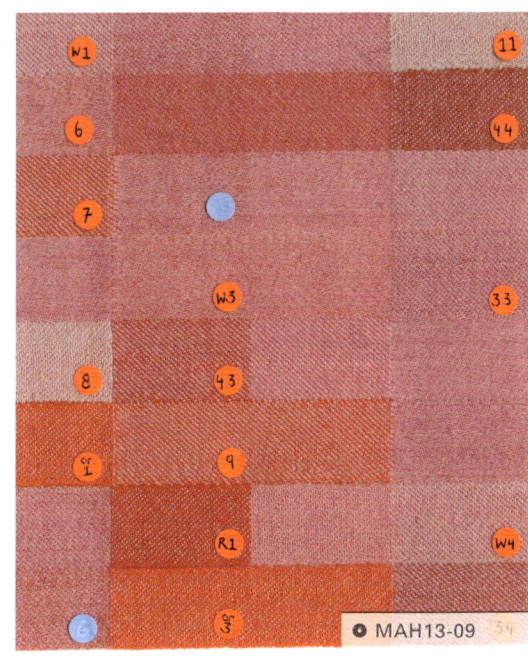

MAH13-09

MAH13-09

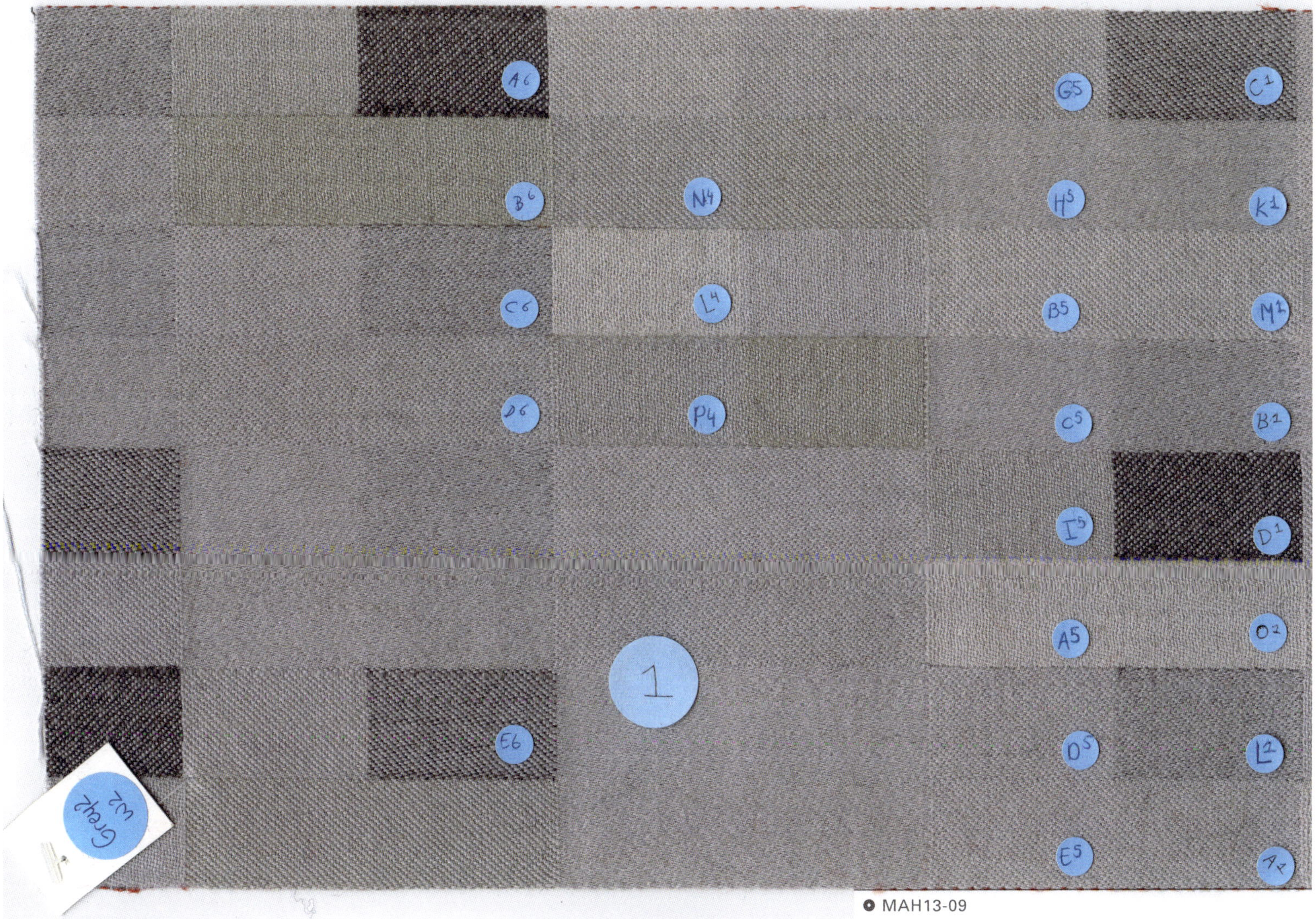

1

MAH13-09

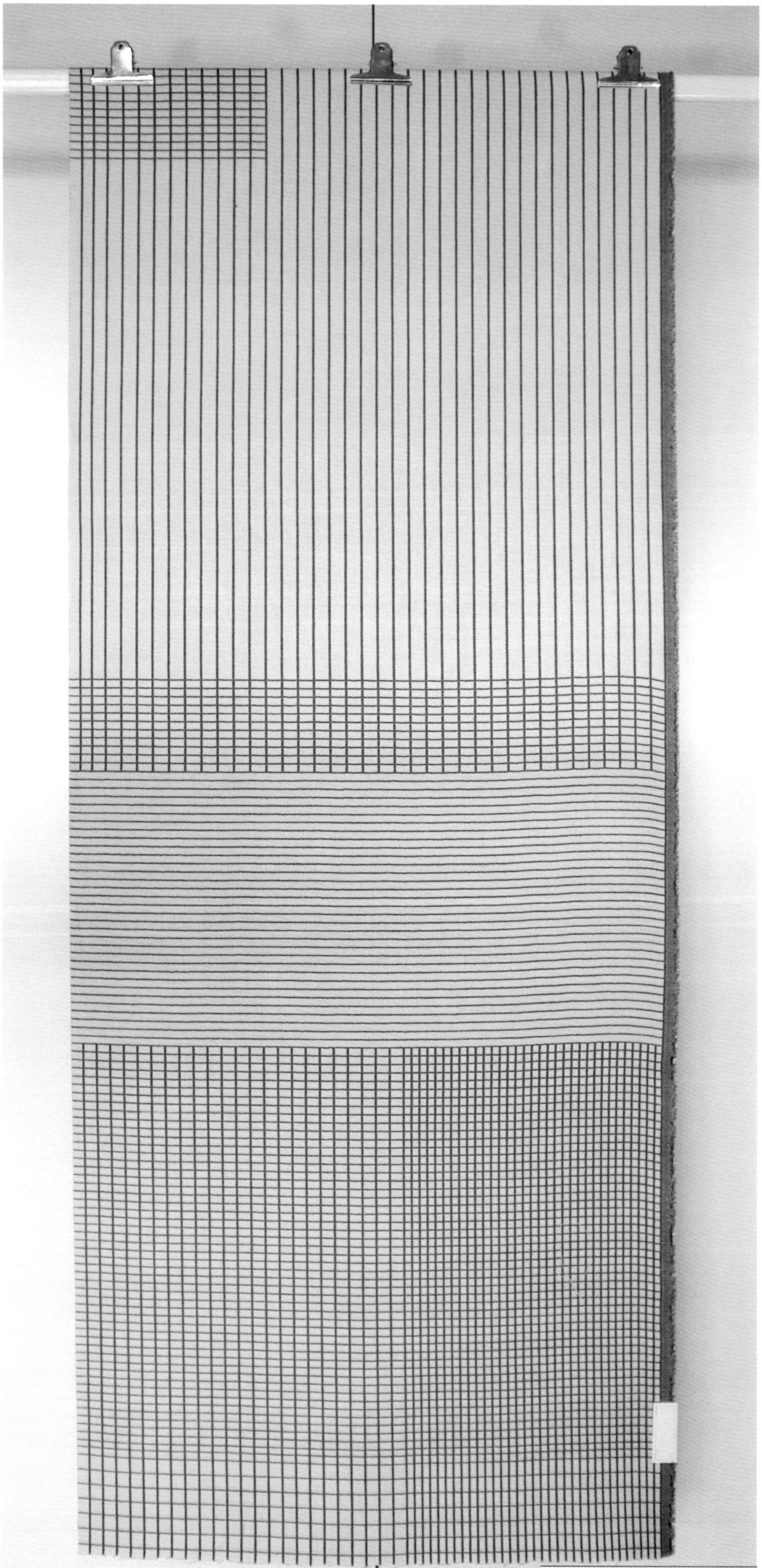

● MAH13-03

● MAH13-05

● MAH13-03

● MAH13-08

● MAH13-08

● MAH13-08

○ MAH12-06

○ MAH12-06

● MAH13-08

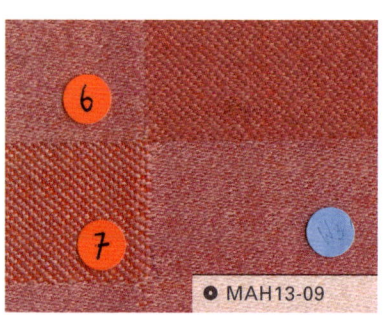

● MAH13-09

● MAH13-10

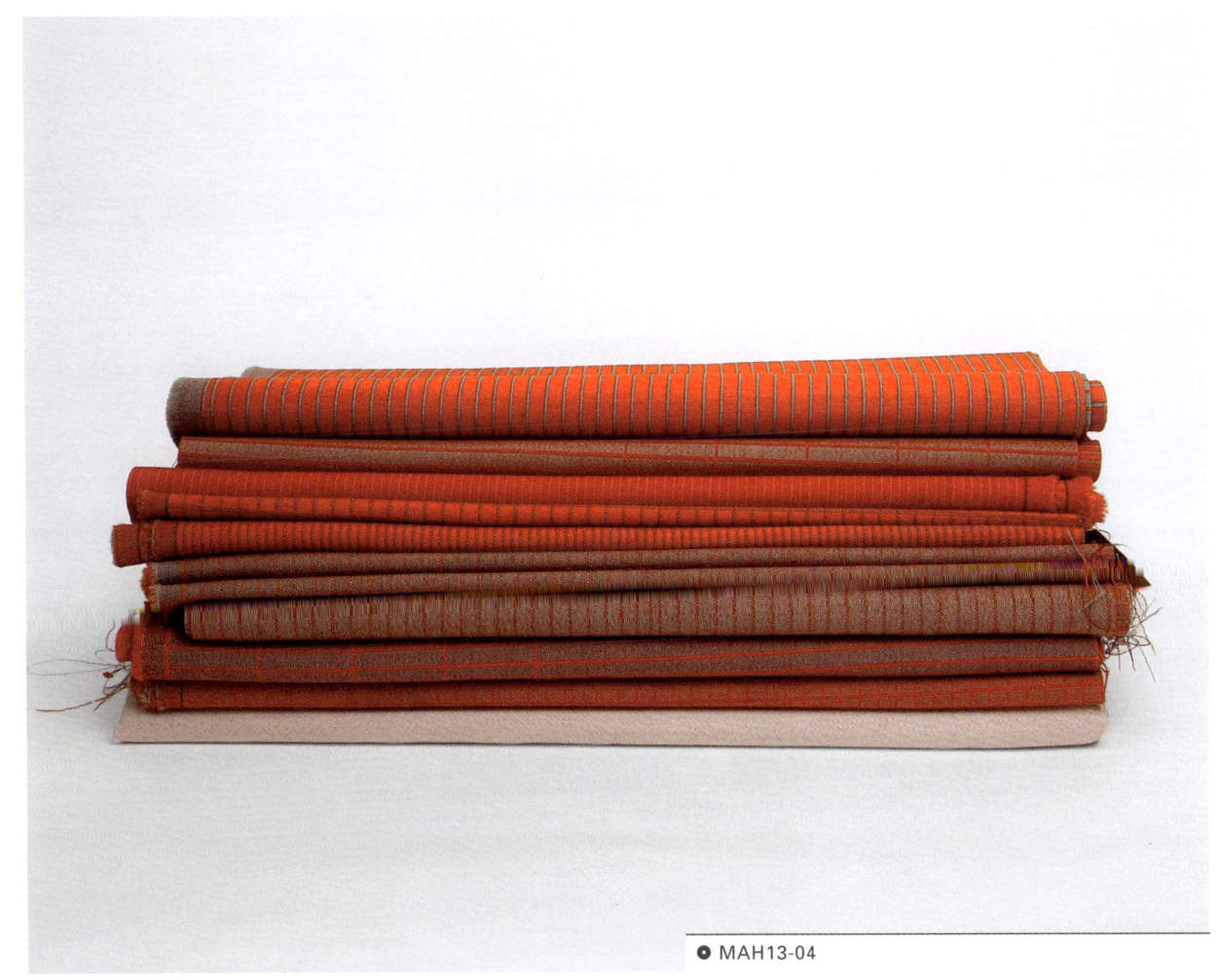

● MAH14-01

○ MAH12-06

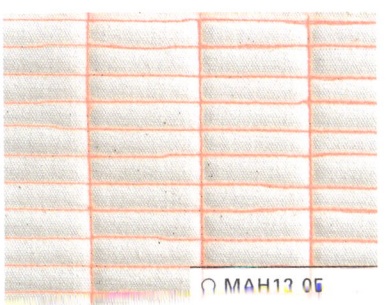

○ MAH13-05

● MAH13-04

● MAH13-05

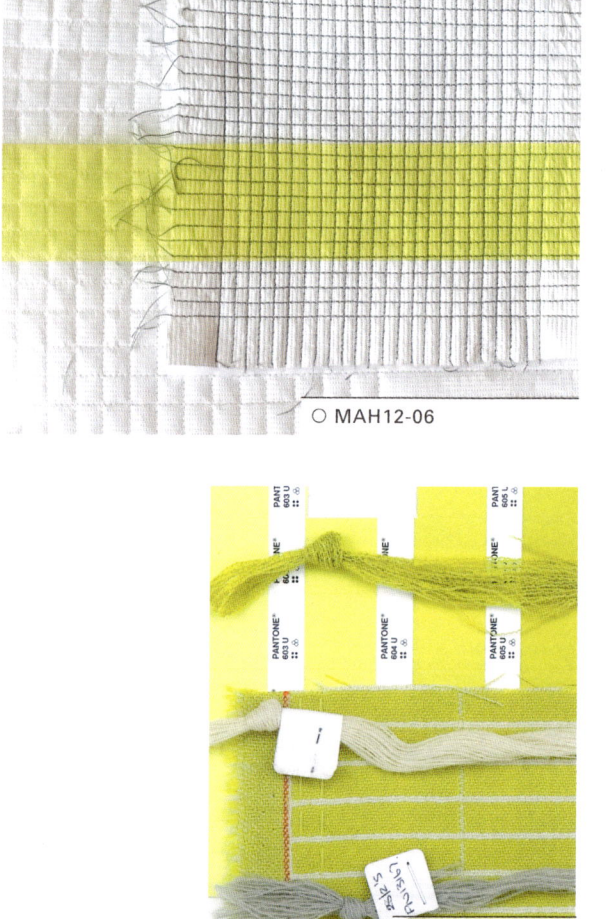

○ MAH12-06

○ MAH13-09

◉ MAH12-11

○ MAH13-01

○ MAH12-12

○ MAH12-09

○ MAH14-01

309

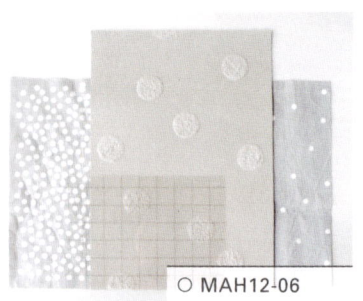

○ MAH12-06

● MAH13-03

● MAH14-01

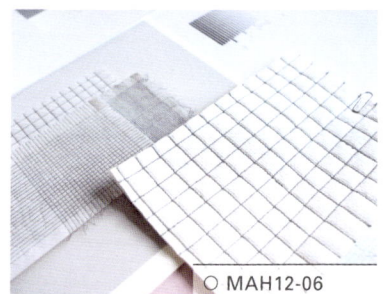

○ MAH12-06

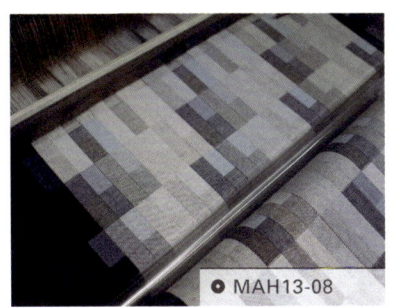
● MAH13-08

● MAH13-04

● MAH14-04

● MAH13-03

● MAH13-08

○ MAH12-06

○ MAH12-08

○ MAH12-07

○ MAH12-08

● MAH14-04

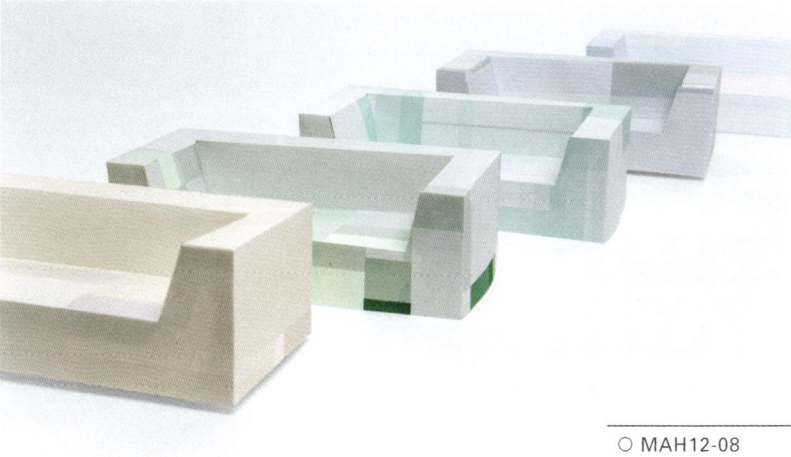

○ MAH12-08

○ MAH12-06

● MAH13-08

○ MAH12-09

● MAH14-01

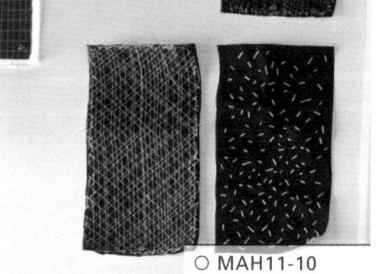

○ MAH11-10

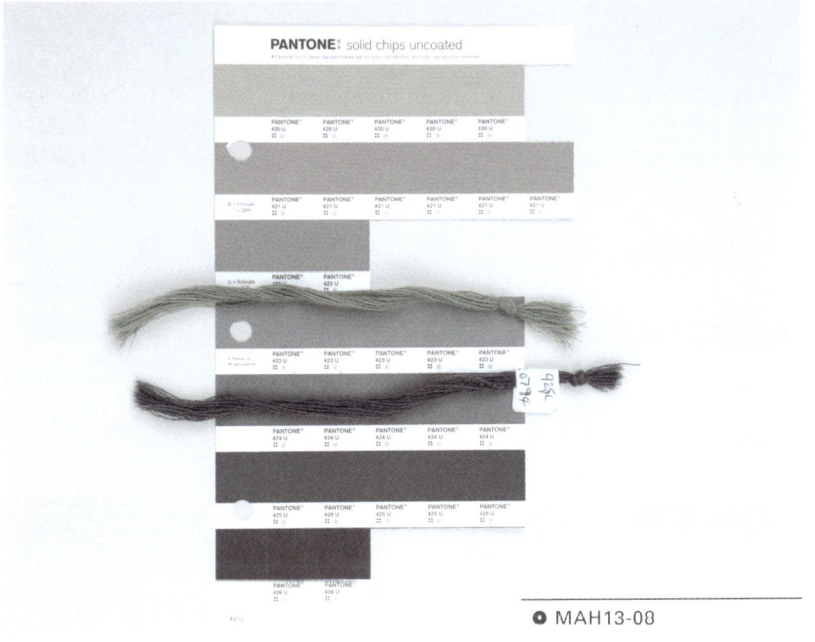

● MAH13-08

● MAH14-01

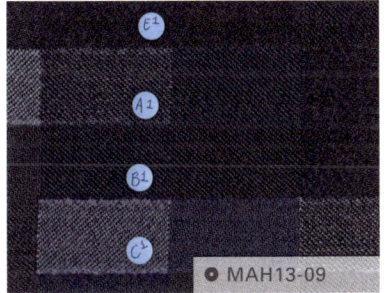

○ MAH13-09

○ MAH12-07

● MAH13-10

315

● MAH13-10

○ MAH12-08

● MAII13-05

● MAH14-01

● MAH14-01

● MAH14-01

● MAH14-01

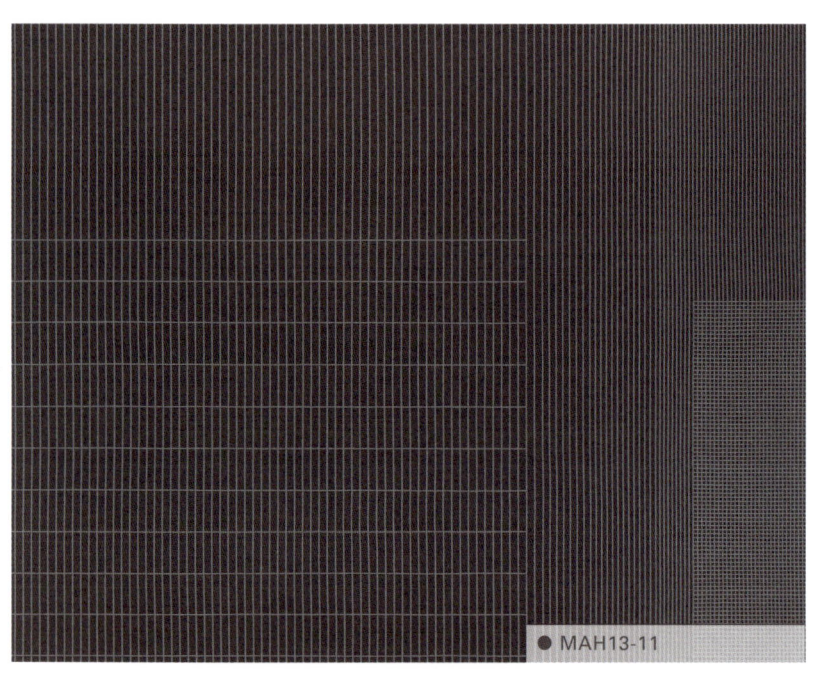

● MAH13-11

● MAH14-04

● MAH14-04

● MAH13-11

● MAH13-11

● MAH13-11

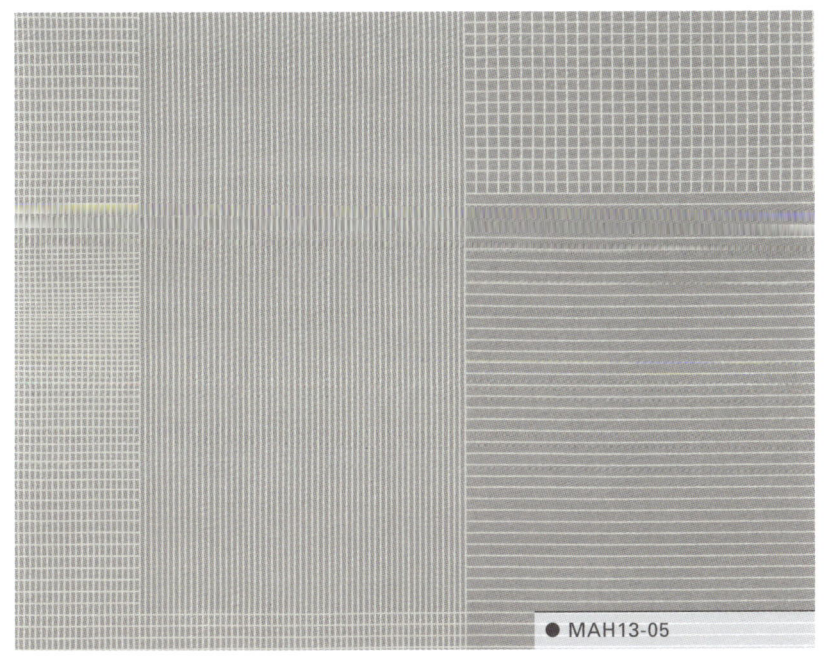

● MAH13-05

● MAH13-11

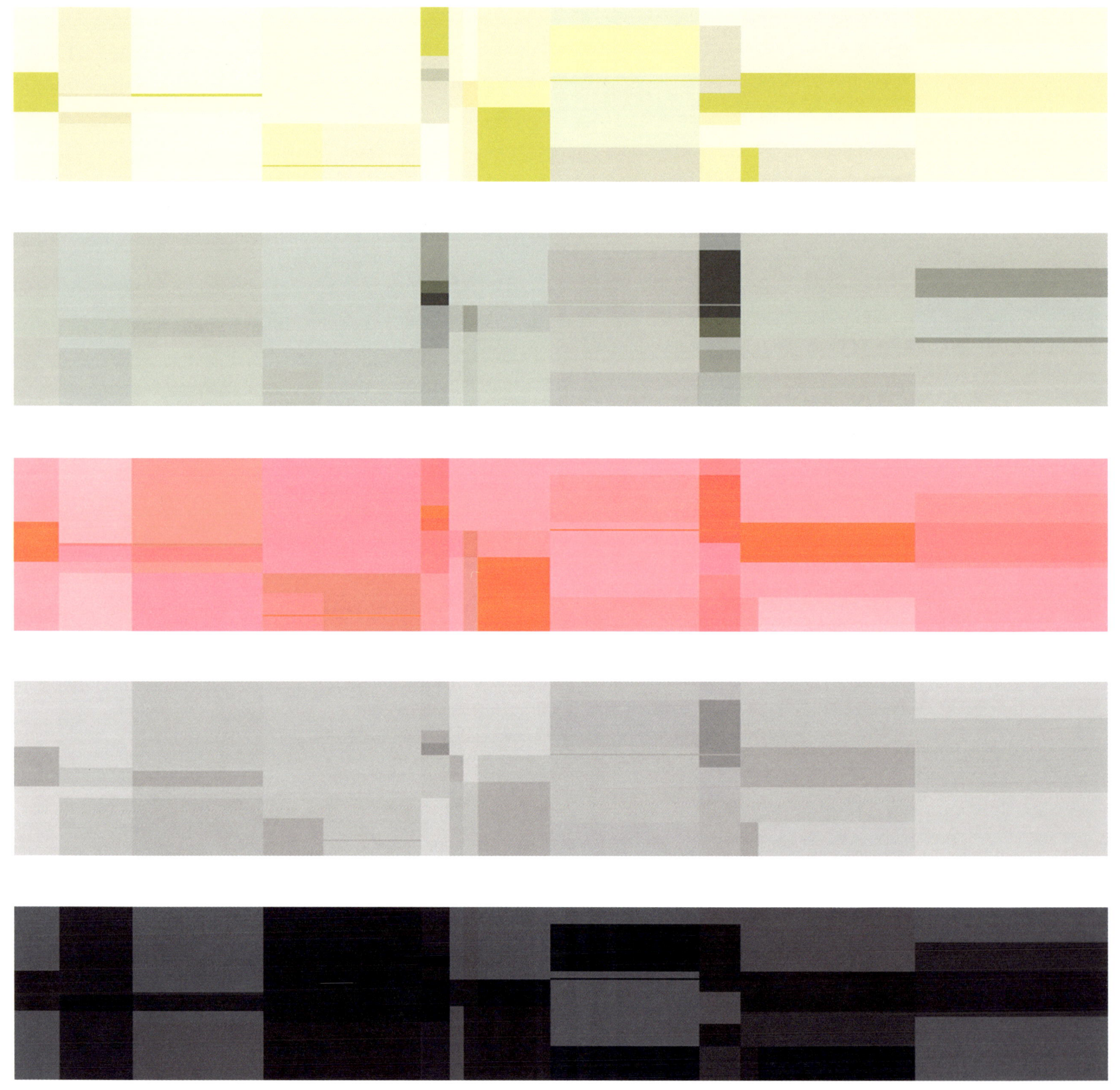

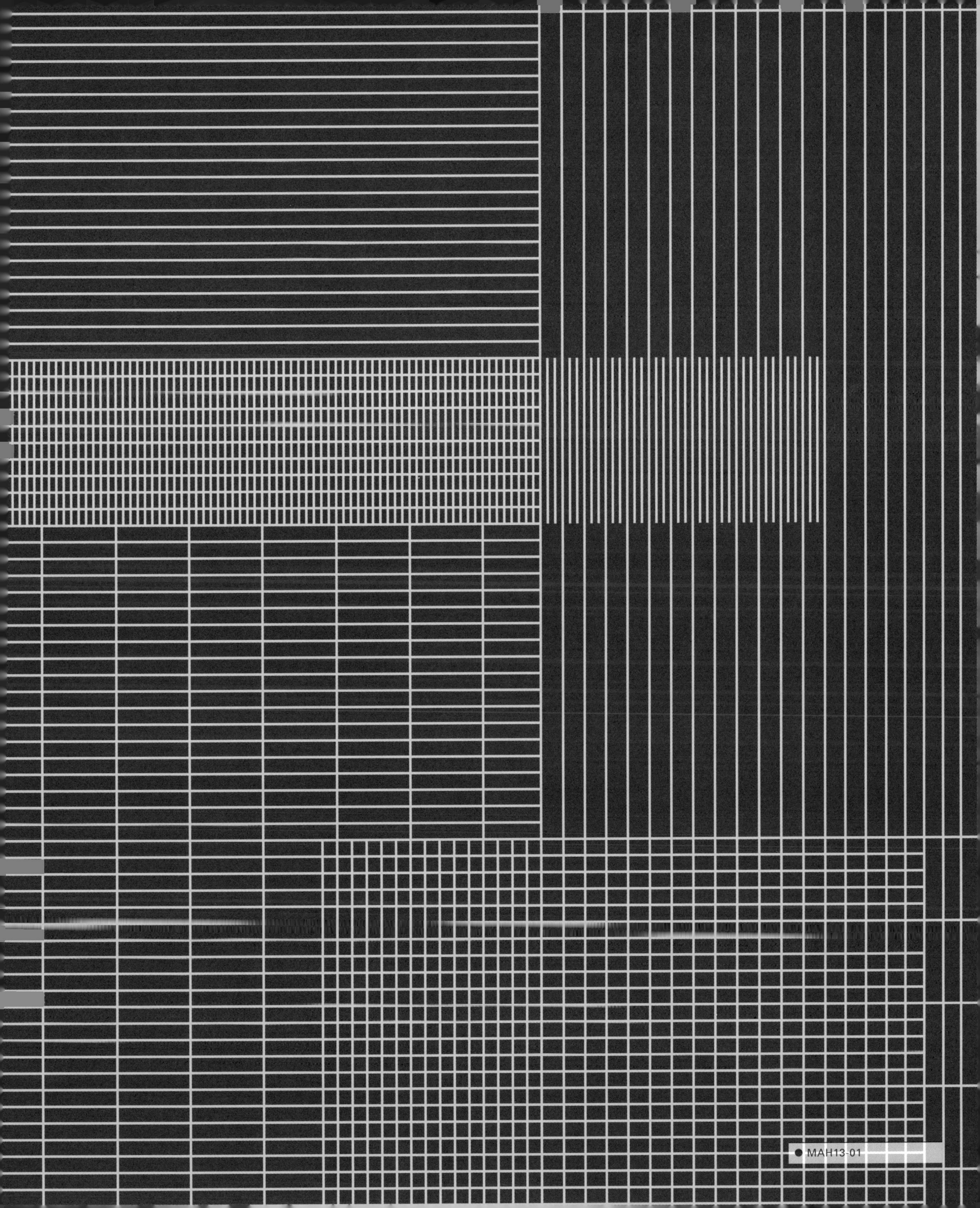
● MAH13-01

● MAH14-06

● MAH14-06

● MAH14-06

○ MAH12-03
Page from sketchbook.
Sketches made using black
pen and crayons on acrylic
and alcohol basis
March 2012

○ MAH12-04
Colour composition.
Printed paper
and colour sheets
April 2012

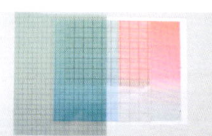

○ MAH12-04
Colour composition.
Printed paper
and colour sheets
April 2012

○ MAH12-07
Composition of layered
printed colour sheets
July 2012

○ MAH12-07
Composition of layered
printed colour sheets
July 2012

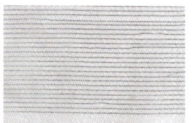

○ MAH12-05
White mesh with
stitched line pattern
May 2012

○ MAH12-05
Fine black Grid,
stitched on white Tyvek
May 2012

○ MAH12-05
Stitched Tyvek
May 2012

○ MAH12-05
Light green Grid pattern
printed on Japanese paper
May 2012

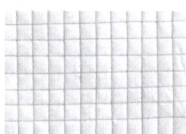

○ MAH12-05
Grid pattern on Tyvek for
selecting the right Grid size
May 2012

○ MAH12-05
White Grid stitched onto
Tyvek
May 2012

○ MAH12-05
3D Grid made of
light-grey cotton
May 2012

○ MAH12-05
Canvas with rectangular
pattern on white paper with
matt foil
May 2012

○ MAH12-05
Grid pattern stitched onto
blue fabric lined with Dacron
May 2012

○ MAH12-05
Fluorescent-orange grid
stitched onto canvas
May 2012

○ MAH12-05
Handmade Grid on paper
May 2012

○ MAH12-05
Paper with holes made
by hand
May 2012

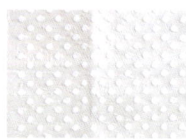

○ MAH12-05
Canvas with glued-on paper
dots and transparent matt foil
May 2012

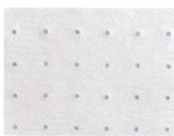

○ MAH12-05
White dyed canvas with
punched-out hole pattern
and an underlying layer
of blue fabric
May 2012

○ MAH12-05
Canvas with glued-on paper
strips and transparent matt foil
May 2012

○ MAH12-05
Processed fabric
with dot pattern
May 2012

○ MAH12-05
White linen embroidered
with fluorescent-yellow yarns
May 2012

○ MAH12-05
Grey fabric with glued-on,
handmade dot pattern
of paper and transparent
organza
May 2012

○ MAH12-05
Dot pattern on canvas
with glued-on paper dots
and transparent matt foil
May 2012

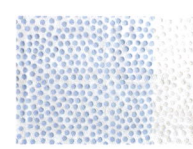

○ MAH12-05
Underlying layer of
blue and white fabric
with hand-punched
dot pattern in Tyvek
May 2012

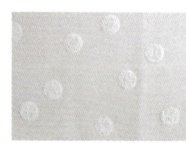

○ MAH12-05
Processed fabric
with large dots
May 2012

○ MAH12-06
Stitched Tyvek, Grid textile
composition printed on paper
June 2012

○ MAH12-06
Printed Japanese paper,
printed & stitched paper,
Grid on canvas
June 2012

○ MAH12-06
Composition of
handmade samples.
Stitched Tyvek
June 2012

○ MAH12-06
Composition of
handmade samples.
Canvas with paper,
stitched Tyvek
June 2012

○ MAH12-06
Composition of handmade
samples. Canvas with paper,
printed Japanese paper,
colour sheet
June 2012

○ MAH12-06
Composition of
handmade samples.
Printed Japanese paper,
stitched Tyvek, colour sheet
June 2012

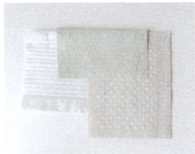

○ MAH12-06
Composition of
handmade samples.
Stitched Tyvek,
canvas with paper,
printed Japanese paper
June 2012

○ MAH12-09
Reference board at the
Scholten & Baijings studio,
made for the first
presentation to Maharam
in September 2012.
Various media
April–September 2012

○ MAH14-01
Selection of printed artwork.
and textile samples,
handmade in-house
January 2014

◉ MAH13-01
Matching yarns for the Blocks
colour scheme at weaving mill
January 2013

○ MAH12-08
Selection of yarns for
the first prototypes
at the TextielMuseum,
the Netherlands
August 2012

○ MAH12-08
Colour selection for
Blocks & Grid
August 2012

◉ MAH12-08
Yarns selected for the colour
scheme of Blocks & Grid
August 2012

◉ MAH13-08
Green and grey warp
on loom at weaving mill
for colour proofs
August 2013

◉ MAH13-08
Individual grey colour proofs
for the final Blocks Grey
colour selection
August 2013

◉ MAH13-08
Grey colour proofs
on loom at weaving mill
August 2013

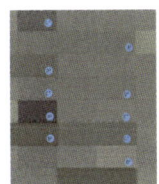

◉ MAH13-09
Final colour selection
for Blocks Green textile
September 2013

◉ MAH13-09
Final colour selection
for Blocks Red textile
September 2013

◉ MAH13-09
Final colour selection
for Blocks Grey textile
September 2013

◉ MAH13-03
Back of first industrial sample
of Grid, hanging at the
Scholten & Baijings studio
March 2013

◉ MAH13-03
Front of first industrial sample
of Grid, hanging at the
Scholten & Baijings studio
March 2013

◉ MAH13-05
Checking the correct
proportions of grid on
Grid textile
May 2013

● MAH14-04
Grid 005, upholstered
on Vitra's Alcove sofa
April 2014

● MAH14-04
Details. Blocks 003,
Blocks 004 & Blocks 005,
photographed by
Scheltens & Abbenes
April 2014

◉ MAH13-08
Red colour proofs on loom
at weaving mill
August 2013

◉ MAH13-08
The fabric's selvedges are
partially cut off during the
weaving process
August 2013

◉ MAH13-08
Check of industrially woven
Blocks 003
August 2013

○ MAH12-06
Grid stitched onto cotton
June 2012

○ MAH12-06
Blocks & Grid design,
Grid print and Grid textile
sample
June 2012

◉ MAH13-08
Red colour proofs on loom
at weaving mill
August 2013

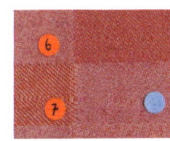

◉ MAH13-09
Final colour selection
for Blocks Red textile
September 2013

◉ MAH13-10
Front and back of Blocks Red
textile, woven to a scale of 1:2
October 2013

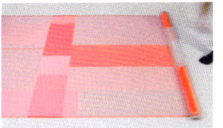

● MAH14-01
Final check of Blocks 003
textile before starting
production
January 2014

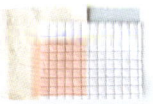

○ MAH12-06
Composition of
handmade samples.
Stitched Tyvek,
treated canvas,
printed colour sheet
June 2012

◉ MAH13-04
Stack of various
Orange-Red Grid textiles.
Industrially woven textile
April 2013

● MAH13-05
Industrially produced
Blocks 001, hanging in
Scholten & Baijings studio
May 2013

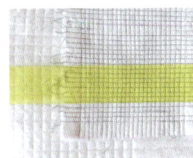

○ MAH12-06
Composition of samples,
handmade in-house.
Stitched Tyvek,
printed colour sheet
June 2012

○ MAH13-09
Selection of final Grid
Yellow-Green colour yarns
for industrial production
September 2013

○ MAH12-11
Prototypes of various
Grid designs woven
at the TextielMuseum
in Tilburg, the Netherlands
November 2012

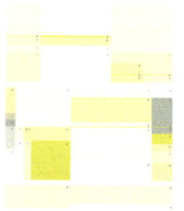

○ MAH13-01
Final design drawing of Blocks
Yellow with colour-coded yarns
January 2013

○ MAH12-12
Woollen Grid textile sample
woven at the TextielMuseum
in Tilburg, the Netherlands
December 2012

○ MAH12-09
Textile sample, linen/cotton,
various Grid patterns woven
at the TextielMuseum in
Tilburg, the Netherlands
September 2012

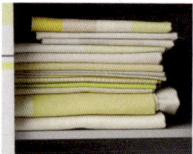

○ MAH14-01
Different versions of Blocks
Yellow and Grid Yellow-Green.
Industrially woven textile
January 2014

○ MAH12-06
Composition of
handmade samples.
Textile with paper,
treated textile,
printed colour sheet
June 2012

○ MAH13-03
First industrial sample of
Blocks Grey textile woven
to a scale of 1:2
March 2013

● MAH14-01
Final check of Blocks 004
textile before starting
production
January 2014

○ MAH13-04
Stack of various colour Grids
April 2013

● MAH14-04
Composition of final textiles:
Blocks 004, Grid 004 and 001
April 2014

○ MAH13-03
First industrial sample of
Blocks Grey textile woven
to a scale of 1:2
March 2013

○ MAH12-06
Composition of
handmade samples.
Textiles with paper,
printed colour sheet
June 2012

○ MAH12-08
Selection of Blocks Green
yarns for prototypes at the
TextielMuseum in Tilburg,
the Netherlands
August 2012

○ MAH12-07
Blocks Green compositions
with printed colour sheets
July 2012

○ MAH12-09
Final Blocks Green
prototype from the
TextielMuseum,
the Netherlands,
presented to Maharam
September 2012

○ MAH12-08
Colour blanket of Blocks
Green made at the
TextielMuseum in Tilburg,
the Netherlands
August 2012

● MAH14-04
Industrially produced Blocks
005, 004 and 002, hanging at
the Scholten & Baijings studio
April 2014

○ MAH12-08
Paper models with first colour
schemes for Blocks textile
August 2012

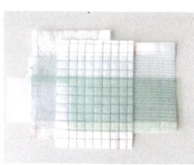

○ MAH12-06
Composition of
handmade samples.
Stitched Tyvek,
printed colour sheet
June 2012

● MAH13-08
Chair upholstered with
Grid 005; in the background
Blocks 002
August 2013

● MAH14-01
Checking the final Blocks 005
textile
January 2014

○ MAH11-10
Textile samples
embroidered
with silver threads
and white cotton
October 2011

○ MAH13-08
Colour selection of yarns
used for the warp in Blocks
Black-Blue
August 2013

● MAH14-01
Final check of Blocks 005
textile before
starting production
January 2014

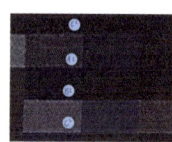

○ MAH13-09
Final colour selection for
Blocks Black-Blue textile
September 2013

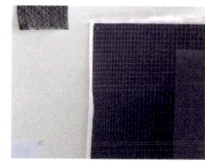

○ MAH12-07
Printed Blocks on paper
with stitched Grid
July 2012

● MAH13-10
Section from complete
colour overview
for Blocks & Grid
October 2013

330

● MAH14-04
Composition of Blocks & Grid,
photographed by
Scheltens & Abbenes
April 2014

● MAH13-10
Complete colour overview
for Blocks & Grid
October 2013

○ MAH12-08
Final Blocks Red
prototype from the
TextielMuseum in Tilburg,
the Netherlands
August 2012

● MAH13-05
Blocks 001
Industrial product
May 2013

● MAH14-01
Blocks 004
Industrial product
January 2014

● MAH14-01
Blocks 002
Industrial product
January 2014

● MAH14-01
Blocks 003
Industrial product
January 2014

● MAH14-01
Blocks 005
Industrial product
January 2014

● MAH13-11
Grid 006
Industrial product
November 2013

● MAH14-04
Composition of Grid 004,
002 and 001.
Industrial products
April 2014

● MAH14-04
Various hanging Blocks & Grid
Industrial products
April 2014

● MAH13-11
Grid 003
Industrial product
November 2013

● MAH13-11
Grid 002
Industrial product
November 2013

● MAH13-11
Grid 004
Industrial product
November 2013

● MAH13-05
Grid 005
Industrial product
May 2013

● MAH13-11
Grid 001
Industrial product
November 2013

● MAH13-01
Full repeat, Blocks 001
through 005
January 2013

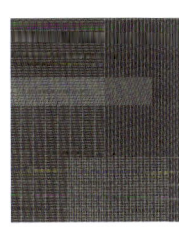

● MAH13-01
Detail of Grid 006
artwork
January 2013

● MAH14-06
Complete Blocks & Grid
collection at Maharam
showroom in Chicago
Photography Dean Kaufman,
courtesy of Maharam
June 2014

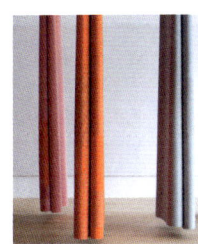

● MAH14-06
Blocks 003, Grid 003
and Grid 004 at Maharam
showroom in Chicago
Photography Dean Kaufman,
courtesy of Maharam
June 2014

● MAH14-06
Selection of Blocks & Grid
collection at Maharam
showroom in Chicago
Photography Dean Kaufman,
courtesy of Maharam
June 2014

SCHOLTEN & BAIJINGS

The designers Stefan Scholten (1972) and Carole Baijings (1973) move fluidly between the disciplines of art and design, and artisanal and industrial processes, to create a visually arresting collection of work which has strong references to the past yet is overtly of the current moment.

The design duo established Scholten & Baijings, Studio for Design, in 2000. They continue to combine minimal forms and balanced use of colour with traditional craft techniques and industrial production in a distinctive, almost un-Dutch design style. The finesse, entrancing colours and subtle use of materials in their work have earned them considerable admiration in the international design world. Their work, both independent and commissioned, is collected and exhibited worldwide.

Scholten & Baijings have been awarded numerous prestigious prizes, such as the ELLE Decoration International Design Award (EDIDA) for Young Designer Talent 2011, a nomination for Designer of the Year at the Wallpaper* Design Awards 2011 and Oeuvre Award Sanoma Woon Awards 2014. Their products and limited editions are presented in museums and galleries such as the Cooper-Hewitt National Design Museum, New York, the Art Institute of Chicago, the Victoria & Albert Museum, London, the Design Museum, London, villa Noailles, Hyères, BOZAR, Brussels, MART, Rovereto, the BMW Museum, Munich, Wilhelm Wagenfeld Haus, Bremen, the Stedelijk Museum Amsterdam, the Zuiderzee Museum, Enkhuizen, the Stedelijk Museum 's-Hertogenbosch, the TextielMuseum, Tilburg, the Museum Boijmans Van Beuningen, Rotterdam, the Centraal Museum, Utrecht, Designhuis, Eindhoven, Elisabeth Leriche's Trend Space at Maison & Objet, Paris, Spazio Rossana Orlandi, Milan, Poldi Pezzoli Museum, Milan, Cibone, Tokyo, Galerie VIVID, Rotterdam, Galerie Binnen, and The Frozen Fountain, Amsterdam.

Industrial clients include Maharam, Established & Sons, HAY, IKEA, Karimoku New Standard, Georg Jensen, 1616/Arita Japan, Moooi, Thomas Eyck, and BMW Group/MINI.

Complete Works

Provided below is a chronologically arranged list of Scholten & Baijings' complete works.

Where applicable, measurements are stated in the following order: height × length × width, or height × diameter.

Eight unique carpets and two pieces of jewellery
2001

Materials: 100% New Zealand woven wool carpet, leather, paint
Techniques: Stitching, embroidery, gluing, shaving, patchwork, blanching
Dimensions: Various
Commission: Initiated by the designers
Production: Scholten & Baijings
Collections: Private collections, designers' collection

For this project we made use of scrap material from the looms of carpet manufacturer M.I.D. One of the residual materials reminded us very much of a Moroccan rug. So we decided to make the patterns, which connect the frequently smallish pieces of scrap material into one larger entity, reminiscent of Moroccan kilims and rugs from the Andes. By hand-processing this residual material using colours, leather and an intricate construction, we were able to create added value. The starting point for making these carpets and jewellery was to turn 'scrap material into gold'.

Divine Glass
2002

Materials: Glass, nickel-plated steel
Techniques: Polishing, gluing
Dimensions: Various
Commission: Initiated by the designers
Production: Van Esch (not currently in production)
Collections: Private collections, designers' collection
Awards: Nominated for the Dutch Design Awards 2004, nominated for Gemeentelijke Kunstaankopen (Municipal Art Acquisitions) 2004

Divine Glass is a series of glass furniture that derives its design inspiration from the traditional Golden Section, also called Divine Proportion. These proportions served as the starting point for Divine Glass. The design is austere, which enables it to blend in well with the space around it. The specially designed hinges, locks and wall brackets – small and almost invisible – are a distinctive design feature of Divine Glass.

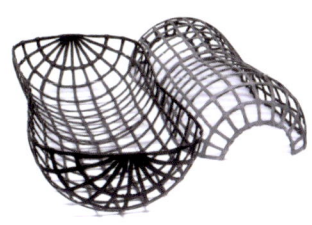

After the Blast
2002

Materials: Earthenware, porcelain, bandage, various glazes
Techniques: Slip casting, 'embroidery' with porcelain
Dimensions: Various / seven different designs
Commission: Initiated by the designers
Production: Developed during a work period at the European Ceramic Workcentre (EKWC) in 's-Hertogenbosch, the Netherlands
Collections: Designers' collection

'After the Blast' was realized during a three-month work period at the EKWC in 's-Hertogenbosch, the Netherlands. The objects created from ceramic grids point to the beauty of that which remains: skeletons of buildings, transformations, textures and colours evolved from extremes.

Styrofoam City
2002

Materials: Porcelain, platinum lustre
Techniques: Slip casting
Dimensions: Various / seven different designs
Commission: Initiated by the designers
Production: Developed during a work period at the European Ceramic Workcentre (EKWC) in 's-Hertogenbosch, the Netherlands
Collections: Private collections, designers' collection

'Styrofoam City' consists of seven different forms. These forms, derived from styrofoam packaging material, are made of porcelain and finished with platinum lustre. By grouping these different forms together, the image of a city emerges.

Forced Mobiles
Colour Machine 'Foliage'
2002

Materials: Computer, aluminium, ABS
Techniques: Electronics, mechanics, silk screen
Dimensions: 37.5 × 180 × 16.5 cm / two different designs
Commission: Initiated by the designers
Production: Scholten & Baijings for 'Smart Alice', Centraal Museum Utrecht / Nike
Collections: Private collections, designers' collection

'Foliage' and 'Water / M2' are mobiles from the 2002 Forced Mobiles series, inspired by the qualities found in nature, such as movement, colour, light and change. Contrary to equilibrium-based mobiles that usually move or change form through air displacement, the principle of Forced Mobiles aims to replace the natural element of wind with a mechanically driven processor.

Flower/Bloom
2003

Materials: Porcelain, glaze, liqueur
Techniques: Slip casting / injection moulding in plaster moulds
Dimensions: 9.5 × 12 × 12 cm
Commission: New Dutch Souvenir for the European Ceramic Workcentre (EKWC)
Production: Erik Jan Kwakkel, A. van Wees Distillery de Ooievaar / Goods / since 2012 made by 1616 / Arita Japan. Only the white matt version without liqueur, called Bloom, is still in production
Collections: Design Museum Ghent, private collections, designers' collection
Awards: Selected for the Dutch Design Awards 2004

This keepsake was produced as part of the EKWC project entitled 'Dutch Souvenirs'. Flower / Bloom is designed and manufactured with the help of a computer. The design is inspired by the colour, texture and shape of various flowers. Flower is made of porcelain and filled with a traditional Dutch liqueur named Forget-Me-Not. The liqueur was first distilled in 1782 by A. van Wees Distillery de Ooievaar in Amsterdam. When empty, Flower and Bloom double as vases.

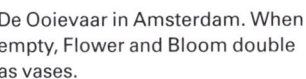

Grid
2004
Solo Exhibition at Galerie Binnen

Materials: Various
Commission: Galerie Binnen, Amsterdam
Production: Scholten & Baijings

The aim of the Grid project is to show the structure of a form. The project explores the possibilities of creating products from, for example, wire mesh fabric. By making use of transparency, the form, construction and function all become visible at the same time. This visual fusion is an important starting point for the work.

Soft Cube
Grid Project
2004

Materials: Open-meshed stainless steel fabric
Techniques: Bending, spot welding
Dimensions: 47 × 47 × 47 cm
Commission: Zetel
Production: Scholten & Baijings
Collections: Stedelijk Museum Amsterdam, Zetel collection, private collections, designers' collection
Awards: Nominated for Gemeentelijke Kunstaankopen (Municipal Art Acquisitions) 2004

Soft Cube is part of the Grid project. Soft Cube is made of an open-meshed stainless steel fabric, bent and spot welded without further construction. This makes the stool both flexible and strong.

Rocks
Grid Project
2004

Materials: Steel, textile mesh fabric / stainless steel wire mesh fabric
Techniques: Bending, welding, mounting, powder coating
Dimensions: Indoor 80 × 140 × 250 cm, outdoor 80 × 280 × 280 cm
Commission: Initiated by the designers
Production: Scholten & Baijings
Collections: Designers' collection

Rocks are spatial objects that offer a place where one can sit with several people in various configurations. These objects come in two versions: an indoor version in a textile fabric and an outdoor version in a fine stainless steel wire mesh fabric. The frames of Rocks are made from powder-coated steel and coloured in off-white and light grey. Both versions are transparent.

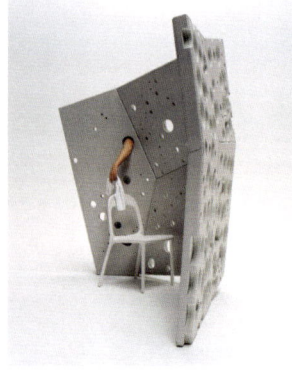

Folding Space
Grid Project
2004

Materials: Textile, foam
Techniques: Water cutting, gluing
Dimensions: 220 × 300 × 13 cm
Commission: Initiated by the designers
Production: Scholten & Baijings
Collections: Designers' collection
Photography: Inga Powilleit

Folding Space is a room divider with two different, randomly applied dot patterns. The screen is three-dimensional but can be folded up into a flat package.

Etch Table
2004

Materials: Aluminium
Techniques: Anodizing
Dimensions: 220 × 76.3 cm
Commission: Initiated by the designers
Production: Scholten & Baijings. Limited edition of two, both with a different line pattern. Every table is handcrafted and therefore unique
Collections: Private collections
Awards: Selected for the Dutch Design Awards 2005

The design's starting point is the creation of a table that subtly changes under the influence of light. Etching is a centuries-old technique, but it's rarely applied to aluminium. The Etch Table is an anodized aluminium table with an etched-in line pattern. Etching changes the structure and texture of the material which, in combination with the pattern, reflects the light in a different way. The table responds with a variety of colour intentions. The soft aluminium and the etching are protected and hardened by means of anodization.

Etch
2004

Materials: Paper, ink
Techniques: Etching
Dimensions: 220 × 90 cm
Commission: Initiated by the designers
Production: Scholten & Baijings, developed at Amsterdams Grafisch Atelier (AGA). Line Pattern 1: Limited edition of two. Line Pattern 2: Limited edition of three
Collections: Private collections, designers' collection

Before the soft aluminium is protected by anodizing the material, the tabletops/etching plates are printed on paper. Etching on aluminium results in a deep black colour nuance and intensity. After printing, the etching plates are sealed by gluing everything together.

Light Tables
2005

Materials: Aluminium
Techniques: Anodizing
Dimensions: 45 × 45 × 45 cm / five different designs
Commission/Production: Van Esch (currently not in production)
Collections: Private collections, designers' collection

They look like robust cubes, but due to their minimalist design they effortlessly blend in with their environment. Depending on the lighting, Light Tables create an attractive interplay between light and shadows. What's more, these aluminium side tables are lightweight and therefore easy to move.

Afrika Museum
2006

Materials: Textile, plastic, aluminium, paint, acoustic panels, laminate
Techniques: Jacquard weaving, anodizing, screen printing
Dimensions: Various
Commission: Afrika Museum, Berg en Dal, Atelier Rijksbouwmeester, Henk de Haan, Architect of the Government Buildings Agency
Production: Scholten & Baijings
Photography: Christiaan de Bruijne

On the occasion of the new construction carried out at the Afrika Museum in Berg en Dal, the Netherlands, Scholten & Baijings received the commission to design a new layout for the museum's lobby area as well as the auditorium. Characteristic features dating from the first extension in the 1950s, such as a sense of space, openness, light and sustainability, were once again key criteria, this time, however, with much more emphasis on elements from African culture. The designs reflect everyday African life and traditional crafts, dominated by the use of primary colours and the simplicity of materials.

Photographs of dancing African people were used for the design of one of the auditorium's two acoustic walls. A coloured grid was superimposed over these figures, so that they appear to be moving more exuberantly. This cloth (10 × 6.5 m) was woven at the TextielMuseum, Tilburg.

Africa Chair
2006

Materials: Polyester
Techniques: Polyester vacuum moulding, CNC milling
Dimensions: 79 × 58 × 55 cm
Commission: Afrika Museum, Berg en Dal, Atelier Rijksbouwmeester, Henk de Haan, Architect of the Government Buildings Agency
Production: Scholten & Baijings
Collection: Afrika Museum, designers' collection
Photography: Christiaan de Bruijne

The Africa Chair was especially developed for the auditorium. The aim of the chair's design was to emphasize the character of the room. In addition, the chairs had to be stackable and joinable. The chair's simple design required the use of polyester.

Still
2005

Materials: Textile: linen, cotton / Trevira, aluminium
Techniques: Jacquard double weaving, stitching / laser cutting
Dimensions: Various / 150 × 157 × 37.5 cm
Commission: TextielMuseum / Royal Ahrend
Production: Prototypes by Scholten & Baijings (currently out of production)
Collections: TextielMuseum, Tilburg, private collections, designers' collection
Awards: Nominated for the Dutch Design Awards 2005

A 'Still' is a room divider. 'Still' is completely machine made. The screen is woven in one operation on a Jacquard weaving machine, including the tunnels for the tubular aluminium frame. This frame gives structural form to the fabric. The outer edges of the screen have been finished using laser technology.
The specific form of 'Still' is attributable to a unique weaving process developed by Scholten & Baijings, which makes it possible to split the fabric. The resulting branches ensure that 'Still' can stand on its own.

The characteristic design elements of the system are reflected in the transparency, texture, colour and the use of patterns. The interaction between the various layers of fabric and the position of the 'Still' in the interior determine the light effects and colour intensity.

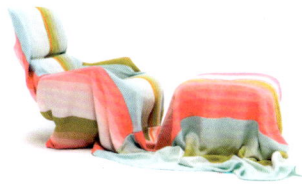

Colour Plaids
2005

Materials: Merino wool, cotton
Techniques: Jacquard double weaving
Dimensions: 180 × 140 cm, 260 × 280 cm / five different designs
Commission: Prototypes in TextielLab TextielMuseum by Scholten & Baijings
Production: Scholten & Baijings
Collections: TextielMuseum, Tilburg, Centre National des Arts Plastiques (CNAP), private collections, designers' collection

The designs of these blankets consist of interrupted colour sequences. It's these vivid stripes and the multitude of colours that make Colour Plaids unique. The blankets are made of Merino wool and cotton, which makes them luxuriously soft. You can use them in countless ways: to wrap around yourself, lie beneath, decorate your bed or sofa, or give an old piece of furniture a new lease of life.

Colour Cushions
2005

Materials: Merino wool, cotton
Techniques: Jacquard double weaving
Dimensions: 33 × 47 cm, 60 × 60 cm and 40 × 88 cm / eight different designs
Commission: Prototypes in TextielLab TextielMuseum by Scholten & Baijings
Production: Scholten & Baijings
Collections: Private collections, designers' collection

The collection of plaids is complemented with a variety of cushions in individual designs.

Armchair 7400
Art Direction Gelderland
2009

Materials: Metal frame, soft inner shell, textile / leather, steel
Techniques: Foam moulding, upholstery, chrome plating
Dimensions: 64 × 81 × 98 cm
Commission/Production: Gelderland
Photography: Alexander van Berge

From 2008 until 2013, Scholten & Baijings were responsible for the art direction of Gelderland, a furniture brand. During this period, the duo also designed furniture for this well-established Dutch brand and attracted young talent. Armchair 7400 is an example of their work for this brand.

Het Appartement/True-to-Life Design
Galerie Binnen, Amsterdam
2005

Materials: Various
Techniques: Various
Dimensions: The entire gallery
Commission: Gelderland, van Esch during ELLE Inside Design
Production: Scholten & Baijings, music by Moritz Gabe, food styling by Yvette van Boven

Visitors might hesitate to walk into the gallery because it looks so similar to a lifelike setting. Books, newspapers, clothes and sneakers are scattered all over the place. The bed is unmade and the

aluminium etch table has not been cleared. The cleaning staff received special instructions to ensure that they didn't tidy up certain parts of the exhibition.

L'Appartamento/True-to-Life Design
Galleria Antonia Jannone, Milan
2006

Materials: Various
Techniques: Various
Dimensions: The entire gallery
Commission: Gelderland, van Esch, Gispen during Salone del Mobile, Milan
Production: Scholten & Baijings, music by Moritz Gabe, food styling by Yvette van Boven

A selection from the furnishings: the display cases that Scholten & Baijings designed for van Esch function as spice racks in the kitchen, while the dish drainer is crowded with dinner service from Dutch fellow designers. Coloured hand-blown glass globe lamps are suspended from the ceiling. The new lounge chair, model 7020 designed for Gelderland, is covered with clothes. A screen serves as a divider between bedroom and living room.

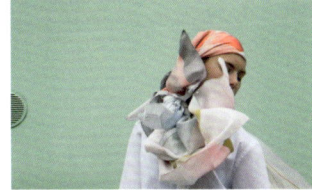

Colour Scarf
2008

Materials: 100% (crepe) silk
Techniques: Printing
Dimensions: 90 × 90 cm, 135 × 56 cm
Commission/Production: Scholten & Baijings
Photography: Viviane Sassen

The patterns of the scarves consist of grids and gradient colours. These soft coloured scarves are made of 100% pure silk and are produced in the Netherlands. They bear the unmistakable Scholten & Baijings signature: colour, transparency, layered patterns, grids – in short, timeless design with an eye for detail.

Light Ball
2006

Materials: Coloured glass, aluminium
Techniques: Mouth-blown glass, glass cutting, sand blasting
Dimensions: Ø 40 cm, Ø 50 cm / two different designs
Commission: Initiated by the designers
Production: Prototypes by Bernard Heesen. Industrial production by Fikelenboom
Collections: Private collections, designers' collection

The Light Ball has a quirky twist. At first sight it seems to be a simple lamp, but the unique details make this lamp just a bit different. Take, for example, the asymmetrical cut of the large Murano glass globe. Or the lustrous exterior that makes the mouth-blown globe literally 'light up'. Attention has also been focused on the lamp's hanging system, whose sand-blasted aluminium finish turns it into an eye-catching design detail. Making visible what is usually invisible.

Woven Willow
2008

Materials: Willow rods, (cristal supérieur) glass, papier-mâché, plastic, textile, paint
Techniques: *Fijnscheenwerk* (fine wicker weave), mouth-blown glass
Dimensions: Various
Commission: Thomas Eyck, t.e.
Production: Unlimited production. 'Garlic Queen' is a limited edition of 10 pieces.
Collections: Zuiderzee Museum, Enkhuizen, the Art Institute of Chicago, private collections, designers' collection

Woven Willow consists of seven different objects based on Scholten & Baijings'

contemporary signature, in perfect harmony with a traditional Dutch 17th-century weaving technique. This technique entails that willow rods are cleaved into very small pieces and used almost like textile. Scholten & Baijings' fresh and innovative approach to this very old technique has resulted in a brightly coloured collection. The wicker as well as the grid of the woven willow inspired Scholten & Baijings to combine several materials in their designs. For the 'Tape Bowl' and the 'Grand Bernard' jug the wicker disappeared entirely, the only reminder being an imprint in the glass.

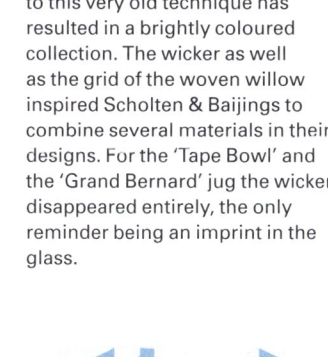

Damask Tablecloth 'Milk Carton'
2008

Materials: 100% cotton
Techniques: Jacquard weaving
Dimensions: Damask tablecloth 285 × 163 cm, napkins 52 × 54 cm
Commission: TextielMuseum, Tilburg
Production: Scholten & Baijings in collaboration with TextielLab at the TextielMuseum, Tilburg. Thomas Eyck, t.e. collection
Collections: TextielMuseum, Tilburg, Zuiderzee Museum, Enkhuizen, private collections, designers' collection

The drawings on Damask 'Milk Carton' have a graphic look. The large milk cartons and the corresponding gaps are an important element in the total composition. The design was motivated by the idea that food in the twenty-first century is equivalent to supermarket food. Consumers no longer make a connection with the way food is obtained, prepared or consumed. Today, our primal necessities revolve around marketing, packaging and convenience. The design was inspired by the Albert Heijn supermarket's milk carton, which displays a small window in the form of an old-fashioned milk bottle.

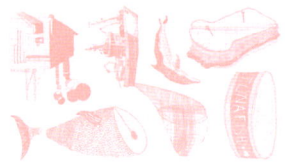

**Damask Tablecloth
'The Life of a Tuna Fish'
2008**

Materials: 100% cotton
Techniques: Jacquard weaving
Dimensions: Damask tablecloth
290 × 160 cm, napkins 53 × 53 cm
Commission: TextielMuseum,
Tilburg
Production: Scholten & Baijings
in collaboration with TextielLab
at the TextielMuseum, Tilburg.
Thomas Eyck, t.e. collection
Collections: TextielMuseum,
Tilburg, Zuiderzee Museum,
Enkhuizen, private collections,
designers' collection

Scholten & Baijings wanted to
transfer the characteristic look
of hand-drawn patterns to the
damask tablecloths, featuring
unique line contours, line
thicknesses and shadings.
The graphic images of the
patterns are traced in actual size
and elaborated with ink. They are
then scanned, converted into
a digital file and translated into
weaves by computer software.
Because the drawings are made
up of varying line shadings,
a variety of textures can be seen
and felt in the woven fabric.

The first damask tablecloth 'The
Life of a Tuna Fish' shows the life
of a tuna in six drawings, from
catch to processing. A thoughtful
reminder that the bluefin tuna
is threatened with extinction.

**Table Glass
2008**

Materials: Cristal supérieur glass
Techniques: Mouth-blown glass,
hand cutting
Dimensions: 15 × Ø 14 cm, 14 ×
Ø 23 cm, 20 × Ø 23 cm, 21 × 11 ×
7 cm, 3.7 × Ø 28 cm, 29 × Ø 14.5 cm /
Limited edition of 8
Commission/Production: Royal
Leerdam Crystal
Collections: Zuiderzee Museum,

Enkhuizen, private collections,
designers' collection

The six-piece glass series is
produced in collaboration with
the master glassblowers of Royal
Leerdam Crystal. The six user
items, with the names Jug, Platter,
Bowl, Platter with Cover, Candy
Dish, and Flower Vase, have been
made from Europe's purest
variety of crystal, cristal supérieur.
Each table object consists of a
pink transparent layer and a white
layer. The two layers of coloured
glass have been brought together
by means of the traditional
glass-blowing technique known
as 'overlay'. After cooling, the
characteristic line patterns of this
series are applied manually with
a small diamond disk.

**Colour Carpets
VIP room TextielMuseum
2008**

Materials: 100% Merino wool
Techniques: Tufted
Dimensions: Various
Commission: TextielMuseum,
Tilburg
Production: Carpet Sign
Collections: Private collections,
designers' collection
Photography: Inga Powilleit

For the VIP room at the TextielMuseum, Scholten & Baijings designed
Colour Carpets that are hand-tufted
of 100% Merino wool. Also on
display are transparent fabrics
produced by the design duo. Each
year, the museum's VIP room is
decorated by different designer.

**Vegetables
2009**

Materials: Textile, yarn, foam, felt,
metal
Techniques: Painting, stitching,
embroidery, sewing, gluing
Dimensions: Various

**Lloyd Hotel
2008**

Materials: Textiles, 100% Merino
wool, glass, chrome, mirror, tiles,
aluminium, pencil lines
Techniques: Hand drawing, glass
cutting, weaving, tufting, gluing,
drawing, anodizing
Dimensions: Various
Commission: Lloyd Hotel,
Amsterdam
Production: Scholten & Baijings
in collaboration with TextielLab
at the TextielMuseum, Tilburg,
Carpet Sign
Photography: Inga Powilleit

Scholten & Baijings designed
a traditional-style room where
everything revolves around
layering, colour and transparency.
There is only a bed; all other
furniture has been removed. One
is surrounded by colour. The most
striking eye-catcher is the carpet,
which has been tufted in harmony
with the shades of the Colour
Plaids. The carpet has a luxurious,
deep-pile texture that invites one
to sit down on the floor and enjoy
a moment of calm and relaxation.
The curtains, specially woven at
the TextielMuseum, Tilburg, come
in a graduated colour scheme.
There is a large mirror on the
ceiling in which the entire room is
reflected. This creates a strangely
fascinating effect.

Commission: Initiated by the
designers
Production: Scholten & Baijings.
Every piece is handcrafted and
therefore unique. Numbered
edition
Collections: Museum Boijmans
van Beuningen, Rotterdam,
TextielMuseum, Tilburg, private
collections, designers' collection
Photography: Yves Krol

The Vegetables series is made of
textile. The work is all about
intensity, colour and craftsmanship.
Every piece is made in-house and
by hand. Over the past few years,
Scholten & Baijings collaborated
with various master craftsmen in
connection with the execution of
many of their projects. The work
always constitutes an interpretation
of their designs, because every
craftsman has a personal signature.
Since their self-made prototypes
frequently come very close to the
ultimate products, a desire grew
in them to also try their hand at
that last part of the design process.

**Colour Wood
2009**

Materials: Chestnut wood,
(fluorescent) paint, textile ribbons
Techniques: Woodwork, realcoat
print, clear coat, painting, woven
textile
Dimensions: 32 × Ø 71 cm,
39 × Ø 60 cm, 45 × Ø 50 cm
Commission: Karimoku
New Standard, Japan
Production: Karimoku Furniture,
industrial production
Collections: Nationaal Historisch
Museum, Arnhem, F.N.A.C. (Fond
National d'Art Contemporain), Paris,
the Art Institute of Chicago, private
collections, designers' collection
Awards: Nominated for the Dutch
Design Awards 2010, iF Product
Design Award 2011, Nominate
for EDIDA 2011 Japan
Photography: Takumi Ota

The Colour Wood side tables
vary in size, colour and pattern.
The objects are the result
of considerations based on the
characteristics of thinned wood as
well as woodworking traditions.
Small-diameter wood is joined
to form a volume. The symbolic
layers of a contemporary view on
traditional shapes and techniques
are achieved by superimposing

different layers of colour shades
and patterns. The texture of the
wood is overlaid with translucent
colour, which in turn is overlaid
with a printed graphic pattern. The
layers balance each other out and
create depth in the stained and
printed chestnut.

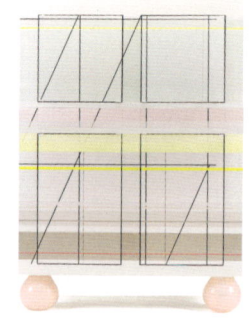

**Truly Dutch
2009**

Materials: Various
Techniques: Hand-painted work, screen printing, willow braiding, glass-blowing
Dimensions: Various
Commission: Zuiderzee Museum, Enkhuizen
Production: Scholten & Baijings in collaboration with Scheltens & Abbenes (photography inside of Amsterdam Amoire), Mathieu Meijers (artwork Tilt-Top Table), Bernard Heesen (glass feet of Amsterdam Amoire), limited editions
Collections: Zuiderzee Museum, Enkhuizen, designers' collection

The Truly Dutch collection can be seen as conversation pieces for the interior. Contemporary, decorated pieces of furniture made by artists and master craftsmen.

The typically Dutch collection comprises five items of furniture that constitute a contemporary interpretation of five masterpieces from the Zuiderzee Museum's collections: *Marker kast* (Marken cabinet), *hangoortafel* (drop-leaf table), *flap-aan-de-wand* (tilt-top table), *butte* (wooden travel case) and *knopstoel* (pegged chair).

The visual images have been applied to the objects using different decorative techniques. The ornamentations reflect the daily lives of the designers of these pieces and depict interiors, objects and landscapes.

Amsterdam Amoire
2010

Materials: Fibre board, HP printed laminate, steel, glass
Techniques: Woodwork, mouth-blown glass
Dimensions: 172 × 121 × 60 cm
Commission: Established & Sons
Production: Scholten & Baijings in collaboration with Scheltens & Abbenes (photography inside) and Bernard Heesen (glass)
Collections: Centre National des Arts Plastiques (CNAP), Paris, private collections, designers' collection

The Amsterdam Armoire is a typically Dutch design, a traditional piece of furniture with a contemporary twist. Made from specially printed 'High Pressure Laminate', the design is both decorative and functional, with upper and lower cabinets and a central drawer across the full width. Special details include two front feet made of pink mouth-blown glass and still life pictures printed on the inside of the cabinet doors. These still lifes were made in collaboration with the photographers Scheltens & Abbenes.

Soft Grid
2010

Materials: Merino wool, cotton
Techniques: Jacquard double weaving
Dimensions: 183 × 137 cm / three different designs
Commission: Established & Sons
Collections: TextielMuseum, Tilburg
Production: Prototypes made by Scholten & Baijings in the TextielLab of the TextielMuseum, Tilburg

These luxurious double-sided Merino wool blankets are a pure celebration of pattern and colour. The Grid that forms part of the textural pattern is woven into the blankets creating a striking graphic effect and fascinating finish. Pastel and fluorescent colours combine with luxurious textures and unique design in these extraordinary pieces of textile work.

Colour Lights
2010

Materials: Opaque glass, steel (ceiling) fixtures, steel suspension cable
Techniques: Mouth-blown glass, etching, spray-painting by hand, powder coating
Dimensions: 35 × Ø 28 cm, 45 × Ø 37 cm / three different designs
Commission/Production: Established & Sons (currently not in production)
Collections: Private collections, designers' collection

Scholten & Baijings' starting point for Yellow Light, Pink Light and White Light was the use of colour in combination with a natural working or reading light. The elegant opaque glass shade is hand-blown, while the paint is applied by airbrush. The colour gradient on the shade creates a special effect that appears to be 'on' when it is in fact 'off'.

Butte
2010

Materials: Oak veneer, black inkjet-printed illustration, paint, UV protective clear matt lacquer
Techniques: Woodwork, inkjet printing
Dimensions: 21 × Ø 16 cm, 16 × Ø 22 cm, 13 × Ø 25 cm / three different designs
Commission: Established & Sons
Production: Scholten & Baijings
Collections: Private collections, designers' collection

A *butte* is a traditional Dutch wooden travel case made from woven willow and wood veneer. This modern take features decorative fluorescent interior paint and hand-drawn printed illustrations. Each tells a story 'The Life of a Tuna Fish', 'The Life of a Turtle' and 'The Life of a Tree', addressing the environmental implications of intensive farming and deforestation.

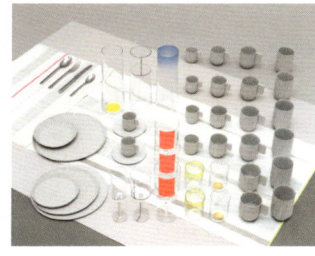

Paper Table
2009

Materials: Porcelain, cristal supérieur glass, stainless steel, textile
Techniques: Various
Dimensions: Various
Commission: TextielMuseum, Tilburg
Production: Scholten & Baijings in collaboration with TextielLab at the TextielMuseum, Tilburg and Royal Leerdam Crystal; Royal VKB
Collections: TextielMuseum, Tilburg, designers' collection
Awards: Dutch Design Award 2010
Photography: Scheltens & Abbenes

In the Total Table Design project Scholten & Baijings present their vision of the art of dining. Royal Leerdam Crystal (glassware), Royal VKB (cutlery) and the TextielMuseum (table linen) joined forces to produce prototypes of the duo's designs. All three partners can boast a long tradition of artisan production, and they regularly work in conjunction with a select group of designers from the Netherlands and beyond. The Paper Table by Scholten & Baijings combines subtlety with elegance.

Paper Porcelain
2009

Materials: Porcelain, (un)glazed, pencil
Techniques: Slip casting / injection moulding in plaster moulds, hand painting, including pencil lines applied by hand
Dimensions: Various
Commission: TextielMuseum, Tilburg, as part of the Total Table Design project
Production: Prototypes by Scholten & Baijings developed at the European Ceramic Workcentre (EKWC) in 's-Hertogenbosch, the Netherlands. Since 2014, part of the collection is being produced by HAY

Collections: TextielMuseum, Tilburg, Stedelijk Museum 's-Hertogenbosch, the Art Institute of Chicago, Cooper-Hewitt National Design Museum, New York, private collections, designers' collection
Awards: Dutch Design Award 2010, 'Best High Tea' Wallpaper* Design Award 2011

The folded cardboard models of the crockery were translated into light-grey, unglazed porcelain cups and plates, delicately playing with the suggestion of cardboard. Scholten & Baijings realized the prototypes of their Paper Porcelain crockery at the EKWC. It took five years before the porcelain went into production.

Colour Glass
2009

Materials: Cristal supérieur glass / crystal glass
Techniques: Mouth-blown glass
Dimensions: Various
Commission: Royal Leerdam Crystal as part of the Total Table Design project
Production: Prototypes by Scholten & Baijings in collaboration with Royal Leerdam Crystal. Since 2013 industrial production by HAY
Collections: TextielMuseum, Tilburg, the Art Institute of Chicago
Awards: Dutch Design Award 2010

The first models were made by hand in thin, transparent plastic and taped to each other. These tape seams are translated on the wine glasses into black and gold lines. Colour compositions are created on the glassware by means of circles and planes: gold dots on the bottom of the water glass and carafe, and a bright-pink rectangle on the red wine glass, the latter hinting at the colour of the red wine.

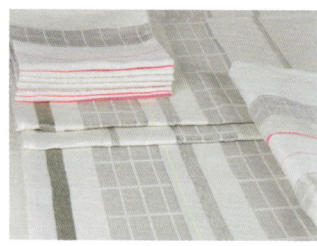

Table Linen
2009

Materials: Cotton, linen, viscose, acrylic/cotton, linen, lurex
Techniques: Jacquard double weaving
Dimensions: 162 × 55 cm, 65 × 45 cm/165 × 61 cm, 68 × 48 cm/ two different designs
Commission: TextielMuseum, Tilburg, as part of the Total Table Design project
Production: Scholten & Baijings in collaboration with TextielLab at the TextielMuseum, Tilburg
Collections: TextielMuseum, Tilburg
Awards: Dutch Design Award 2010

For Table Linen, the duo came with a contemporary solution: they designed two sets comprising table runners and napkins that can be used in various combinations. Table Linen was developed in the TextielLab of the TextielMuseum, Tilburg, and was executed on the basis of paper designs. An eight-person set consists of three table runners and eight napkins. Table Linen is characterized by a paper-like structure and a variety of weaves.

ID / Cutlery
2009

Materials: High-quality stainless steel
Techniques: Cutting, metal spinning, polishing
Dimensions: Various
Commission: Royal VKB as part of the Total Table Design project
Production: Royal VKB, industrial production

Collections: TextielMuseum, Tilburg
Awards: Dutch Design Award 2010

The design of the cutlery is inspired by the effect produced when paper is folded. The application of numerous small indentations creates fluid shapes. The final design is a reflection of modern times: clear, minimalist and elegant.

Scholten & Baijings
Winner of the Woonbeurs Pin
2010

Materials: Various
Dimensions: Various
Commission: Woonbeurs Amsterdam
Production: Scholten & Baijings
Awards: Woonbeurs Pin 2010

Every year, Woonbeurs Amsterdam awards a trade prize to a person or company that has made an outstanding contribution to Dutch interior design. In their distinctive, almost un-Dutch design style, Scholten & Baijings combine minimalist forms and balanced colour schemes with the application of traditional craftsmanship and industrial production techniques. Scholten & Baijings always translate this wide variety of working methods into functional and, at the same time, highly individualistic products. In the jury's view, the duo has succeeded in enriching the Dutch design landscape and was therefore declared winner of the Woonbeurs Pin 2010. By invitation of the Woonbeurs, the Woonbeurs Pin winner will be represented at the fair with a personal exhibition.

Tea Towels GRID
2011

Materials: Cotton mix
Techniques: Woven textile
Dimensions: 75 × 52 cm / five different designs
Commission/Production: HAY, industrial production
Collections: TextielMuseum, Tilburg, the Art Institute of Chicago
Awards: Dutch Design Award 2011, 'Best Home Product' Sanoma Woon Awards 2011

Cold Forest, Box, Gradient, Kitchen Tiles and Hanging Grid are the names of the tea towels, all of which are woven. The use of bright fluorescent yarns is recognizable as work by Scholten & Baijings. The towels are sold as sets of two pieces of one design: always including a neon version.

Colour Block / Minimal
2011

Materials: 100% satin cotton
Techniques: Rotation screen printing
Dimensions: Available in various sizes, differing per country
Commission/Production: HAY, industrial production
Collections: TextielMuseum, Tilburg

Awards: Dutch Design Award 2011, 'Best Home Product' Sanoma Woon Awards 2011

Scholten & Baijings developed two collections of bed linen: Colour Block and Minimal. Colour Block, with complex coloured designs, is a collection available in the colours Red, Pink, Yellow or Green. The Minimal collection is a more simplified version of bed linen with the following names: Lemon, Sand, Syrup and Moss. For both collections, the colours have been carefully screen printed on beautiful satin cotton.

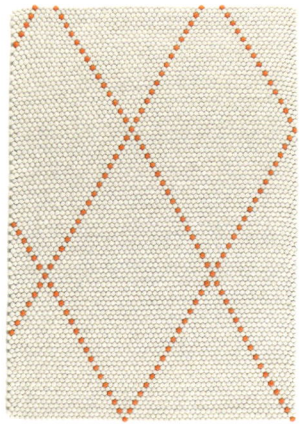

Dot Carpets
2011

Materials: 100% pure new wool
Techniques: Felted balls stitched together by hand
Dimensions: 80 × 100 cm, 120 × 170 cm, 150 × 200 cm / eight different designs
Commission/Production: HAY
Collections: TextielMuseum, Tilburg, the Art Institute of Chicago
Awards: Dutch Design Award 2011, 'Best Home Product' Sanoma Woon Awards 2011

Each of the Dot Carpets consists of thousands of felted, pure-wool balls, stitched together by hand. Each carpet is named after its Grid colour, such as Hot Pink, Electric Green, Glacier Silt or Poppy Red.

Colour Carpets
2011

Materials: 100% New Zealand wool, 100% cotton backing
Techniques: Tufted
Dimensions: 240 × 170 cm / six different designs
Commission/Production: HAY, industrial production
Awards: Dutch Design Award 2011, 'Best Home Product' Sanoma Woon Awards 2011

All of the Colour Carpets are highly defined and richly coloured. Scholten & Baijings created optical transparency by using colour gradients. The result: a variety of different carpet designs in a beautiful array of colours. Six distinct identities with their own unique colour scheme and graphic expression.

Flare
2012

Materials: MDF, metal, mirror
Techniques: Lacquering, printed colour gradient, powder coating
Dimensions: Various / eight different designs
Commission/Production: Schönbuch, industrial production

The idea was to transfer the subtle colour gradients familiar to them from fabrics as a restrained *dégradé* print to the front panels of the cupboards, wall-mounted units and sideboards. The colours – light grey, blue or rose pink – change gradually to pure white. The programme is notable for its well-thought-out interiors and stylish details. The coat storage element, shelf and wall mirror (the latter can be easily tilted to the desired angle) have a back panel with a neon-yellow surface finish.

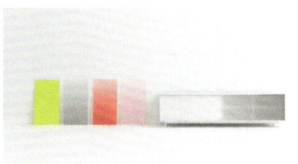

Shift
2012

Materials: MDF, translucent acrylate, metal
Techniques: Lacquering, printed colour gradient
Dimensions: 160 × 45 × 45 cm, 210 × 45 × 45 cm / Colour collection of six designers' choice colours, frame or wall mounted
Commission/Production: Pastoe, industrial production
Collections: the Art Institute of Chicago
Awards: Nominated for EDIDA 2012 Netherlands, nominated for 'Möbel des Jahres Raum und Wohnen 2012', 'Best Domestic Design' Wallpaper* Design Award 2013

Shift combines a minimalist shape with an expressive use of colours. By working with translucent sliding doors in different colours in combination with a colour gradient, an intriguing play of colours is created when the cabinet is opened and closed. The look of Shift is characterized by two sliding doors made from translucent acrylate, the reverse of which have been coloured. When the doors move across each other, the colours mix, fade or are enhanced. The name Shift is derived from this interplay of colours.

Colour Stool
2011

Materials: Itaya maple wood, opaque and transparent colour, paint, clear coating
Techniques: Milling, (hand) painting
Dimensions: 43 × 45 × 31 cm
Commission: Karimoku New Standard
Production: Karimoku Furniture, industrial production
Collections: the Art Institute of Chicago
Photography: Takumi Ota

This stool is a direct reference to the traditional way of sitting in Japan. Colour Stool shows the wide range of woodworking options in great detail. A modern version of a very traditional piece of furniture has been created through the minimal use of colour in the grids and the transparency of the colours. The stool is made using one of the most advanced woodworking machines available today

Colour Platter
2011

Materials: Chestnut, realcoat print, clear coat
Techniques: Woodwork, inkjet printing
Dimensions: 4.5 × 45 × 45 cm (stacked)
Commission: Karimoku New Standard
Production: Karimoku Furniture, industrial production
Collections: the Art Institute of Chicago
Photography: Takumi Ota

Colour Platter is a set of three different-sized serving dishes, designed to present and serve exquisite food, or to be used as a fruit bowl or attractive centrepiece. The different sizes, in combination with the varying patterns and rich colours, make it possible to create exciting compositions. Colour Platter is made of Chestnut wood and provided with a high-tech print. The design was inspired by the traditional Japanese style of presentation, where the material and layered colour application play an important role.

Blush – Design in Full Colour
Solo exhibition at Stedelijk Museum 's-Hertogenbosch, 2011

Materials: Various
Dimensions: Various
Commision: Stedelijk Museum s'-Hertogenbosch
Production: Scholten & Baijings
Photography: Inga Powilleit

The exhibition at the Stedelijk Museum s'-Hertogenbosch was the first large retrospective of Scholten & Baijings' work. The unique presentation focused on their highly individual approach. It traced their career from the first self-initiated products like Colour Plaids to later industrial designs for companies such as Karimoku New Standard and HAY.

Colour Bin
2012

Materials: Chestnut wood, translucent colours, (fluorescent) paint, clear coating, leather
Dimensions: 10.1 × Ø 7.8 cm, 25.8 × Ø 18 cm, 33.6 × Ø 22.4 cm / three different designs
Commission: Karimoku New Standard
Production: Karimoku Furniture, industrial production
Collections: the Art Institute of Chicago
Awards: Nominated for the German Design Award 2015
Photography: Takumi Ota

Colour Bin comprises a series of coloured containers made of Chestnut wood. These round bins are available in three different sizes and can be used in various places in the interior. All containers have their own colour palette, ranging from soft pastels to fluorescent pink. The bins are made with utmost precision, using traditional woodworking joinery techniques. A special lacquering technique enables the application of a transparent, exceptionally high-quality colour finish to the wood.

Colour Wood Dining
2012

Materials: Chestnut (tabletop), oak (leg), realcoat print, clear coating
Techniques: Woodwork, paint, inkjet printing
Dimensions: Ø 95 × 74 cm, Ø 120 × 74 cm / two different designs
Commission: Karimoku New Standard
Production: Karimoku Furniture, industrial production
Collections: the Art Institute of Chicago
Photography: Takumi Ota

Colour Wood Dining is an extension of the successful Colour Wood side tables. The symbolic layers, representing a contemporary view of traditional shapes and techniques, are achieved by superimposing different layers of colour shades and patterns. The tabletop is embellished with a dotted pattern, Gray Dot, and is also available in a pale natural version.

Colour Porcelain
2012

Materials: Porcelain, various glazes, transfers
Techniques: Injection moulding in plaster moulds, hand painting
Dimensions: Various
Commission: 1616 / Arita Japan
Production: Momota-Touen
Collections: Museum Boijmans van Beuningen, Rotterdam, the Art Institute of Chicago
Awards: Dutch Design Award 2012, Public Award of the Dutch Design Awards 2012, ELLE Decoration International Design Award 2013, nominated for Designs of the Year 2013, Design Museum London
Photography: Inga Powilleit

Scholten & Baijings designed a porcelain service at the request of 1616 / Arita, one of the oldest (1616) Japanese porcelain manufacturers. The collection consists of three series: Minimal, Colourful and Extraordinary. On behalf of the collection, Scholten & Baijings prepared a colour analysis involving historical masterpieces. Even though these colours have been used individually in the new designs, together they form the specific Arita colour spectrum.
This resulted in layered colour compositions, executed in different shades of glaze, in combination with the natural porcelain colour.

Colour One for MINI
Conceptual Concept Car
2012

Materials: Carbon, polyester, polyurethane
Techniques: Resin moulding, 3D printing, CNC milling

Dimensions: 1.43 × 3.61 × 1.67 m
Commission: BMW Group / MINI
Production: BMW Group / MINI,
Scholten & Baijings
Awards: Best of Best Awards
German Design Council
Automotive Brand Contest 2012,
iF Communication Design Award
2013, nominated for German
Design Award 2015

The 'Colour One' installation
explores the design of a MINI
One by examining its composition
down to the smallest detail and,
in so doing, dissecting the design
process per se. The upshot is
a thought-provoking and inspiring
new interpretation that draws
on Scholten & Baijings' familiar
stylistic devices – colour and
material – to query the rules
of automotive design and shed
new light on them.

**Colour One for MINI
Presentation at Salone del Mobile
Milan
2012**

Materials: Metal, transparent PVC
screen, wood
Dimensions: Pavilion 6 × 21.4 ×
12.2 m / total installation 30 × 30 m
Commission: BMW Group / MINI
Production: Scholten & Baijings

The 'Paddock' installation 'Colour
One' for MINI was exhibited at
Interni Legacy during FuoriSalone
2012. Scholten & Baijings peeled
the MINI One like an onion, layer
by layer, while analysing the car
as such and its individual
components. Applying their highly
conceptual approach, the
designers questioned virtually
every aspect of design along the
way, extracting the essence of
each component, whether this
was revealed at its core or during
the dismantling process itself.

**Colour Blend
2013**

Materials: Urea powder
Techniques: Hydro dipping
Dimensions: 44.9 × 38 cm
Commission/Production: Pressalit
(not yet in production)
Photography: Wyne Veen,
especially for Wallpaper*

In collaboration with Scholten &
Baijings, Pressalit Seats has
developed a designer collection,
Colour Blend, which sets new
standards for bathroom design
thanks to its unique combination
of flawless minimalism, fused
patterns and high-quality
functionalism. The new dotted
toilet seats have been designed
so they can be installed in four
widely differing universes of
colour, shape and style.

**Tea with Georg
2013**

Materials: Stainless steel,
synthetics, porcelain, transfers,
silver lustre, glaze
Techniques: Forced deep
moulding, etching, laser welding,
glazing, colour gradients applied
by hand
Dimensions: Various
Commission/Production: Georg
Jensen, industrial production
Collections: the Art Institute of
Chicago
Awards: Best of Best Interior
Innovation Award 2014

Scholten & Baijings designed
a tea and cake collection entitled
Tea with Georg. The title is a nod
to the company's Danish founder,
Georg Jensen. The design for this
everyday tableware is based on a
study conducted into the Japanese
tea ceremony, freely interpreted
for Western use by Scholten &
Baijings. The starting point for the
design process was the symbolic
value the Japanese attach to the
tea ceremony, as well as their love
of aesthetics, the appreciation of
traditional handicraft and the
beauty of the material in general.

**Towels
2013**

Materials: 100% cotton
Techniques: Weaving
Dimensions: 140 × 70 cm, 70 × 50 cm,
33 × 33 cm, 90 × 55 cm
Commission/Production: HAY,
industrial production

With eye-catching textures and
colours, this series of towels, bath
mats and washcloths by Scholten
& Baijings is high in contrast and
sensuous appeal. Striking a
perfect balance between subtle
and loud in a distinctive design
where the terrycloth waffle weave
is the perfect base for the
unconventional colour range.

**Colour Tape
2013**

Materials: Paper, ink, glue
Techniques: Rotation printing
Dimensions: 3 m × 1.5 cm / five
different designs
Commission/Production: HAY,
industrial production
Collections: the Art Institute of
Chicago

The designs of Colour Tape are
not purely practical and
functional. They are minimalist,
but with a poetic twist. Colour
Tape is available in five stripe
designs and a variety of colours.

**Colour Notes
2013**

Materials: Plastic, ink, glue
Dimensions: Ø 5.5 cm / five
different designs
Commission/Production: HAY,
industrial production
Collections: the Art Institute of
Chicago

These geometric plastic stickers
make it possible to bookmark
passages in books and magazines.
Colour Notes are available in five
designs and assorted colours.
The small section of the sticker
is used to precisely indicate
a relevant passage on a page, while
the larger section marks the page
itself.

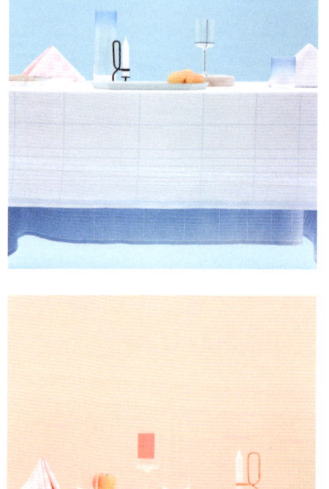

**Tablecloth with Napkins Double
Grid/Dot
2013**

Materials: Cotton
Techniques: Jacquard weaving
Dimensions: 290 × 140 cm,
240 × 140 cm, 50 × 50 cm
Commission/Production: HAY,
industrial production

Collections: Tablecloth with
Napkins Dot is part of the
permanent collection of the Art
Institute of Chicago

Scholten & Baijings have
revitalized the tablecloth as
a modern home accessory by
balancing the positive-negative
interplay of colour and absence
of colour with simple graphic lines
and dots. The stark grid design
and the dots cover the full width
and breadth of the tablecloth and
appears as a subtle ornamentation
in a delicate colour code.

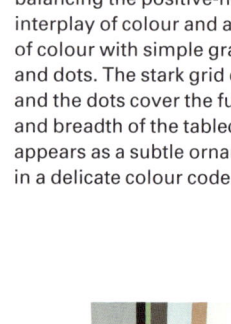

**Paper Carpets
2013**

Materials: 100% paper, rubber
coated
Techniques: Hand weaving
Dimensions: 200 × 80 cm / six
different designs
Commission/Production: HAY,
industrial production
Collections: the Art Institute of
Chicago

The designs are made with
self-mixed colours painted on
cardboard in a harmonious
composition of planes, lines and
vibrant colours.
The carpet is made of woven paper,
has a non-slip backing, and each
carpet comes in a unique colour
combination.

**Colour Binders
2013**

Materials: Canvas, cardboard,
chrome rings

Techniques: Printing
Dimensions: 31.5 × 26 cm
Commission/Production: HAY, industrial production
Collections: the Art Institute of Chicago

The Dutch design duo created optical colour modules with this mini series of ring binders that delight with a delicate interplay of colour patches. The five colour schemes are kept in a toned-down expression and engage in a mutual dialogue when the binders are placed side by side on a shelf.

The Dinner Party / True-to-Life Design
Installation at the Victoria & Albert Museum, London
2013

Materials: Various
Techniques: Various
Dimensions: 5.36 × 6.20 × 9.99 m
Commission: London Design Festival
Production: Scholten & Baijings, music by Moritz Gabe & Henning Grambow
Photography: Inga Powilleit

In galleries and museums, design objects are frequently displayed on pedestals or in glass display cases, but rarely in something resembling the everyday living environment for which they were conceived. For a period of nine days, Scholten & Baijings transformed the Norfolk House Music Room in the V&A Museum into a true dinner setting in a lived-in home.
The objective of the presentation was to let people see things in a different way. More adventurously, because many designs are only discovered at a second glance. More objectively, because there are no nameplates, so that the boundaries between exclusive design and mass-produced products become blurred and prejudices disappear.

Colour Installation
Exhibition at the Art Institute of Chicago
2013

Materials: Wood, steel, photo prints, various products
Dimensions: 3.5 × 7.85 × 7.14 m
Commission: the Art Institute of Chicago
Production: the Art Institute of Chicago, Scholten & Baijings, Scheltens & Abbenes

Colour Installation has been custom-designed for this exhibition and re-envisions the presentation of Scholten & Baijings' work by making connections between their design practice and their multiple collaborations with artisans and manufacturers. The large-scale images integrated into the installation were produced by Scheltens & Abbenes and were specifically commissioned for this exhibition. The meticulously composed images capture specific moments and relationships, and frame connections and the various lines in Scholten & Baijings' work, while emphasizing the duo's ability to generate beautifully creative expressions of quotidian objects.

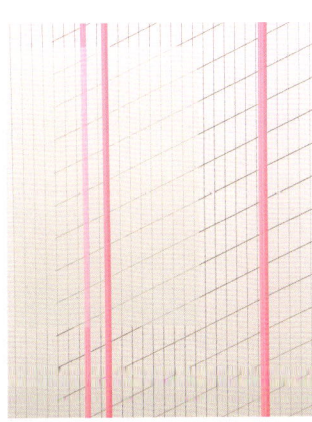

IKEA PS14 Posters
2014

Materials: Paper
Techniques: Offset printing, fluorescent printing, embossing, spot lacquer
Dimensions: A3, A2, A1 / four different designs, sold in sets of two
Commission/Production: IKEA, industrial production

The poster collection consists of four posters in three paper formats, and combined with each other they can create different compositions. The posters are much like views that give rooms an extra dimension. The quality and treatment of the paper – using colour, (matt) gloss, gradients, grids and embossed sections – turn the posters into playful, layered products that bear the distinctive Scholten & Baijings signature.

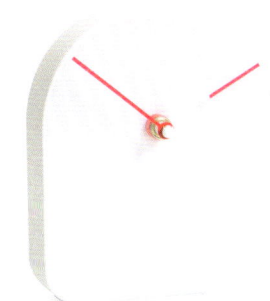

IKEA PS14 Clocks
2014

Materials: ABS plastic, polyester paint, rubber / textile ribbon
Techniques: Injection moulding, woven textile
Dimensions: Ø 19 cm, Ø 20 cm, 4.5 × 12 × 10 cm
Commission/Production: IKEA, industrial production

Scholten & Baijings designed three clocks: two different-sized wall clocks and one table clock. The clocks are not just purely practical and functional time pieces. The designs are minimalist, but with a poetic twist. The large hand is screen printed onto a transparent, patterned revolving disc. A clock is meant to be an ornament for the home, just like a watch can be an ornament for the body.

Place Mat & Runner Dot
2014

Materials: Cotton
Techniques: Jacquard weaving
Dimensions: 45 × 35 cm, 140 × 55 cm
Commission/Production: HAY, industrial production

Place Mat & Runner are an extension of the textile tablecloth Dot, which Scholten & Baijings launched for HAY in 2013. Place Mat & Runner are perfect for creating an attractive, informal table setting.

Elements
2014

Materials: Crystal glass
Techniques: Mouth-blown glass, hand cutting, sand blasting, polishing
Dimensions: 59 × Ø 85 mm, 77 × Ø 85 mm, 144 × Ø 63 mm, 175 × Ø 73 mm, 102 × Ø 67 cm, 105 × Ø 53, 122 × Ø 98 mm, 308 × Ø 85 mm, 206 × Ø 104 mm
Commission/Production: J. HILL's Standard
Photography: Tom Brown

J. HILL's Standard, a new manufacturer of mouth-blown, hand-cut crystal glassware from Waterford, Ireland, has launched its first collection designed by Scholten & Baijings. For the Elements series, Scholten & Baijings created an extensive range of geometric cuts and built these up on individual glasses and across the range of glass types. Each glass in the Elements series has a different design, allowing the customer to create collections of glasses that are matched or unmatched, restrained or exuberant. The glass sizes are not prescriptive and suit a multitude of uses, from whisky to wine to water. An elegant jug and decanter completes the series.

Colour Globe
2014

Materials: Coloured glass, steel, LED electronics
Techniques: Mouth-blown glass, paint, transfers
Dimensions: 28 × 16.5 cm, Ø 40 cm, Ø 50 cm
Commission/Production: Moooi, industrial production

The Colour Globe lamp consists of two layers of mouth-blown glass that run parallel in a rounded embrace of playful details and colourful contrasts that optically blend into each other. A bright LED lamp, enclosed and protected by an opal shrine, shines through the glass layers. Colour Globe's lively shapes, shiny colours and see-through patterns portray Scholten & Baijings' exuberant, extrovert character in a lamp that tickles our imagination with entertaining geometric games and light-hearted reflections.

Strap Chair
2014

Materials: Metal frame with polyester straps
Techniques: Powder coating, hand weaving
Dimensions: 62 × 60 × 80 cm
Commission/Production: Moustache, industrial production

The Strap Chair is a stackable, lightweight chair with armrests. The straps are designed especially for this seat. The way the straps are wound around the tubular frame gives the upholstery its unique structure. The strength of the material, very strong polyester yarn in combination with this specific type of braiding, render foam and other upholstery materials superfluous. The special polyester fabric and powder-coated metal frame ensure that the seat is ideal for both inside and outside use.

Colour Notebook
2014

Materials: Canvas, cardboard, paper

Techniques: Printing
Dimensions: 20.5 × 13 cm,
26.5 × 16.5 cm
Commission / Production: HAY,
industrial production

Colour Notebook is the new
member of Scholten & Baijings'
Colour series, where five ring
binders in different colour
combinations create new pattern
and colour constellations in
a bookcase. Colour Notebook
consists of a stylish cover with
a replaceable pad.

Chromos, Iris & Pastel
2014

Materials: Coloured glass, metal
Techniques: Mouth-blown glass,
silvering inside, metallic coating
outside, powder coating
Dimensions: Chromos: 24.8 × 11.7
cm, 7.5 × 8.1 cm, Iris: 26.6 × 10 cm,
8.5 × 7.9 cm, Pastel: 22 × 30.4 cm,
14 × 16.9 cm, 7.2 × 30 cm,
4.1 cm × 25.9 cm, 22 × 14.5 cm
Commission: Verreum
Production: Gaia & Gino,
industrial production

Three different collections of
hand-blown coloured glass with
metallic coating, consisting of two
decanters with matching glasses
and a series of five table pieces.
The production of the collections
was preceded by extensive
experiments involving a library
of skills. For instance, Scholten &
Baijings combined coloured glass
with gradients, silvering inside

and metallic coating outside, all of
which were in perfect harmony
with their design language, marked
by layering, mixing of colors
and surprising finishes. In order
to create timeless pieces, the
contemporary shapes and colours
were enhanced with unique
silvering techniques.

Solid Patterns
2014

Materials: Different kinds of
marble
Techniques: Three-dimensional
band saws, five-axis CNC-
controlled milling machines,
water-jet cutting machines,
a 4-m-high robot for spatial
interventions
Dimensions: 35 × 137 × 97 cm,
40 × 128 × 106 cm, 74 × 115 ×
106 cm, 74 × 134 × 109 cm,
74 × 193 × 140 cm
Commission: Luce di Carrara
Production: Henraux. Numered
edition
Collections: Private collections,
designers' collection
Photography: Scheltens & Abbenes

Scholten & Baijings created five
unique marble tables. Each form
was designed in one of the finest
types of Italian marble. The design
process was all about expressing
the various characteristics of the
marble in a single shape. The
addition of patterns to the designs
created a contemporary look that
enhances the contrast between
the graphics and the crystalline
marble patterns. The rock was
processed with an advanced CNC-
controlled, 4-metre-high robot
milling machine.

Tilt-Top Table
2011

Materials: Oak wood, steel
Techniques: Inkjet printing, paint,
powder coating
Dimensions: Ø 90 × 74 cm
Commission/Production: HAY,
industrial production

At the invitation of HAY, Scholten
& Baijings translated their Tilt-Top
Table - initially designed for the
Zuiderzee Museum, Enkhuizen
– into an industrially produced
product. Tilt-Top Table folds
completely flat against the wall
and has decorations on the
underside of the table. Scholten &
Baijings applied their bright
signature colours, here in three
versions of varying impact,
in tone-on-tone powder-coated
steel. The result is a contemporary
artistic interpretation of
a charming piece of furniture
history.

Tea Towels Dot
2014

Materials: Cotton / cotton with
polyester
Dimensions: 52 × 75 cm
Commission/Production: HAY,
industrial production

Tea Towel Dot is a new collection
of tea towels by Scholten &
Baijings, which uses the dot as
a geometric archetype to create
constellations and outlines in a
new and more subtle colour scale.
Five contemporary designs
in several colour schemes are
packaged in sets of two, in two
different colour combinations:
always including a neon version.

DOT Chair
2013

Materials: Polypropylene plastic,
maple wood and powder-coated
steel
Techniques: Injection moulding
Dimensions: 68 × 66 × 45 cm
Commission/Production: HAY,
industrial production
Collections: the Art Institute of
Chicago

How can a plastic chair take on
a sensuous dimension? In the
case of the Dot Chair, it can be
attributed to the more than 1,300
perforations in the organic and
inviting plastic seat, which seem
to add extra layer to the plastic
and gives the material a new
tactile quality. The tiny holes give
the chair a characteristic aesthetic,
where transparency and a play
of light and shadow add to the
chair's expression.

Blocks & Grid
2013

Materials: 92% wool, 8% nylon
Techniques: Jacquard weaving
Dimensions: 8.38 × 1.40 m
Commission/Production:
Maharam, industrial production
Collections: the Art Institute of
Chicago, Cooper-Hewitt National
Design Museum, New York
Photography: Dean Kaufman,
courtesy of Maharam

Scholten & Baijings approached
the project by embarking on an
investigation into modern colour-
blocking. That led them to develop
two large-scale compositions
based on the amount of fabric
typically required to upholster an
entire sofa. The resulting textiles
both have massive 9-metre
repeats – the length of fabric
before the pattern begins again
– and a more standard width of
142 centimetres.

Over the Rainbow
Solo exhibition in villa Noailles,
Hyères
2014

Materials: Various
Dimensions: 14 × 8.55 m
Commission: villa Noailles
Production: Scholten & Baijings
Photography: Lothaire Hucki

At the invitation of villa Noailles,
Scholten & Baijings custom-
designed an exhibition for Design
Parade 9. It consisted of a
multilayered assemblage of work
selected from across the life of the
studio. The virtuoso employment
of colour, which characterizes
their work, infused the swimming
pool at villa Noailles. This colour
palette had been created
especially for the exhibition and
took its inspiration from the
surrounding landscape and sky.

INDEX

THANK YOU!

We would like to dedicate this book to our son, Rem Martin Scholten, so that he can have a better understanding of everything that has gone into, or been a part of, our work so far.

Our special thanks go to Michael Maharam. Michael is not just a successful entrepreneur, but a man who thinks and works from his heart—a rare and incredibly stimulating attribute. Alongside his inspiring questions and innate understanding of the market, it is his work philosophy that truly reveals his passion for the design process, watching a product grow from idea to reality. Michael, Stephen and their team's confidence and trust in us have encouraged a deeper drive and expectation of ourselves as designers, both for the Maharam brand and in daily life. For that, as well as their generosity in making this book possible, we will be forever grateful.

We want to pay tribute to Louise Schouwenberg for her sharp analysis and clear translation of our personal stories and methods and for placing our work within the context of contemporary design. We would like to thank Joost Grootens for the creation of a conceptual grid that renders a beautiful and detailed portrait of our 'Atelier-way-of-working'.

In particular, we would like to express our gratitude to our current team: Yildith Della Coletta (our personal assistant & studio manager), Roel Deden (CAD specialist), Niels Heymans (designer), Aukje Fleur Janssen (hands-on designer), Jody Kocken (designer & our right hand), Iwan Pol (junior designer), Sanne Schuurman (junior designer), Bastiaan de Nennie (intern) and last but certainly not least all the designers and interns who have worked at Scholten & Baijings and are not mentioned in this list.

Freelancers: Willem Derks (CAD specialist), Denise Gons (designer), Brit van Nerven (designer), Claartje van den Oever (textile designer), Emilie Pallard (designer) and Thijmen van der Steen (designer).

And also to our former team members: Oskar Peet (designer), Dominique Pluer (designer), Lex Pott (designer) and Mieke Verhoef (designer & PA).

We wish to express our sincere thanks and appreciation to all the photographers for creating such inspiring images of our work, including: Paul Barbera, Alexander van Berge, Merel van Beukering, Nico Bick, Koos Breukel, Tom Brown, Christiaan de Bruijne, Freudenthal/Verhagen, Lothaire Hucki, Ariko Inaoka, Dean Kaufman, Yves Krol, Anne-Sophie Markus, Marie-Pierre Morel, Alberto Novelli, Jouk Oosterhof, Takumi Ota, Viviane Sassen, Jaap Scheeren, Maarten Schets, Ami Sioux, James Stokes, Wyne Veen, Qui Yang, Nobuo Yano, Aisha Zeijpveld and all the other photographers we have worked with, who are not mentioned in this list. Special thanks go to Inga Powilleit for traveling the world with us and documenting the way we work. We would also like to express our gratitude to Scheltens & Abbenes for their unique and abstract portrayal of our projects.

346

We are grateful for all the beautiful assignments we were fortunate to receive over the years. Our special thanks go to ABN AMRO Bank, AEGON, Afrika Museum, Ahrend, 1616 / Arita Japan, Amsterdamse Fonds voor de Kunsten, Amsterdam Museum, the Art Institute of Chicago, Bar L'Europe, Bijenkorf, Blickfang, BMW Group/MINI, BOZAR, Centraal Museum Utrecht, Ceramica Bardelli, Cityhall 's-Hertogenbosch, Cooper-Hewitt National Design Museum, Craft Council Gallery, Designhuis, Design Indaba, Design Museum London, DutchDFA, Eikelenboom, Established & Sons, Estate Internet, The Frozen Fountain, Gaia & Gino, Galerie Binnen, Galerie VIVID, Galleria Antonia Jannone, Gelderland, Georg Jensen, Gispen, Goods, the Government Buildings Agency, Gras communiceert, HAY, IKEA, J. HILL's Standard, Juul, Karimoku New Standard, Llove Hotel, Lloyd Hotel, the London Design Festival, Luce di Carrara, Mabeo, Maharam, Ministry of V&W, Moooi, Moustache, Museum Boijmans Van Beuningen, Netherlands Embassy Tokyo, Nederlandse consulaat-generaal Milaan, Nationaal Historisch Museum, Nike, OeO, Pastoe, Pressalit, Provinciehuis Overijssel, Rossana Orlandi, Rotero, Royal Leerdam Crystal, Royal Marine, Royal VKB, Samsung, Schönbuch, Stadsschouwburg Amsterdam, Stedelijk Museum Bureau Amsterdam, Stedelijk Museum Amsterdam, Stedelijk Museum 's-Hertogenbosch, Stedelijk Museum Roermond, Stichting Regentenkamer, TextielMuseum, Thomas Eyck (t.e.), Ir. PRJ Toornend, Tommy Hilfiger, Toyo Kitchen, Valerie Traan, Van Esch, Velux, Woonbeurs Amsterdam, Zetel, VPRO Zomergasten, Zuiderzee Museum.

We also would like to express our sincere appreciation to everyone who was instrumental in our success: Fredric Baas, Caroline Baumann, Christiaan Bastiaans, Annette Baumeister, Jean-Pierre Blanc, Gilda Bojardi, Caroline Boot, Anne-Marie Buemann, Coppens & Alberts, Saskia Copper, Ilse Crawford, Dick Dankers, Marianne van Dodewaard, Lidewij Edelkoort, Ad van Esch, Simon van Esch, Thomas Eyck, Philip Fimmano, David Glaetti, Arjan Gras, Marva Griffin, Chantal Hamaide, Gen Harada, Mette Hay, Rolf Hay, Bernard Heesen, Mary Hessing, Esmé Hofman, Adrian van Hooydonk, Laura Houseley, Connie Hüsser, Jeroen Junte, Hiroshi Kato, Annemartine van Kesteren, Ryuko Kida, Gerrit Komrij, Aad Krol, Andrea Lipps, Thomas Lykke, Michael Maharam, Stephen Maharam, Tony Manzari, Jack Meijers, Mathieu Meijers, Paul van de Meulengraaf, Stef Miero, Mary Murphy, Noriyuki Momota, Henrik Most, Ravi Naidoo, Ben van Os, Alex Otten, Suzanne Oxenaar, René Pingen, Els van der Plas, Vincent de Rijk, Ingeborg de Roode, Cok de Rooy, Helen van Ruiten, Jacqueline Schaap, Erik Schilp, Suzan Russeler, Zoë Ryan, Tecla Temmlnk, Emilia Terragni, Pilar Viladas, Nick Vinson, Adri Vlasblom, Bernardine Walrecht, Anders Warming, Till Weber, Veerle Wenes, Alasdhair Willis, Paul Wyber, Koichiro Yamaguchi, Teruhiro Yanagihara, Koji Yokoi.

Much love and gratitude go to our families who have believed in us from the very beginning, and continuously provide us with good advice and assistance.

Phaidon Press Limited
Regent's Wharf
All Saints Street
London N1 9PA

Phaidon Press Inc.
65 Bleecker Street
New York, NY 10012

www.phaidon.com

First published 2015
© 2015 Phaidon Press Limited

ISBN 978 0 7148 6871 4

A CIP catalogue record for this book is available
from the British Library.

Commissioning Editor
Emilia Terragni

Project Editor
Joe Pickard

Production Controllers
Sue Medlicott, Nerissa Vales

Printed in China

Concept and graphic design
Studio Joost Grootens/Joost Grootens with Hanae
Shimizu, Tine van Wel, Silke Koeck

Text
Michael Maharam, Louise Schouwenberg

Art direction
Scholten & Baijings

Project coordination
Jody Kocken at Scholten & Baijings

Photography
Alexander van Berge, Merel van Beukering, Nico
Bick, Tom Brown, Christiaan de Bruijne, Lothaire
Hucki, Ariko Inaoka, Dean Kaufman, Yves Krol,
Alberto Novelli, Takumi Ota, Inga Powilleit, Viviane
Sassen, Scheltens & Abbenes, Wyne Veen

Translation
Dagmar Speer, Michael Meert

Final editing
Dagmar Speer

Louise Schouwenberg studied psychology (Radboud University Nijmegen), sculpture (Gerrit Rietveld Academie, Amsterdam), and philosophy (University of Amsterdam). After establishing a career as visual artist, since 2000 her focus has been on theory, and incidentally, curating exhibitions on the cutting edge of design and art (i.e. gallery Fons Welters Amsterdam, 2012; Museum Boijmans Van Beuningen Rotterdam, 2010; Textile Museum Tilburg, 2006). She writes for various magazines and websites, including *Domus*, *Frame Magazine*, *Dezeen*, *Metropolis M*, and has contributed to a range of books, including a monograph on artist Robert Zandvliet (Nai Publishers, 2012), and two monographs on designer Hella Jongerius (Phaidon Press, 2004 and 2010).
Schouwenberg is course director of two master departments: Contextual Design at Design Academy Eindhoven (MDes), and Material Utopias (MFA/MDes) at the Sandberg Instituut/Gerrit Rietveld Academie Amsterdam.

Joost Grootens studied architectural design at Gerrit Rietveld Academie in Amsterdam. As a graphic designer he is self-taught. His studio designs books in the fields of architecture, urban space and art specializing on atlases.
Among his clients are Nai010 Publishers, Lars Müller Publishers, gta Verlag, Phaidon Press, Van Abbe Museum and Boijmans Van Beuningen Museum. Grootens has won numerous prizes for his designs. Among them the Goldene Letter and two Gold Medals in the Best Book Design from all over the World competition in Leipzig. In 2009 he was awarded the Netherlands' most prestigious design award, the Rotterdam Design Prize.
A monograph about his work titled *I swear I use no art at all* was published in 2010 by 010 Publishers. Grootens is head of the Master Information Design at Design Academy Eindhoven. He has also lectured at various institutions in Asia, Europe and North America.

ISBN 978-0-7148-6871-4

9 780714 868714